Jacket painting by Penny Corradine, Wolfpack Studio, Turner Valley.
Unless otherwise captioned, all photographs are from the Patterson collection.

We acknowledge the financial support of the Government of Canada through the Book Publishing Industry Development Program (BPIDP) for our publishing activities.

The author wishes to thank the Alberta Historical Resources Foundation for a grant to assist with the completion of this project.

Printed and bound in Canada by
Friesens, Altona, Manitoba

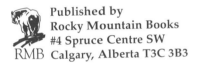

Published by
Rocky Mountain Books
#4 Spruce Centre SW
Calgary, Alberta T3C 3B3

Canadian Cataloguing in Publication Data

Finch, David, 1956-
  R. M. Patterson

Includes bibliographical references and index.
  ISBN 0-921102-75-5

1. Patterson, R. M. (Raymond Murray), 1898-1984. 2. Frontier and pioneer life--Canada, Western. 3. Authors, Canadian (English)--20th century--Biography.* 4. Ranchers--Alberta--Biography. 5. Canada, Western--Biography. I. Title.
FC3675.1.P37F56 2000   971.2'03'092   C00-911180-8
F1060.92.F56 2000

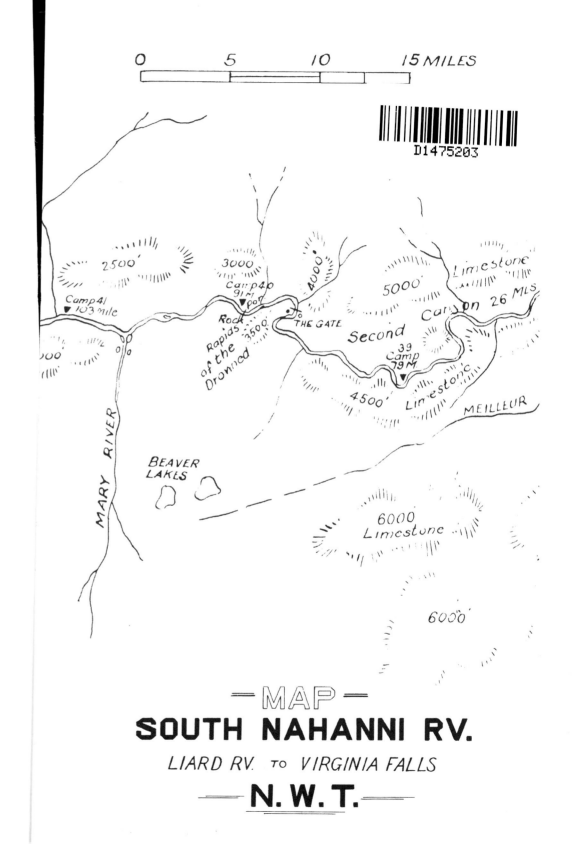

R. M. PATTERSON
A Life of Great Adventure

David Finch

Rocky Mountain Books, Calgary

Contents

R. M. Patterson on Holy Cross Mountain, 1940.

Foreword

DAVID FINCH has done us a great service in completing the biography of a fascinating, unique Canadian. Raymond Murray Patterson, an international man of letters, published in London and New York, with translations in Spanish and Dutch, enjoyed a worldwide readership. But we only knew him from his books and articles.

When I became his Canadian publisher we were neighbours on Vancouver Island in British Columbia. We shared a common bond in our experiences as war veterans and ranching in the foothills of southern Alberta. For nearly a quarter century we were close friends, working together with mutual delight in creating *Far Pastures* (1963), republishing his *The Dangerous River* (1966) and exchanging confidential correspondence when he was travelling abroad. But I never knew the whole man.

Four years ago David visited us at the start of his quest. I showed him my Patterson file from which he drew out additional memories from Eleanor and me.

From here David set out to follow R. M.'s trail into the Nahanni country where his youthful adventures resulted in *The Dangerous River* (1954). He rode into the high valleys at the headwaters of Sheep Creek, not far from the source of the Elbow River; *The Buffalo Head* (1961). He went overseas to R. M.'s home in England, visited his public school and his college at Oxford.

Then he started to write with the assistance of Janet, R. M.'s daughter. What we have here is a definitive work that demands a place beside the Patterson titles, in libraries and schools, tracing the life of a classical scholar discovering the wonders of our Canadian wilderness.

David Finch deserves our gratitude as he opens our eyes to a broad canvas of the man Bruce Hutchison described as "a mixture of Thoreau and Jack London."

Gray Campbell, Deep Cove, 1999

(Author note: Gray Campbell passed away June 10, 2000, at his home in Sidney, British Columbia, at age 88.)

for Jeannie

The subtitle comes from the dedication page in R. M. Patterson's book, *Far Pastures*: "To the memory of a great Canadian, Sir Edward Peacock, G.C.V.O., the man who pronounced a blessing on this Odyssey, many years ago, with the words: 'I think that it will be a great adventure.'"

The Early Years
1896 to 1916

RAIN pelted the thin man as he slogged up the canyon, pulling a heavy canoe on the end of a waterlogged rope. And then it happened. "I fell with an awful crash in amongst these pointed rocks, lay there and groaned for a minute but nothing was damaged. A thing like that could lead to a bad accident."[1]

With months of travel and many tough rapids behind him, Raymond Patterson lay flat on his back in the Third Canyon of the South Nahanni River in Canada's Northwest Territories. The year, 1927; the month, August. For a hundred days he had been on the trail. And now this. Except for Albert Faille, Patterson was the only white man on the South Nahanni. The Minnesota trapper was ahead, somewhere, headed for the Flat River to build a cabin, run a trapline and prospect for gold.

"What in the blazes am I doing here?" Patterson probably wondered. "I could be home in London with Mother or at the bar with friends in Peace River, Alberta. This must be one of the loonier things I've ever done."

But he had his reasons. Life was moving on. Marriage, a family and a settled existence seemed inevitable. The North had beckoned him since childhood and this had seemed like the perfect summer to follow the siren call. Quitting was not on his mind; not yet. Before turning his canoe downstream he had to see the famous Falls of the Nahanni and find the legendary gold. In almost every bay of black sand he saw the alluring yellow twinkle, proof of wealth untold.

Time was the adversary that summer. He would have to turn back by the middle of the month. It would take until winter to return to Edmonton by canoe, on foot, horseback, riverboat and train. Even with the best of luck, he might run into trouble. As it turned out, disaster, disguised as starvation and a timber wolf, almost caught him that fall. His name nearly passed into history as yet another crazy Brit who had pushed his luck too far in the Canadian North.

So what was he doing on the South Nahanni? Perhaps it began in a British nursing home when Dr. Stott pulled his tonsils and told him to take it easy for the summer. Or maybe it was the result of the Great War? Could it have been the view of distant hills from the little attic window in his grandfather's mansion? Or was it those Canadian cousins and a great uncle who convinced him to head for the North? Perhaps the wanderlust was hereditary or maybe it came from surviving to the ripe old age of twenty-nine after most of his boyhood chums had died in the Great War.

PATTERSON'S story began when he came into the world on May 13, 1898, at Darlington, County Durham, in northern England. He was the only child of Henry Foote Patterson and Emily Taylor Coates who were married in 1896.[2] It was a volatile marriage, a partnership of two people that one relative said was like "fire and fire."

Emily was the eldest of seven children. Her father, Thomas Coates, was an engineer. In 1891, he took charge of the Whessoe Foundry Co. Ltd., turning around a declining business and making it a progressive industrial force in the new century. On the home front, the foundry provided ironwork for the London Underground. It also built large steel tanks to hold natural gas and many other vessels used in natural gas processing facilities throughout Europe and as far away as Canada and New Zealand. Later, Coates expanded the business by making oil storage tanks for Standard Oil and Shell Oil facilities around the world. Skilled craftsman that he was, he cared about his product and his employees. He knew workers by name and took a personal interest in their fortune. Thomas passed along the management of Whessoe to his son Alfred, who ran the company until his death in 1924. From her father Emily learned to befriend strangers, but she also inherited a strong family preference for financial security. She could be forceful and opinionated; someone who knew her own mind.

By contrast, Henry Patterson was "a Scot from the valley of the Tweed." He worked for several newspapers during his brief marriage to Emily, serving for a time as editor of a pro-English newspaper in Dublin, Ireland—an occupation guaranteed to create enemies. He once sat atop a printing press with a loaded revolver to ensure the publication of his opinions. For this stunt he was roundly beaten by a mob, the turning point in his career that encouraged him to head to South Africa as a correspondent.

Young Raymond picked up his father's politics by osmosis. Prompted by his father, the two-year-old crashed a party where Mother was serving a tea to Irish friends. "Damn Oom Paul! Damn Oom Paul!" Screaming slogans against the president of South Africa did little to ingratiate Raymond to adults, so the nanny yanked him from the room, his backside smarting.[3]

Raymond's earliest memories of his father relate to his love of distant mountains. Sitting on his shoulders, the little boy peered at the horizon as Henry pointed across Killiney Bay in Ireland to the Wicklow Hills. Even though they

Raymond Patterson and his mother, Emily Taylor Coates.

were little more than shadowy lumps in the distance, the 2000 foot-high mountains captured the young boy's imagination.[4] In 1901 Raymond's father left to report on the war in South Africa, and except for a brief visit two decades later, the link between father and son was broken for life. Henry Foote Patterson died penniless in South Africa in 1935.

No one knows why the marriage ended. Henry invited his young wife along on the South African adventure, but Emily chose to stay home. As much as she loved her footloose partner, she simply could not give up a stable English life to chase around Africa. Once Henry left, Emily erased his memory: photographs of Henry disappeared and he was never mentioned again. Mother and son moved to the Coates' family home in Darlington. From the upper windows of the ivy covered, red-brick house that seemed a castle to the small boy, Raymond would gaze at the hills to the southwest. No adults shared his attraction for the high country, so he kept his dreams to himself.[5]

His father's absence left a huge hole in his life, one that Raymond's adoring mother filled as best she could. Financially, her family supported the boy's education, while she managed the household for her aging parents, became his only confidant. His long letters home from school and

Canada reveal a deep affection for the strong woman who served as the only constant in his life for more than forty years. Her letters to him always began: "My Very Dear Raymond." Through tough times and many adventures she believed in her son, listened to his dreams of a fantastic life and nurtured him constantly.

Amid the bustle of the Coates' household, that included entertaining engineers from around the world, young Raymond made a world of his own. Treats from Canadian relatives and books about the North fostered an appetite for the life of the voyageur, the trapper, the native and the coureur des bois. He once tied tennis racquets to his feet and stomped around the family yards on a thin layer of snow. The ruined racquets, discovered the next spring, pointed directly at Raymond.[6]

Other adventures attracted less adult attention. His bicycle took him many places, but try as he might, he never found the road into the distant hills that beckoned from the upper window. Decades later he wrote: "Which is, perhaps, as it should be, for it still has for me, today, all the charm of the unknown, and it still leads, as it always did, to who knows what hidden pleasance in what lost valley of the hills."[7]

After a few years in a small local school, the time came for further education. As was the English custom at the time, young Patterson went to

The Coates' family home in Darlington.

public school. Ostensibly, one sent one's offspring to these privately funded institutions for an education. Besides academic learning, young boys also received instruction in the ways of society. Because most came from comfortable homes with servants and nannies, public school also provided these youngsters with hard knocks as a preparation for the harsher realities of life.

While Rossall School helped young Patterson become a man, its influence was not entirely positive. Born the same year as Patterson, author C. S. Lewis berated the British public school. He believed it taught youngsters to grasp social status through every possible method: intellectually, socially, through sports and every other conceivable method of deviousness. The intent of this total reordering of life was to make small boys "normal."[8]

Patterson's own experience in the public school system barely surfaces in his books. He only credits it with teaching him how to stay warm in cold weather and almost killing him with a bout of double pneumonia.[9] Rossall, however, taught him much more than he realized at the time. In the spring of 1951, while helping manage the Big Coulee Ranch in the foothills of the Rockies west of Fort Macleod, Alberta, he reflected on his youth while reviewing letters he had written Mother while at Rossall. Patterson edited the letters, which dated from 1911 to 1917, excerpted them, added comments, then self-published seventy-five copies of a booklet he titled "Dear Mother."

One lonely letter home from the early days stated "and I brewed alone." Afternoon tea was a "brew" and with a few treats from his tuck box or the tuck shop, he kept starvation at bay. As an only child, he missed Mother desperately and it took until his second term to begin making friends in his own dormitory, called the Maltese Cross House.[10]

From Darlington a train took him across the Pennines to Rossall, located near Fleetwood, Lancashire, beside the Irish Sea. "It was a lovely journey, and I always enjoyed it, going or coming. You followed the Tees for nearly twenty miles, and then crossed Stainmoor and the headwaters of the Eden—finally coming down to Lancaster, through the great fells, by the valley of the Lune."[11] Travelling by train allowed him the luxury of bringing a healthy stock of food. "I got here alright and nothing in my tuck box was broken." Thus began at least eighteen letters during his Rossall days. Later he recalled: "It was a magnificent tuck box, stoutly built, iron grey, and one of the largest in the House. No space was ever wasted, and the railway's charges for excess baggage were invariably shattering."[12]

That tuck box was an important public school fixture. Although fees were steep, precious little money was spent feeding the growing young men. As a result, they were always hungry, especially after meals that were barely palatable. Virtual starvation set in after the boys refused, en masse, to touch some of the plates set before them. Protein was sometimes unrecognizable. "The meat was the greatest curiosity. I have seen particularly refractory pieces of this material—of a greyish colour, and frequently shot with bright, iridescent hues of blue and green—slowly curling and uncurling themselves as they lay there on the dish, surrounded by a watery mess of vegetables, à l'Anglaise, colourless and sodden. Tortured, reptilian squirmings—ugh!"[13]

Food requests figured prominently in letters to Mother. At times he merely asked for more biscuits, cakes or whatever treats were at hand. Other times he was more creative: "I should think pheasants and sausages will be awfully cheap by next Sunday, don't you?"[14] "...I wish I was at home today. But I will eat a jolly big dinner when I do come. Can you send me the cakes you always send me this week as the biscuits have given out at last? I suppose there wouldn't be any mince pies yet that you could put in?"[15]

Strong opinions were not only reserved for food. As long as he lived, Patterson always knew where he stood on a topic. Shortly after arriving at school his political conservatism caused him to state: "In our dormitory 2 chaps snore and 2 are Liberals."[16]

A keen observer, he often described specific fellows. Some became fast friends, older ones he fashioned into role models. Sadly, many of them died in the next few years at battles in the Great War at Gallipoli, Flanders, Suvla Bay, Tiflis, and in many other places in France and in other theatres. "No luck at all...," Patterson commented in 1951. A haunting refrain kept appearing in his letters home. Even before the Great War broke out in 1914, his schoolmates were dying in battle. In a letter dated July 5, 1912, he mentions another fellow from the school killed in action. On July 21, another.[17]

During the second year at school he acquired some important skills, such as avoiding needless expenditure of energy. Early each morning the boys ran half a mile. "I used to go as I was in my pyjamas straight out of bed, out to the sea wall and then back to bed again. It saved an awful lot of bother but it has been stopped as, when it had rained in the morning, we used to find our pyjamas still wet at night."[18] Likewise, Patterson and a few others reduced another morning ritual—going to chapel—to its barest essentials. "It was a picturesque sight—the hardier souls from each house going all out, putting on collar and ties as they ran, with Sergeant Shepherd cutting across the line of travel, note book on high. It taught us to sprint and, in its small way, it was adventure."[19]

Whatever else he absorbed in those hallowed halls of learning, Patterson learned the best methods to find and enjoy adventure. It was to stand him in good stead. In later years he sought its rewards everywhere and found them where others encountered only boredom, misery or death. It helped that he often possessed the financial resources to take advantage of opportunities that arose, but the independent spirit of the wanderer and explorer set him apart from many of his generation and financial status.

By 1912, as a fourteen-year-old, Patterson's letters were filled with themes that became common in later years. His extraordinary powers of observation were already at work; school comes alive through his recollections. Once, the Head of the school gave the boys a half-day off to celebrate the arrival of his newborn son. He called it a "Happy Event" but Patterson added: "The extra half was appreciated, but B. E. Craigie voiced boyhood's base ingratitude when he said, 'How much better would have been Twins and a Whole Day.'"[20]

Leisure activities were an important part of the curriculum. Besides playing bridge in their rooms, the boys partook in organized sports. For some, Patterson was only an observer. "The boxing was last week. One boy has just come out of the sanatorium. He was knocked out three times, and the last time the other fellow was so exhausted that he fell on top of him."[21] Cricket, however, appealed to the young man and he became a great bowler. His skills as a batsman were also renowned. "I made one of my rare connections with a half volley, and Hunt, on the centre net, stopped it with his skull. I can hear the awful crack now, [1951] and still see that burly figure crumple to the earth."[22] Chasing the ball around the soccer field was not one of Patterson's favourite sports, but in the early years he participated in all aspects of the game. "Feeling between the two Houses ran high over this match—and, in addition to the central combat, a number of subsidiary fights and scufflings broke out amongst the onlookers along the touchlines. The House Brew was a roaring success."[23]

Organized sports aside, his eyes still wandered to the horizon. Three times during his six years at Rossall the weather cleared enough to provide a glimpse of distant mountains on the Isle of Man, seventy miles away. To the young man, trapped in a school yard, they were "an unattainable paradise." For the remainder of his life he retained "a distaste for the lowlands, and a delight in the high alpine places that endures and will never fade."[24]

Patterson's health was not good at school. Although fairly rugged, he caught colds regularly and often found himself in the school sanatorium. "My cough is getting better and that rotten feeling has gone. They are absolute idiots over at the sanatorium, though—they think Corlett and I are shamming, they are so stupid that they can't tell when anything is wrong with you.... It is most annoying, when you are ill, to be told you are not by a red-headed lunatic. Cold, cough, sore throat, headache or stomach ache—you get the same medicine for each, and for most other things as well, as Corlett and I have discovered. However, I am better now; how, I don't know—certainly not through the 'cure-all' as it is called—the remedy for everything from ear ache to a broken neck."[25]

A letter shortly after his fifteenth birthday described a twenty-mile march called a "field day" in hot weather. Upon arriving at their destination, Patterson threw himself into the river. At a nearby spring he drank until he "nearly burst" and then filled his water bottle with clear, cold water. After gorging on ginger beer from a nearby farm, the boys cooled off by "walking about with wet handkerchiefs on our heads, gasping like fishes."[26]

The same letter mentions another former Rossall student lost in battle. The "field days" were, of course, a euphemism for combat training, an integral part of public school culture. As hostilities increased, marches lengthened and the trench digging became more serious. But luck sometimes smiled on Patterson's house. In late 1913 he wrote: "The field day was pretty decent—they forgot all about us and we lay under a hedge for three hours." His 1951 perspective on this event read, "Some perspiring militarist's brain had gone haywire, and Kingsford's were left to have their sleep in peace."[27]

Not content to hide in the hedge every day, the boys created diversions for themselves. When a big sea washed over the sea wall, the boys got thoroughly drenched playing in the pools. As a result, school officials forbade games by the barrier. "And with that was included the companion sport—rafting about the Sandy Hoy on unfastened agglomerations of driftwood, ships timbers and the like, riding the waves caused by the inrushing sea waters. That was a loss, for we had taken much innocent pleasure in watching Gibson's frantic efforts to hold one of these contraptions together in about five feet of water, and the look on his face as

Photos David Finch.

Rossall School, May 1998.

Janet Blanchet and assistant principal Mr. Pengilly at the chapel door, Rossall, May 1998.

the last two spars parted company and he sank, fully clad, beneath the waves, more than rewarded us for our patience."[28]

During these middle years at Rossall, his personality developed in some unbecoming ways. In addition to requests for food and clothing, obnoxious demands also arose. "Would you put my tweed trousers in the press in what is more or less the right crease?"[29] "Don't forget about any of the things I asked you for and don't send my suit too soon as it will only get in the way. If it comes by next Saturday it will do but not later, perhaps Friday because of the Xmas rush. I am sorry I sent a letter without a stamp but I forgot."[30] Luckily, with time, the take-all attitude moderated.

Patterson was often in trouble. "On Thursday night I got 500 lines from Mr. Kingsford for being caught wrestling in the dormitory."[31] "Being caught" seems to have been the offense, not wrestling. On another occasion he was tardy returning from a brief holiday from the school. "My exeat [leave of absence from school] seemed to unfit me for school…. I was late for P.T., got my Latin grammar to say again, and ended up with two hours punishment school for doing an essay while that ass, Mr. Sykes, was talking about Poland. I thought he was such a fool that he couldn't see what I was doing. It seems I was mistaken."[32]

Horsing around is common enough in boarding school but part of the game is to avoid getting caught. "Gibson and I are exiles from the house-room since last Sunday. A. B. K. [Housemaster Kingsford]

15

kicked us out. After chapel we were fighting in there and I put Gibson on the floor and piled some rugs, heavy books, six chairs and a small table on him meaning to leave him there till prep. I was just arranging the last chair when in came A. B. K. and snorted at me, 'Who is under there?' Then he said, 'Get out whoever you are.' Gibson thought he could not be seen so he lay still and tried to look like a pile of furniture, but alas his great beastly feet were sticking out into the fire place and he was caught and I had to undo him in a dead silence and help him up and get out. And we are out still...."[33]

By 1915 the dark cloud of war overshadowed schooling. In January, while playing hockey, the boys heard the deep rumble of explosions nearby. "Of course we didn't stop as we could do nothing." It turned out to be German submarines sinking ships on the Irish Sea. The hockey game continued.[34]

The boys increasingly found their non-scholastic hours occupied with preparation for trench warfare. Once Patterson forced his housemates into a hard four mile run—"rather fun especially as they thought they were only going to the End of the Lane...."[35] Three days later he wrote that he and another lad skipped out of a run by dodging off into a hay stack and hiding while the others finished the run. Much to their surprise, they found fresh eggs in their hideaway and smuggled them into the house— a rare and expensive treat during the war. In 1951 he mused: "It wasn't that we couldn't run seven miles—it was rather that the feat of 'cutting out,' with the attendant difficulty of getting back to Rossall, especially when hampered by a load of eggs, plus the risk of a monitor's caning, had an irresistible appeal."[36]

He was not always so lucky. Later that year, he was promoted to the rank of corporal. "To celebrate that, we had another awful route march on Tuesday on packed snow and ice—I have never been so tired since I came here." Although all were in good condition, their leader, a man they called Pup, forced the pace while wearing a pair of "well nailed moun-taineering boots." The boys, meanwhile, struggled to keep up in their smooth bottomed army boots, carrying greatcoats and rifles. "I must say the action of walking tautly braced so far over the ice, sought out coy and hidden muscles which, so far as I was concerned, had hitherto lived in retirement and complete seclusion."[37] Digging trenches added another dimension to the torture. By some stroke of genius, Patterson landed the job of field cook. "Corlett was jealous and said it was wonderful how near I always got to any food."[38]

In March he joined another fellow in a mud bath. Years later he remembered the details: "That was Gibson, and the occasion of this disaster was some manoeuvres in the direction of Larkholme Farm. The performance dragged its incomprehensible way towards a close, and at long last came the order to charge. Glad of any diversion, the two of us tore off with well simulated zeal and, yelling like Apaches, topped a low dike and jumped. The tune changed swiftly when we saw, all too late, what awaited us—bubbling, manurial slime with a fine, healthy green scum overlaying its surface—a specialty of those lowlands of the Fylde.

"The rest of the House Squad, Platoon…had got sedately and soberly off the mark, as was its custom—just fast enough to escape The Pup's eye, and not one jot more—and consequently had a grandstand seat for the show. They started talking about skunks, and begged us to get to leeward of them; they held their noses and made other rude gestures; and the more erudite, who happened to be 'doing' Macbeth that term, fell to misquoting the more apposite sayings from the sleep-walking scene of that play: 'All the perfumes of Arabia…,' they said, and 'Out damned spot…' and much more of that sort, making a great parade of their poor wit. That little affair took some living down, in more senses than one."[39]

His seventeenth birthday found him digging trenches regularly. "By now the Corps was well in the saddle, and—if I may be permitted to confuse horse and rider—feeling its oats. No longer could we call our souls our own, and every spare moment of the day was devoted to the study of some already obsolete weapon, or to instruction in Boer War tactics."[40]

On the first day of August 1915, the young men were at Barnacre Camp, Garstang. Wrapping blankets over their clothes, they slept as best they could in the open on Beacon Fell, 900 feet above sea level. He later recalled the weather as "beastly cold, and the night was showery into the bargain…. We bivouacked in a big upland pasture, and six of us lay down in a row for mutual warmth and protection. I slept: the others, apparently, tossed about restlessly, getting colder and colder, and finally, after a few periods of nightmarish unconsciousness, gave it up as a bad job and wandered around in the grey light of dawn, trying to get a bit of warmth into themselves. As each one departed he chucked his blanket over me and I slept on, warm and comfortable under this extra covering.

"I was finally aroused by the groans and curses of a vast suffering going on all around me, and especially by a strange voice from another House saying 'My God! Don't tell me somebody can still sleep in this devilish place!'

"I sat up and looked about for the others. There they were, not far away, in a little hollow and strangely occupied. They had met with a most unusually placid and good-tempered cow and were leaning against her—Powell and Parry on one side, and Goodwin, Howl and Gaulter on the other—warming themselves against her body while the gentle beast relaxed, as all cattle do, in the first rays of the morning sun."[41]

Perhaps as a result of this training, Patterson decided to enlist for the war. Late in 1915 he wrote a very excited and forceful letter home, informing Mother and Uncle of his plans. "I suppose you are aware that I intend to join the army as soon as I am eighteen and I am jolly glad conscription is coming because now you and uncle can't keep me out if you do want to and I am working hard to try and get a scholarship for Oxford so that I can leave and go and if you think you are doing me a kindness you aren't because I'm not going to be laughed at all my life and Roberts is doing just the same, he is going to try soon. All my friends have gone except P—and he ought to, so you must make up your mind to it...."

In latter years he explained this outburst of youthful exuberance. With training behind them and daily accounts of the action on the front lines, the fearless young men were determined to get into the trenches before the Great War was over and their chance at glory disappeared.[42]

Onto this headstrong young man the school bestowed a leadership role shortly before his seventeenth birthday. "I am a house monitor, now that Corlett has gone, and have the dormitory that I was in my first term to look after, and fags and all that sort of thing. I think as I am a monitor I had better have my grey suit to go home in, but I will let you know later." A preoccupation with clothing and physical appearance made itself conspicuous in his letters once he achieved status in the house.[43]

Along with duties as a monitor came the opportunity to do unto others as had been done unto him. "I gave four chaps...100 lines each yesterday for throwing bread about, and I made them do them out of the book that Chamier gave me my first lines from." C. K. Chamier, Head of the House when Patterson arrived in 1911, was killed in action in France on April 24th, 1914.[44]

As commodities in England grew scarce, authorities began rationing water. For their part, school officials removed the handles from the shower spindles. First among equals, Patterson used pliers as a handle and continued showering as before.[45] Creative he might have been, but all such things are eventually revealed. A few weeks later his letter home complained: "Now when they have come to put handles on again they found the thread of the screws worn away and so we were found out and nine of us have to pay for new spindles and have been stopped pocket money, brewing, the tuck shop and the house room for today (Saturday) so I think I had better keep the War Loan interest. I am writing letters as I have nothing else to do with all this [time]. What it comes to is that the nine cleanest boys in the house have been punished for washing. (I was one of them.)" By 1951 his attitude toward the incident had changed and he added: "Punished for washing? or for being completely irresponsible?"[46]

Undoubtedly, Housemaster A. B. Kingsford of the Maltese Cross House doled out suitable punishment to the nine young men, including the newly appointed house monitor. In the years to come Patterson continued in positions of responsibility even though he often found himself in the wrong. Kingsford was the same man who looked in on him in his first days at school and found him brewing alone. With a smile and a word of encouragement, he helped young Raymond through a lonely moment.[47] As a result, Patterson dedicated the edited version of his letters home to Kingsford in 1951.

Without a father, young Patterson took a liking to Kingsford and told Mother he didn't "intend to do anything mad beyond what is prompted by a natural disposition to kick up a row or tumult…and hideous luck in smashing things which A. B. K. must have got used to by now."[48] Patterson was nearly caught several times. In November, 1915, "Mr. Kingsford came upstairs about eleven p.m. when I was still fully dressed, and I had to rush into bed as I was and with my boots on while a loyal dormitory snored loudly."[49] Patterson was not only quick, he had trained his unruly house to protect his skin.

The war continued to affect their lives. They perused the morning papers daily, often finding "there the name of a friend or of someone we had known." With the typical bravado of youth, Patterson counselled Mother to ignore the bombing raids that the Zeppelins mounted over her house and stay in her warm bed rather than shiver in the cellar.[50]

In a way, life was just an adventure for the boys. In June 1916, four of them were nearly swept out to sea. "About midnight on Friday night I and three others got out of our bedroom window in the sick house and tore down the seafront and over the links and race course in pyjamas. We took a boat out on the Esk by moonlight, and came back at two a.m. with a couple of policeman after us, running heavily—I have never enjoyed myself so much."

The rest of the story came out in 1951. "The boat episode on the Esk very nearly gave us more than we bargained for: either the river was still in semi-flood, or else a strong ebb tide was running—I forget which— and for a time we seemed to be headed for the open waters of the Firth of Forth and, for all we knew, the North Sea....

"But we made it back upstream by rowing like galley slaves and making use of the shore eddies, and it was then, as we urged the bateau towards the boathouse with an old French Canadian voyageur song that I had picked up, 'J'ai du bon tabac dans ma tabatière,' that we attracted the attention of two solid Caledonian coppers. I suppose that in the flush of victory we were kicking up rather a row!

"We disposed of them by making a feint landing—then landed and ran for it. Lumbering along in their heavy boots they never had a chance against four boys in perfect condition and burdened only with pyjamas, sweaters and gym shoes. Silently we drew ahead and vanished into the shadow of the trees."[51]

That fall Patterson returned to school with a minor cold. During a house run, he took the boys along the ocean. Hijinks followed and they returned soaking wet. In 1951 he recalled that "taking the House into the sea in the last days of a very cold September did not prove to be, oddly enough, the completest cure for a cold."

It was not as though he went swimming intentionally in the cold Atlantic that blustery day. Patterson was in the habit of taking the House for a run and bringing along hockey sticks and a ball to use on the frozen ponds. Inevitably someone knocked the ball into the surf and the boys followed, thrashing their sticks, missing the ball and soaking each other. Some food treat was the reward for the one who proved lucky enough to actually bash the ball out of the surf.

Upon returning to school, Patterson found his shirt-sleeves frozen solid. With a stiff upper lip, he refused to admit that his cold was getting worse until Kingsford ordered him to sit by the fire. There, he shivered under a mountain of blankets. When he refused tea, Kingsford became alarmed and dispatched him to the sanatorium. And none too soon. Patterson developed double pneumonia and pleurisy. As his temperature soared past 106° Fahrenheit, a host of new friends and strange apparitions entered his room and did acrobatic tricks beside his bed, culminating in a fantastic disappearing act through the ceiling. Mother arrived to console her delirious son. At his bedside stood oxygen cylinders. When all treatments failed, the whole school took the unprecedented measure of praying for Patterson in Chapel.

(Four years later, he used the story of this experience to win a tall tales contest and convince his fellow contestant to pay for tea.) Because of, or perhaps in the face of this last remedy, the thin young man survived.

He returned from death's door a changed person. While bedridden, Patterson read every Jack London book Mother could find. "They fascinated me, those stories of the North, and I made up my mind that I, too, would hunt and drive my dogs in that blank space on the map, the Yukon-Mackenzie Divide."

The pneumonia excused Patterson from participation in sports. "This was probably just as well, as I only had a month remaining in which to set my brain in some sort of order for my scholarship exam at Oxford. But it was a peculiar kind of existence—in the school, but hardly of it, and free from so many of its rules that one hardly felt like bothering to keep the rest of them."[52]

C. S. Lewis also sat the Oxford entrance exam that December 1916 in the Hall of Oriel. Hundreds of hopefuls swarmed into the university town, shivering as they considered the consequences of failure. Low temperatures added to that chill. The young men, huddled in greatcoats, mufflers and gloves, wrote until their arms ached, then returned home to await the results.[53]

Patterson's force-fed brain rose to the challenge. The exams went well enough, though they were harder than he expected. He didn't hold out much hope for a scholarship. To relieve the tension, he visited a Canadian aunt and uncle in London. Vast quantities of food and two theatre tickets each day distracted him from the inevitable consequences of the Oxford test results. Luck visited him again, though, and a telegram brought good news of acceptance into St. John's College at Oxford and an "exhibition"—a junior prize—of sixty pounds. Suddenly, Patterson was a scholar with a bright future.[54]

After Christmas holidays he returned to a most unusual term at Rossall, almost a respite between storms. Sitting in front of a blazing fire, Patterson and his chums wiled away the hours with quiet games of chess. Academically he did "more or less the same work as last term so I see no need for me to overwork myself." Decades later he reminisced, "My particular case was aggravated by the fact that nobody really cared what I did, or did not, do. I had won my exhibition at St. John's, and that was that as far as Rossall was concerned. All I had to do was to make complete my recovery from pneumonia, and await my summons to a cadet unit—'so I see no need to overwork myself.'"[55]

During that last term he took on a position as an editor of the school newspaper. "I have to write the editorial for The Rossallian and do the school news, and I also go to Fleetwood fairly often to see the printers—of the three Editors I have the best job."[56]

Part of his personal preparations for the army involved picking a skill to hone. He became a bombing specialist since it seemed a safe occupation. In retrospect, he said it also "relieved the monotony of corps work and provided me with a military use for my one accomplishment—heaving things where they belonged."[57]

A stunt just before his nineteenth birthday landed him in virtual house arrest. "The four of us are gated and can't go to the tuck as, on Sunday, we hired an awful old growler and drove round and round the square in it, and then up to Big School door just before roll call. Half the school was there, yelling with laughter and cheering—the cabby of course couldn't see anything particularly comic in his old horse and hearse—he went wild with fury and swiped around with his whip. The Head had me up. I pointed out that there was nothing in the rule book against taking a cab to roll call and he said it was difficult to make rules that would cover all emergencies—there was also no rule in it against murdering your form master, but one shouldn't do so simply on that account."

Such was the unprecedented nature of the event that it became part of the school mythology. "This effort was known, I was told, for some years after we had all departed, as 'The Cab Turn,' and no doubt lost nothing in the telling. We had found the old cabby washing down his dreadful vehicle in some yard or other near Cleveleys—and were so fascinated by the tatterdemalion aspect of the pair of them that we promptly hired them both.

"The Head undoubtedly had reason on his side—and even he, he admitted to me, had watched from behind his curtains and laughed. Otherwise, official Rossall made no comment: after all, they would be rid of us in a month's time forever. Only Mr. Gibson (housemaster of Pelican) over a friendly coffee and biscuit, said his little say: 'If you had arrived in a taxi, it would have been merely vulgar. But to find a thing like that, and then to conceive the idea of driving up to roll call in it—that is Great Art!'"[58]

By April Patterson was gone from Rossall and in training for the artillery. "I said goodbye to Mr. Kingsford and to some of the other masters, and was not very sorry to leave, as I was getting a bit tired of it all." "I got the history prize as I promised you, but only got second prize this year in the cricket ball with a throw of 92 yards. I won it last year with a much longer throw—must be still feeling that go of double pneumonia. On the whole, it has been a good six years."[59]

Patterson always remembered Rossall fondly. He later claimed it had provided "an education that enabled us to appreciate beauty in nature, and in man-made things. These things we carried away, each according to his nature and individual tastes, together with a memory of certain masters who showed us the way to live like men—and in the forefront of these I, for my own part, would place A. B. K."[60]

Learning to be a man was important to Patterson. Without a father to act as a guide or a foil, he looked to his grandfather, his uncle and the older boys and the masters at Rossall. His grandfather and uncle taught him to value craftsmanship. The system at Rossall taught him to survive institutional life and instilled in him many British middle-class values and a loyalty to the Empire. His instructors honed his intellect and spurred him on to higher learning by preparing him for the Oxford exams.

As a result, by 1918 Patterson was beginning to meld these disparate influences into a unique identity. Passing the entrance examination for Oxford before setting off to war assured Mother he would find a proper place in British society when or if he returned from battle. His career as an artillery officer would allow him to share his quixotic father's wanderlust, this inherited trait conveniently disguised as patriotism. Going overseas would also give him a chance to become an adventurer and a man of mystery like his father. Only time would tell if he would be able to balance his parents' competing expectations and create a place for himself in a changing world.

War and a Sort of Peace
1917 to 1923

THE WAR that generals promised would not last until Christmas, 1914, dragged on four more years. Initial surges of willing recruits disappeared into trenches and the war demanded more. Shortages, conscription and a sense of desperation set in as Canadians supported the Allies in a war that would not end. Children weeded potato plants in victory gardens while their parents built guns and assembled ammunition. Civilians watched as brothers, fathers, husbands and sons boarded trains for the battlefields. They returned weeks or months later, war weary, some missing limbs, others in caskets.

Canadians never feared invasion like their British cousins. Bombed from the air in disorienting night-time attacks, Britain was also vulnerable to direct attack after Germany conquered France. Submarines sank the supply ships laden with everything the British needed to survive. Food rationing began in July 1917. Coupons were necessary for the weekly half pound of sugar and for meat, margarine, bacon and cheese. Eventually, even tea was rationed. Bread was never rationed, but coarse dark loaves replaced white bread. Clothing became scarce.

British society surrendered all its men to the war effort except the oldest, youngest and those in essential services. When the Allied offensives of 1917 failed to conquer the Germans, 30,000 farmers left their fields and headed into the trenches. Schoolboys and women took over the potato harvest. The munitions industry gave up 100,000 men and the coal mines sacrificed 50,000 of their best workers. Finally, men aged forty-two to fifty-five put on uniforms and headed for France.

Rain, sleet and bone chilling cold awaited the lucky ones in the trenches. Daily life included mud, rats, poor food and the constant threat of an enemy charge. Earth-shaking explosions demolished trenches, killing some instantly, wounding others, leaving all feeling mortal. Poisonous gas crept across the line, attacking lungs and blinding eyes. Boring days passed slowly, with no comfortable place to sleep. When the call came to charge the enemy line, soldiers flung themselves from the trenches and ran across no-man's-land, shooting as they went. Twisted masses of barbed wire greeted the unprotected soldiers. The air was full of shrapnel and bullets thwacking through the fetid fog. Men cried out in pain and died quietly in a living hell. Those that rose from the trenches often met death at enemy lines where machine guns riddled their unprotected bodies.

Success in reaching the German trench only gave the men a chance to die from pistol shots, bayonets or from knives, shovels or clubs in hand-to-hand combat. The stench of rotting corpses filled the air as the screams of the wounded mixed with the cacophony of artillery and rifle fire. Even in the relative safety of field hospitals, infection killed quietly in the days before antibiotics. Many who recovered returned to fight in deteriorating conditions.

Mother and R. M. Patterson in uniform.

Patterson arrived in this cesspool in early 1918, a few months after leaving Rossall. Like his school-mates, he was blind to the dangers, only exhilarated to be involved in the greatest adventure of his times. Reality descended a few weeks later when he fell captive to Prussian soldiers in the Spring Offensive of 1918. Both sides knew a massive assault was inevitable, but the Germans had lulled the Allies into complacency by announcing their impending attack repeatedly in the fall of 1917, each time postponing the inevitable. Both sides strengthened positions, added reinforcements and artillery, expanded the trenches and improved communications systems.

As the build-up continued, the Royal Flying Corps flew reconnaissance missions over the battlefields, recording troop movements and gun posi-

25

tions. One airman winging over Patterson's head was Gordon Matthews. He and Patterson would later become close friends, winter on the South Nahanni River together and godfather each other's children. Providing valuable information for the ground troops, the RFC helped plan the defence against the massive German assault. However, cloud, thick fog and rain prevented the RFC from observing the German build-up in March 1918. Under cover, the Germans moved in so many guns their artillery outnumbered that of the Allies four to one.

Finally, in the early hours of March 21, 6,000 German guns began bombarding the Allied forces. One large gun supported every ten German solders. High explosives and poisonous gas rained down across the lines for nearly five hours, some shells landing fifty miles behind the front. Intending to soften the enemy positions, the artillery attack destroyed communications lines and trenches. Then came the troops, screaming across the no-man's-land in a line forty miles wide. Supported with troops from the recently conquered Russian front, the German attack seemed invincible. Heavy fog and mist veiled the assault and made defence futile. By mid-morning the forward observation posts were overrun or surrounded. By noon the front lines were straining under the attack. During the afternoon the Allies began a sluggish retreat that lasted until April 5. With incredible effort they kept the Germans from their goal at Amiens.

Patterson was in the unit responsible for holding 125 miles of that line. The Spring Offensive of 1918 found him in a forward observation post in a bombed-out farmhouse. Darkness and fog obscured the terrain and prevented him giving directions to his gunners. So he settled in for a rest. The attack came at exactly 4:30 a.m. When he poked his head out to look for the cause of the commotion, he found "the air full of screaming metal...."[1]

Unable to direct his battery of gunners, he led his telephone operator and sergeant back to the guns by compass. How anyone survived the retreat amazed Patterson. All life seemed to have been obliterated by angry steel. When the German guns moved on to bombard the territory behind the artillery battery, everyone knew the infantry attack was imminent. After a quick attempt to render their own guns useless, the Brits ran for safety. All except Patterson. In the hustle of loading, firing and emptying the artillery guns, he dropped his revolver. Going back for it took only a few seconds but two Prussian infantrymen grabbed him as he made his retreat. Thus, Second Lieutenant Raymond Murray Patterson of the Territorial Force, Royal Horse and Royal Field Artillery became a prisoner of war.

Back home, his mother opened the dreaded envelope early the next month. The letter did not announce her Raymond's death, but it did not promise much hope either.

9/4/1918
Dear Mrs. Patterson,

I am sorry to have to inform you that your Son, 2/Lt. R. M. Patterson was taken prisoner on the 21st. ult. He was attached to this battery not very long before, and it was very rotten luck to be taken prisoner so soon. He was perfectly well at the time and we all feel sure that he would not come to any harm. The Captain and the other Officers join me in sending their deepest sympathy in these anxious times, but we wish to assure you that we think he is quite well. When you hear of, or from him, we should be greatly obliged if you would send us the news.

I am sorry I have been unable to write you before, but all papers had to be destroyed and letters have been very much delayed, so that we have not had your address to write to. I am returning by this mail some letters and parcels.

Of course, all his kit, with sure, are missing.

With kind regards,

Yours sincerely,

(Sgt) Harold J. Rabon. 2/Lt.

C/83 R.F.A.[2]

Once again, Mrs. Patterson had cause to worry about her only child. She would have been horrified to learn he almost took a bullet in the head from his own captain while being captured. When Patterson did not return from collecting his revolver, his commanding officer stopped just long enough to see the young artilleryman fall captive. Losing off a round from his pistol at the Prussian holding Patterson's arm, he just missed his friend's ear. Near misses would become a recurring theme in Patterson's life.

There followed nine long months as a prisoner. Nothing in his childhood quite prepared him for this life of sloth, but he took to indolence quickly. In later years he commented upon his ability to turn complicated tasks into easy ones by dint of his intelligence. He never shied from hard work but was always quick to find shortcuts and use the extra time for more pleasant tasks.

His daughter Janet recalls he "joined the artillery because he liked the boots." He hated the Cadet Corps intensely "because it was run by idiots." But cadet life was part of Rossall so he had made the best of it. Patterson's formal artillery school training began on April Fool's Day, 1917. There he met a horse for the first time in his life and became its servant and groom. Some of the training was easy for the youngest man in the school. As part of the Officers Training Corps at Rossall, he had marched in all weather, dug trenches, slept everywhere, commanded troops of Rossallites, thrown bombs, shot rifles and lived in trenches.

Using twenty-year-old artillery and strategy from the Boer War in South Africa, the men did their best. Much of their theory derived from Napo-

R. M. Patterson, bottom right, with fellow officers.

leon: they studied his battles. Their squad leader, Jessop, bellowed constantly that this Colonial Squad was "the worst squad ever." "Oh, God give me patience" was his refrain as he trained his men to handle the horse, the wagon, the eighteen-pound field gun and the 4.5 inch howitzer. This must have been some challenge. His new charges were from all parts of the Empire; Canada, Australia, New Zealand, South Africa and the United Kingdom. Most were seasoned soldiers. Patterson was one of the raw recruits.[3]

An accident nearly ended his brief career as an officer in training. While riding his horse downhill, Patterson got kicked in the head and ended up in the hospital. Friends from the Colonial Squad, A. S. Mitchell and E. P. Hill, visited him as he recuperated and later borrowed him from his visiting mother. Promising not to let him drink too much wine, they took him to town and plied him with liqueur brandy. As they entertained him with stories of their far away homes in Australia and Africa, Patterson regaled them with his imitations of mannerisms and accents.

For the remainder of 1917 they learned to move guns and ammunition with six-horse teams and wagons. One rider rode a horse in each pair. From that position they controlled their mounts as the screaming steel wheels and grunting horses combined in cacophony.

It was not always chaotic. Arriving at their destinations, they positioned their guns and grazed their horses. Map reading and plotting the complicated formulas necessary to send artillery shells to their destinations stretched their mathematical skills. These times were particularly peaceful for the youngest man in the group. His eye deciphered maps at a glance and he found calculations a breeze. So Patterson often snoozed in the grass, listening to the faint sounds of real war across the English Channel. He finally graduated, received the Second Lieutenant's single star, and bought the most impressive boots and riding breeches that London could supply to augment his immaculate uniform. In his heart of hearts, Patterson recalled decades later, "at last, I fancied that I was a somebody."[4]

Although life in the trenches was hell, the young Second Lieutenant probably withstood the hardships better than most. Under the cover of darkness, he and his fellow artillerymen moved guns and delivered ammunition. These forays tested his skill with horses; packing explosives onto the animals and trailing them in the dark over hellish terrain required constant attention. After a busy night he rested during the day in a bunker.

The Spring Offensive of 1918 changed everything. By sunset on March 21 Patterson was a prisoner. Casualties lay everywhere, some writhing in pain. Sleep deprived and aggressive from battle, jumpy German soldiers smashed anyone who made a wrong move. The British prisoners themselves had gone without sleep for thirty-six hours. In his understated way, Patterson said that his tin hat was dented "where a German rifle butt had made contact."[5] Actually, a vicious German guard had knocked him unconscious with a savage blow to the head. All were bruised and bleeding from close contact between prisoners and guards. And then, from nowhere, a buzzing bullet struck the meanest German guard dead.

The first days of captivity meant endless marching and rides in cramped cattle trucks with little food or drink. The Germans finally dumped them into an old Russian pub on the Rhine River. In the first fourteen days alone, Patterson lost twenty-eight pounds. Luck of a sort visited him when he won a lottery and cashed a cheque through the army bankers. He gorged himself on food and drink only to regain consciousness in the hospital with a high temperature and a bad case of mumps.

The hospital was a comfortable place to wait out part of the war. Clean surroundings and reasonable food were pleasant. In one room French officers played interminable games of cards, while in another their Portuguese counterparts used blades of grass to egg on their favourite in frog races. Patterson prolonged his stay by mimicking mumps symptoms: he puffed out his neck muscles and elevated his temperature with a bar of soap tucked into each armpit. Penned up with far too many men, he decided solitude was not something to fear and promised to "greet loneliness forever afterwards with a smile."[6]

Then came a slow train ride across Germany to a fortress town called Schweidnitz in modern-day Poland. Patterson and his fellow officers from the hospital commandeered a large room and soon had the best digs. Patterson volunteered as camp librarian, set up shop with a few books, then requested more volumes about the area. When they came, complete with maps, he turned them over to the escape committee. He also bribed one guard to bring him more maps in exchange for tobacco and chocolate.

All the while Patterson kept himself well supplied with adventure books. Under trees and a blue sky, he could have been anywhere. His daydreams took him back to England and to far-off lands. From the upper reaches of the house his gaze settled on distant hills that continually beckoned. Some prisoners escaped, but all except one were recaptured. Patterson also made escape plans but postponements and interruptions prevented his attempt. Finally, the events of November 11, 1918, released him from captivity.

At war's end, passionate life broke out everywhere. Liberated men spent money freely in local pubs and restaurants. Patterson and four others wandered farther afield, taking wonderful meals at inns within walking distance. During these treks, he visited Napoleon's tomb, "a lonely mausoleum on a little hillock amongst the pines…the sword and the cocked hat lying on the tomb."[7] Finally, they headed home by train. The vast forests and unending horizons of Europe convinced the recently released young officer that the world was much larger than his experience. It was a place he would have to see.

The next official letter the Patterson family received was on Royal stationery from Buckingham Palace. Hand-written, it celebrated good news.

R. M. Patterson
Second Lieutenant
Territorial Force
Royal Horse and
Royal Field Artillery
2.1.18
Buckingham Palace
1918

The Queen joins me in welcoming you on your release from the miseries & hardships, which you have endured with so much patience & courage.

During these many months of trial, the early rescue of our gallant officers & men from the cruelties of their captivity has been uppermost in our thoughts.

We are thankful that this longed for day has arrived, & that back in the old country you will be able once more to enjoy the happiness of a home & to see good days among those who anxiously look for your return.

George R. I.[8]

"What a wonderful life," thought Patterson. He loved the army: learning new skills, dressing up in a fancy uniform and tall boots, being treated as an officer. It all went to his head. He returned to England with fantastic plans for an army career. The entire world beckoned and if the army wanted to pay his way, he was anxious to go. But his dream did not meet with approval in England. His mother wanted him closer to home. Finally, his guardian uncle, Alfred Coates, set him straight: there was no future in the army. So Patterson went to St. John's College at Oxford to take advantage of his scholarship and become educated.

Although Oxford offered everything a young man could want intellectually, Patterson was not really ready to buckle down and learn. Diversions were everywhere. The pubs, gardens and countryside provided entertainment without end. Oxford relaxed its rules for the veterans, so for seven terms Patterson's class lived life to the full. Following the lead of other students, he went off to Switzerland for winter sports and there fell in love with high mountains. Attempting to justify his Europeon trips, he took French lessons with the idea of taking the Diplomatic Service exams. Personalized instruction from young women in cafes soon replaced the formal language lessons.

Back in England, he studied political science and philosophy but his heart remained in the mountains. Books on the Alps soon filled his studies. Quite by accident, perhaps, he was honing his research skills. He also entertained himself playing golf and cricket, punting on quiet rivers with pretty women friends, pursuing archery, tipping the wine cup and dazzling young girls with tales of his adventures.

Although scholarship seemed a secondary occupation at St. John's, Patterson managed a respectable grade considering his seven terms of sloth. During the last few weeks he memorized everything in sight, especially anything to do with Napoleon's 1806 Jena campaign. He later wrote that his "highly creditable second" put him into the category of a student who "had tried for a first and failed, either because he was incapable of using his brain or because he had allowed the locust to consume his days."[9]

The walls of the Bank of England loomed large the day he entered its gates as a probationer. If only he had learned French, German and Spanish he could have pursued a diplomatic career. But that was in the past, so he entered the bank prepared for a life in business. How he managed to learn anything about financial affairs at the Bank of England, Patterson never knew. Sacks of cash came and went. Cheques made their mysterious rounds through offices with no apparent reason. Gold bars from sunken ships appeared on some days. Strange customs and costumes dominated the entire system. He was eventually invited into the council room and commended for his work. A director of the bank later told Patterson's wife he had "done very well at the Bank of England."[10] He never knew why he had deserved such praise. Somehow he had earned the prospect of a promotion and could look forward to a long, illustrious career with the bank. According to Patterson, his only major contribution was a game. Each morning a few men threw a round of darts in the gallery of the chief accountant's office. Lunch at the George and Vulture awaited the arm with the greatest skill at launching the dart at the target. Then it was back to work.

When not at work, Patterson wandered the countryside in pursuit of adventure. He rode horses and lunched with friends at Doctor Butler's Head and at the George and Vulture. The gang once purchased a five-ton sloop that gave them less trouble than the rented horses. After work they often took a train to Oxford where they punted on the rivers Cherwell and Isis, drank and returned sleepless in time for work the next morning. Many were the days when the bank was short-changed for its investment in Patterson. Time passed in a pleasant haze.

R. M. Patterson at Oxford, 1919.

Then came the day when a strange envelope arrived in the mail. Posted from South Africa, it announced that Henry Patterson, his long lost father, was coming to London to visit on "mining business."[11] After an absence of twenty-three years, a stranger was dropping into his life, professing to be the father who took a sliver out of his thumb twenty-four years earlier.

Young Patterson chose to meet his hero at the Cock Tavern on Fleet Street. Sure enough, it reminded his father of his early days as a young newspaperman. Over the next few weeks they became fast friends: Father told stories about Africa and they visited the geological museum together on Saturdays. Gradually, Patterson was absorbing his father's lust for prospecting and world travel.

Patterson was taking Spanish lessons at the time with plans for visiting Central and South America, but quit when Father suggested he should explore the Empire instead. Finally, the elder Patterson left the "grey desert of stone"[12] in London and returned to South Africa. The son considered following his father, but could not hurt his mother's feelings. He never

33

told her of his father's visit. Father and son corresponded for a time, then the letters stopped. More than a decade later, after chasing down an obscure reference in an article, Patterson learned his father had died penniless in Johannesburg.

The time for making decisions arrived when Henry Patterson returned to South Africa. Raymond took a holiday in the north of England where he read Stefansson's *Hunters of the Great North*. The Mackenzie and Athabasca rivers came alive to the city man. In contrast, the train back to gloomy London only depressed him.

He decided a full life was not measured in years but by adventures. Walks in the countryside only served to bolster his resolve. He was nearly twenty-five years old. It was time to get on with life before it was over. He later told his daughter Janet that although there was much in the old city of London that amused him, in the end he "could not face a future of regular hours, train schedules and concrete."[13] It was "time to get away from the ant heap before I succeeded there and before it held me through my active days."

With great trepidation, Patterson asked for a meeting with the director of the Bank of England who had nominated him as a probationer. In an intimidating office, Patterson stood stiffly and informed Sir Edward Peacock of his plans to leave for Canada. Silence greeted his announcement. Finally, the dignified Canadian looked up. "I think that it will be a great adventure" came his reply as he stood, smiled and offered his handshake.[14]

Homesteading
1924 to 1926

GREAT adventures began almost the moment Patterson stepped on Canadian soil. Within months of arriving, Patterson found himself benighted in northern Alberta. As darkness fell the ex-employee of the Bank of England headed for a copse of trees. Travelling light, he carried only a bit of food, the makings for tea, a book and a blanket. He pushed over dead trees for firewood, dragged them into camp and lit a roaring blaze and settled in for the long winter night. On a mat of spruce branches he ate bannock—an old voyageur's flour and baking soda bread—cheese and raisins. Sweet tea washed everything down and warmed his body. He read himself to sleep. The temperature dropped to -33° Fahrenheit that night. Morning snapped him to attention with a cold start and off he set again. That first cold winter had forced him to begin "learning the ways of a new and strange country."[1]

Patterson spent a carefree half-decade in Canada from 1924 to 1929. He laboured on a farm, in a lumber camp and on his homestead, learned to survive cold winters and bug-infested summers, and spent many beautiful days in spring and fall exploring the new land. Settling down was far from his mind. Marriage, a family and a responsible business life were even more distant. These were his years to live as he pleased. Good financial fortune allowed him to pursue diversions as they arose.

This immigrant came with more than a few extra pieces of baggage. In the trunk with work clothes and woollens he packed fancy dress duds, more suitable for life in the bank or a party in an English castle. Putting on the ritz was easy for him. He also brought books and magazines. Although the Oxford degree was not of the highest calibre, it impressed his neighbours. Old-world clothes, books and an education, however, had not prepared him for the wild nature of the Canadian west. From books he had learned the myths, but not the reality. Immigration agents had also provided information, which was usually misleading, of endlessly fertile lands and temperate winters.

Public relations schemes did not influence Patterson's choice of Canada over Australia or New Zealand. As he recalled fifty years later, relatives had turned his attention to Canada. "I had a great uncle in Ottawa and cousins in Toronto. They always came over, bringing Canadian presents, Canadian books, some Indian trophy, sweetmeats or maple sugar with cranberries inside them, and I began to think Canada was a wonderful place."[2]

The Canada that greeted him as he walked off the S.S. *Lancastria* at Montreal was everything he imagined and much, much more. Coming from a small island nation, Patterson was impressed by the size of the country. He crossed the continent by train to reach his first job on the west coast. It took two days to span the Canadian Shield from Toronto to Winnipeg, "Gateway to the Canadian West." Another travel day took him across the prairies to Calgary, another through the Rocky Mountains to the port of Vancouver.

Patterson already had a job near Abbotsford before he left England: the Soldier Settlement Board had placed him on a dairy to learn the ropes as a hired hand. Generally, British migrants did not do well as farmers in the Canadian west. Most came from cities and innocently believed the false advertising sponsored by the railways and the Canadian government. Many quit farming and moved to town. Others demanded return passage to England.

Situated on recently drained land in the Sumas Lake area near Abbotsford, the dairy supplied milk, butter and eggs to neighbouring communities and to Vancouver. Just as Patterson arrived from England, Roy Scott from Prince Edward Island was also hired on at the farm. They found learning to milk by hand a painful process. Hands are not shaped for milking. With a most unnatural action, one must squeeze fingers and the thumb together around the teat, not all at once but in a sequential manner that coaxes the milk out. The milker must tug gently, avoid the swishing tail and the flying hoof, keep track of the pail and stool, and milk quickly enough so the cow does not withhold her milk in disgust.

Patterson and Scott worked for a "down-trodden relic of a good-looking man; and his wife…a woman with a soul above cooking." It was not that she didn't know how to cook, because guests always ate well, but she was often too busy with flower shows to cook edible food for the hired men. Other quirks of the place irked the wage labourers so much they quit in disgust, confirmed in their determination to end their days doing anything but coaxing milk from ornery stock. The weeks before Patterson and Scott left in late 1924 for greener pastures included many adventures. A letter home provides details.

British Columbia is now living up to its guide book reputation…I am now a hearty brown & my arms brick red & now, at the end of a long day, I have the living room of Scott's & my house in sole possession & am writing by lamplight at the open window in my breeches, stockings & khaki shirt—a clean one as I had a bath in the dairy last night—poured buckets of cold water over myself & felt much refreshed. I haven't worn a collar or tie since I came here for which relief much thanks.

Today has been gorgeous. I roused up about 5:15 a.m. owing to the hooves thundering past the window of my room & on looking out I saw Kate doing wanton destruction in the flower garden so I sallied forth & led her captive back to the stable. I fed the horses, calves & pigs, milked my cows—I have four now to cope with, morning & evening—& generously allowed a guest of the house to drive the milk to the stations inwardly thanking the good Lord for implanting this strange desire in his heart. Then Scott & I cleaned & dressed ourselves nicely & set off to the mountain with my well travelled Sussex haversack containing chocolate, beef & bread & butter sandwiches, eggs, apples & a large bottle of milk. We roused a lot of pheasants & an enormous eagle from the roadside & then started to climb & took the old trail, blocked every few yards by fallen trees but now used again by the bootleggers, for the Columbia Valley. At 500 feet, about, we stood on the frontier, a slash forty feet broad through the forest & a wire fence on the plain below dividing the fields & running away far as we could see—running across all America for that matter—& then crossed over into Washington State. We had our lunch & lazed on a little alp 1000 feet above the Sumas valley & looking down both into that & the Columbia Valley."

From that vantage point they gazed on a scene where forest fires had burned much of the land. Mosquitoes were noticeable by their absence.

…we reached home in time to see the bull do a stampede all on his own. Highly interesting. He smashed up a gate, a fence & himself & now is in stall—a saddened animal, bearing no malice but obviously cursing himself for a fool. As Scott observed, theatres & picture shows are superfluous on a farm.

Friday was the notable day of the week. I began by driving Kate & the milk cart, fully laden, over a milk pail which the breeze rolled playfully down hill. Kate, the cart, the milk & I were reversed with a resounding crash. I retrieved three whole cans from the wreckage—about 12 gallons went west entirely—leaving Kate, who is reliable, to fend for herself. She, however, was unable to avoid breaking up the harness & I never expected really to reach the station that morning. After that I retired from public life till lunch time & spent the morning with Kate & Florrie ploughing with the walking plough. Scott took his turn at the chores & just had the stables & the barn nice & smart when the boss had all the cows brought in for an inspection & Scott apparently asked him how in hell he expected his stables kept clean & nice if he brought his cows in at any old minute of the day. They then had words on other matters while the cows seized the golden opportunity to get into the pot garden. When brought out of this they stampeded madly round & round the barn—Canadian cows seem to be more energetic than their English forbears. I saw the pandemonium from afar & wondered if rabies had broken out…. Finally a young pigling died on us & Scott dropped half a dollar in a ten gallon can of cream & lacked the time to retrieve his coin.

This sounds like comic opera but I only give you a few outstanding incidents. My first day on the plough I laboured far into the sunset, hatless & bent on keeping the accursed weapon from turning either to the right or to the left. I have the art in mastery now—also that of milking, though indeed I did tonight have words with my Jersey cow—an animal misnamed Darling. I can't yet think what she wanted but anyhow she was very cross-grained over something….

I am well & having the time of my life & like the work. I shall not of course spend all my time in this small farming district but, before I come home in the fall of next year, shall take in a harvesting on the prairie….

Be sure & write & tell me all the news.

Scott & I are becoming pretty good friends—we hope not to lose sight of each other.

Love from Raymond[3]

Scott and Patterson were not typical hired hands: they sent laundry to Abbotsford with the mailman for his mother to wash. Socks they rinsed out every second day. For diversion they once hiked to Whatcom Road and spent a dollar on ginger ale and tobacco. Scott noted, "one of the main blessing of the Sumas Valley is that the hired men are totally unable to get rid of their earnings."

At this stage Patterson still retained his English values. Informed that his mother's maid banged the silver, was deaf and had bad manners, he insisted she be replaced: "…I can't imagine anybody less suited to you. I wanted you to have a nice, smart, up to date maid who would impart a certain amount of tone to the proceedings. I do hope you will have one when I come home. I can rough it with anybody when I am out for roughing it but when I come in to civilisation my idea of hardship will be, as someone has aptly put it, to be compelled to ring the bell twice for a water. For heavens sake don't have any more oddities in the house & in the meantime don't let this one run riot over my things."[4]

Late in May came the first chance to shoot pigeons. Patterson's nose had just recovered from London's pollution and he had not sneezed for weeks. Then, while shooting at a bird, he got clobbered on the nose by the cranky old weapon. But despite the problems with the gun, roast pigeon graced the dinner table.[5]

Patterson and Scott left for Alberta a few days later, enticed by a brochure extolling the virtues of the Peace River country in northwestern Alberta. After giving the dairyman two weeks' notice to hire replacements, they boarded the train for Alberta in early June 1924. The trip east through the Rockies was spectacular. Winter was only just beginning to give up its stranglehold on the Rogers and Kicking Horse passes. Through snowsheds and the Connaught and Spiral tunnels the train strained on steep grades, and sped above precipitous drops and through massive snow banks. At Field, passengers stretched their legs and admired incredible peaks. While some stayed at Mount Stephen House or visited nearby Emerald Lake, the dairy escapees hurried on to the prairies where homesteads prospered and grain grew without fail.

The Peace River country was the "last best west" in Canada. Originally, the Canadian Pacific Railway planned to send its tracks through Fort Edmonton and over the Athabasca Pass to the Pacific. Cost cutting in the early 1880s forced the CPR to choose a more direct and shorter route through Calgary in the southern prairies. As a result, settlement land in northwestern Alberta lay untouched for another half century. The Peace River area had to wait for another transcontinental line to put track through Edmonton before developers could extend the Edmonton, Dunvegan and B.C. Railroad to the northwest.

In the 1920s, ten years before the Depression of the 1930s that caused worldwide hardship, a drought in the southern Canadian prairies began. Wheat prices plummeted from $2.31 per bushel in 1919 to $0.77 in 1922.

As southern Alberta dried up and blew into Montana, thousands of settlers abandoned homesteads and flocked to the Peace River country. The frontier's population more than doubled during the 1920s to 44,000, almost a tenth of Alberta's inhabitants.

The Alberta to which Patterson and Scott immigrated was agriculturally based. A farmer's government, the United Farmers of Alberta, ruled provincially. The oil industry, based in the Turner Valley oilfield southwest of Calgary, was still young. Coal was the king of fuel. Alberta was desperate for immigrants to develop its resources. Although not the best settlers, the British were the socially preferred immigrants at that time. Also, Great War veterans could receive a Soldier Settlement of 320 acres of free land and a $1500 loan toward machinery, stock and construction supplies.[6]

With these incentives buoying their spirits, green homesteaders Patterson and Scott walked out of Peace River town, headed northwest. Patterson intended to reach Fort Vermilion in the far reaches of northern Alberta near the Northwest Territories, but Scott convinced him to choose land in the Little Prairie region of the Peace River country. The lure of the North had to wait a bit longer.

After paying his five-dollar filing fee on 320 acres at the land office in Peace River, Patterson bought supplies and building materials and freighted them to the homestead. There he and Scott threw up a sixteen by thirty-two foot log cabin on a ridge just as the full fury of a northern summer hit. Thunderstorms alternated with hot weather and the legendary hordes of insects made collecting timber for the cabin a trial. The report to Mother read, "…These trees usually grow by streams & in swamps & muskeg & consequently as I wallowed about I raised a cloud of mosquitoes, sandflies, botflies, bulldogs & any other kind of insect that felt like coming along with me—which they all did & did meal very heartily off me & raised a many lump…."[7] They slaved on until August, then headed for town, anxious to earn harvest wages.[8]

A drink changed their lives when friendly George Macrae bought their beer at Macnamara's Hotel in Peace River and convinced them to work at his lumber camp at Driftpile on Lesser Slave Lake. There they worked ten-hour days for three months. Twice Patterson narrowly avoided death or serious injury at the hands of the machinery.[9]

Back at the homestead they finished the cabin and settled in for a cold winter. In many ways the year 1924 had not yet arrived in the Peace River area. Primitive transportation systems made it feel much more like the 1890s. Creaking wagons followed plodding oxen along the trails that snaked over virgin prairie. Except for a "scattering of rampant individualists" in widely separated cabins, the land was uninhabited and remained in its natural state. Open prairie alternated with patches of forest. Hills and bluffs, creeks and coulees all gave cover for plentiful game such as moose, deer and bear. An afternoon saunter with a shotgun readily put a prairie chicken on the dinner table.

R. M. Patterson and Roy Scott at Macrae's Lumber Camp, 1924.

Oxen pulling walking ploughs broke the native grass for crops. Settlers seeded small fields with hand-cranked broadcasters worn around the neck. If rain and sun came on schedule, grasshoppers ate elsewhere and fall waited until its time, homesteaders got a good crop. They threshed grain by hand, tossing it into the air with a shovel to separate the kernels from the chaff. Oats were the crop of choice as feed for horses and oxen.

Patterson was happy in the sparsely populated frontier. For most settlers, land was an investment. Summer toil and residency were necessary to meet the homestead agreement with the government. Settlers worked as wage labourers part of each year. In winter, trapping tapped the abundant fur supplies and provided extra income. The system worked well for the footloose English bachelor. With a total tax bill of $4.50 on his 320 acres, Patterson's land investment did not drain his pocketbook.[10]

Opportunities for amusement were surprisingly varied. Casual visits with neighbours were typical of country life. Dances drew a full house. Home brew was more common than store-bought liquor. Basket socials offered a way for the young to court, with women auctioning off a picnic meal—and the opportunity to eat it in their charming company—to the highest bidder. July Sports Day was another annual highlight. When all else failed to entertain, an expedition to the town of Peace River, 80 miles away, promised diversion at the bar.[11]

Sometimes the amusement came unsolicited. A letter home in the fall of 1924 reviewed the Duke of Devonshire's visit to Peace River. Unfortunately, his host was off on a drunk, "...so the Duke came unwelcomed to the Waterhole &, not liking to make a fuss, went to a hotel kept by a Chink. He pleaded at least for clean sheets but the Chink said 'Last man him no complain. You no like can go.' Finally, the truth leaked out & the married women of the place rallied round & fixed him up."[12]

Housewarmings also filled everyone with good cheer. After a few final touches to the cabin on the ridge, the residence Patterson named "Hardfire Hill" was ready for a party. First, the neighbours moved everything outdoors to make room for flying feet. The cookstove roared to life in the open, heating pots of coffee and steaming away like a runaway caboose. Inside, candles and lamps shone with festive brilliance through the windows and the open door. Whites, natives and Métis all mingled in one great crush of humanity. Stomping feet kept time with the scratchy fiddles as George Robertson called the square dances all night long. Supper break came at midnight and then they were back at it again, stomping with gusto about the sturdy plank floor, testing the strength of the cellar trapdoor to its fullest. Finally, when dawn began to brighten the eastern sky, they closed the door, blanketed the windows and danced on until daylight flooded the land. Then the guests acted as house movers once again, refilling the cabin with furnishings.[13]

Patterson's most exciting escapade as a homesteader came while mounted on a wildly galloping horse, charging through a dark night into "some Fifth Dimension where demigods could fly and horses went on forever."[14] His mount was a fine mare he named The Urchin. This cranky animal bucked without notice, or chose any unsuspecting moment to "rear up and fling herself backwards" in an attempt to impale her rider on the saddle horn.[15]

The other participant in this adventure was called Johnny Arnold, although his actual surname, Arnault, linked him to French and Cree parents of voyageur days gone by. One day he offered Patterson a drink, but first they had to ride for the Englishman's own bottle of Scotch from another settler. Drinks with a house full of Norwegians, the Russian and others followed. Then dancing broke out, and food appeared along with an unlimited supply of coffee. When Arnold and Patterson finally left, darkness was upon them. As their horses bolted for home, Johnny challenged Patterson to a race, trying to convince him to sell the spirited mare. Lashing their mounts on with quirts and yelling at the top of their lungs, they sped through the night, crossing bridges with a thunder of hooves on the planks. A shotgun blast from an irate settler renewed their vigorous flight. At one place they stopped to buy eggs. Off again, with his rider carrying a dozen fragile orbs in a small cloth sack, Johnny's mount surged forward and crushed two of the eggs on his rider's nose. As they began to ooze from the sack and drip, Johnny held them out to the side of his body where the sticky bag only added to the frightened steed's anxiety. Urged on by adrenaline and fear, the horses raced to Johnny's cabin. Eggs and rum whipped up into eggnogs polished off the night. A brief morning sleep by the creek refreshed a bleary-eyed Patterson, and after tea and leftover cake from the previous night The Urchin and her master went home, very, very quietly.[16]

The end of October found Patterson in Edmonton, staying in the Hotel Selkirk, "second hotel here after the [CNR Hotel] Macdonald." From there, he purchased supplies for the coming winter. "I have been preparing— hard. All yesterday & today I have been buying & my room looked like pandemonium. A large wooden box is up there that I have caused to be made & the place is just stiff with stuff—I came out of the bush with a goodly wad of dollars, fortunately."

Among his most notable purchases were six egg cups, "a beautiful .303 Lee Enfield Canadian Sporting Model rifle," a year's supply of toothpaste, Pickwick Papers, Vanity Fair & Lord Jim, "traps & a housewife." Not a companion, this last item was a small sewing kit. "These are a few of the oddments—& I haven't finished yet by any means. The strain is beginning to tell upon the accumulative Scotch part of me but at 3:30 on Monday I leave this city for the edge of the North &, if all goes well, I shall not see Edmonton again till I am on my way home…."

While shopping, he found his appetite was down considerably from his usual consumption. His menu for Friday, October 24, 1924, consisted of an apple upon rising. At 8:45 he breakfasted on porridge and cream, Finnan haddie and fried potatoes (a terrific helping), two poached eggs, five slices of toast, two cups of coffee and cream. Lunch at 2 p.m. began with deep apple pie and whipped cream and a pot of cream and vanilla ice cream, all drowned in coffee and still more cream. Another apple snack late afternoon rounded out the diet. Dinner at 6:45 p.m. began with rolls and butter, a bowl of chicken broth, liver and bacon and potatoes in jackets, deep apple pie and whipped cream as well as coffee and cream followed by still more apples just before turning in. "Of course breakfast <u>was</u> a bit large. The food is beautifully cooked & served—it seems to be so all over Canada. Cream is a thing of no account—they almost give it away. If the menu seems a little odd & barbarous you must remember that I have been for some time removed from A la carte...."[17]

A month later, back at the cabin with his haul, he wrote of winter's beauty. "I saw a funny thing a few weeks ago when it was very cold—a complete arch of light in the sky the shape of a horseshoe magnet, passing over the sun & coming straight down to the horizon on each side—I have seen it on the covers of Jack London's books & other novels of the north. Little Dunk said it was a Far-hand Arch & that people said 'Far-hand Arch, near-hand storm.' It usually means a change in the weather & is a lovely thing to see. What with the Sun Dogs, the Aurora & the Far-hand Arch my education is progressing....

"The Indians say this open weather will last a bit yet. There is a bare powdering of snow that fell the other night—nothing more."[18]

December can be a long month in a lonely log cabin. Chopping wood and hauling water from the creek consume only a small part of the day. Letters home mention idle time for chores, and chances to hone skills and pursuits often overlooked during warmer days.

"I have been lazy in letter writing these last few days as I unearthed, in my unpacking, Joseph Conrad's 'Lord Jim' which I had bought in Edmonton & had started in the train on the way in. Perfect English, which one so rarely meets nowadays, & draws on all the time—I keep saying 'Just one more chapter & then I'll go to bed'—which is as it used to be when I was little & you read to me. I shall finish it tonight & know the ending of it....

"I am getting a master in the figures of the square dance. The music of the fiddle & the rising & falling notes of the caller make it a thing apart.

"I put on one more pair of socks this morning, making three now. One of those lighter kind that Carpenter makes I wear next to me—then a lovely thick Hudson's Bay sock on top of that & then another Hudson's Bay over both. In these & a moccasin walking is beautifully soft & easy....

"Thank heavens I can cook a little—there must be men who would be utterly helpless if confronted suddenly with an uncooked bean."[19]

When holidays rolled around, Patterson was once again in the most civilized surroundings the town of Peace River could provide. From a base at Macnamara's Hotel, he visited and wished all a Merry Christmas. On December 21 he danced with Mrs. McLeod. The next day he watched an ice hockey game and the curious sport called curling, where otherwise respectable people sweep ice with a broom after hurling a rock down a sheet of ice. "Got a little Christmas grubstake—almonds & raisins, cheese, candies, jam, marmalade, Worchester sauce, pickles, lime juice (lemons would freeze solid) Scotch, Jamaica rum & herrings."[20]

During the next two days he travelled from Peace River town through various frontier landmarks including Horseshoe Slough and The Muskeg on the Christmas trail toward home.

A photograph taken at Clear Hills Post on Patterson's first Christmas Day in Canada shows quite the character, one he named the Greenhorn Homesteader: shirtsleeves rolled to his elbows, a striped tie, a tall Tom Mix hat and woollen trousers tucked into heavy woollen socks inside moccasins. Only a skiff of snow covered the ground outside the trading post where he celebrated with his new friends.

The Greenhorn Homesteader at Clear Hills Post, Christmas Day, 1924.

Undoubtedly, many others descended on Clear Hills Post that winter day. As the only general store within a day's ride, it accepted furs on trade and provided meals at any hour. The Stonehewer family farmed there, having acquired it sight unseen in trade for a fruit farm. Although commerce was one draw, the biggest attraction was the gorgeous school teacher from Calgary. Suitors from every direction swarmed to the trading post, ostensibly to shop. Business boomed during the two years she taught school. Try as they might, the diligent bachelors could not convince the lovely young city girl to trade an urban future for a lonely log cabin on the edge of the wilderness. Indeed, only two white women lived in the entire area and both were married to settlers.[21]

As 1925 drew near, Patterson's eventful first nine months in Canada also came to a close. In exchanging his fancy surroundings at the Bank of England for a rough-hewn shack on the frontier, Emily Patterson's only son had carved out a new life for himself. During the next few months he roamed far and wide throughout the community, visiting and generally entertaining himself and others as he got to know his small part of Canada.

His abilities as a quick study, willing worker, smart businessman and good storyteller were appreciated and much admired. He even tried out his internal furnace and slept in the trees on a cold winter's night while walking to town.

Although Patterson learned much from his neighbours, he was also an education to them. A Brit with an Oxford degree in the Canadian west was unusual. Interest in his story grew with the telling and his reputation expanded far beyond that which a strict interpretation of the facts might allow. One version had him a wealthy heir to a grand estate and castle in Scotland. But first, he had to homestead in the new country to prove himself worthy of the title and position that awaited him. Another story made him a fancy lawyer, recuperating from a mental collapse. The one Patterson liked best gave him a double first from Oxford, instead of the "highly creditable second" that he received for his last-minute memorization marathon. But perhaps the best fabrication rose from his lumber camp sojourn. After Patterson told off the foreman's son in very colourful language, the foreman threatened to put the Brit in his proper place. But Patterson's milking buddy Scott warned the foreman that Patterson was none other than a vicious criminal, wanted for a villainous murder. Together the stories mixed and propagated a reputation that most people came to respect.[22]

Mother on Summerhouse Hill, 1926.

Another side to this most unusual of homesteaders was his connection to the Old Country. Most settlers left Europe with only a few possessions and a small nest egg. For years they struggled to survive, eking out a marginal existence on the land. Winter traplines augmented by wage income from working on threshing crews or in lumber camps barely kept the small farms afloat. By comparison, Patterson was relatively affluent. His reputation as a man of money was not totally deserved because he never had much cash. But his clothing, manners, education, manner of speech and frequent forays to Peace River and cities all pointed toward financial backing. Few other settlers invested in shares in the Company of Adventurers and Explorers Trading into Hudson's Bay (the Hudson's Bay Company), or bought shares in other promising companies. Patterson did all these and also corresponded with Mother about investments. For the most part, he considered his Canadian adventure as self-supporting and did not rely on either his British investments or Mother's wealth to finance his homesteading venture and other Canadian exploits.

One major extravagance was his annual voyage to England. As an only son, Patterson's strong ties to his mother made it a priority to visit her often. His photo collection indicates he set sail from Halifax harbour in late winter of 1925. Back home, he lived life to the fullest: hiking with Mother and visiting Clovelly, Wells, Sonning and Marston Ferry with friends dressed to the nines. One photo shows him in top hat and tails, accompanied by a lovely young woman fashionably dressed and carrying a bouquet of flowers.

These social events were not just innocent fun. Mother, who wanted him married and soon, had begun matchmaking for a suitable partner. Patterson was also eyeing the prospects, but was not ready to settle down quite yet. For a time he dated an attractive, outgoing American woman. But Mother and the mother of another young woman conspired to arrange a proper relationship for their children. According to Marigold Portman, Patterson's future wife, they met at an afternoon tea at Mother's house, but the story of their first date is much more fun.

Dressed in their best, they attended the Covent Garden opera with their mothers on May 19, 1925. The tall, thin, good-looking wanderer with a smart moustache sat next to a radiant and cultured blond woman five years younger than her date. The opera was Tristan und Isolde and, according to Patterson, he could not understand why Kurneval stood at the window, singing for hours as he looked for an overdue ship. His date says he nodded off, snoring as he slept through the howling onstage that passed for the highbrow entertainment that his future wife found most pleasing. In spite of this ignominious meeting, affection developed between Miss Portman and Mr. Patterson. However, the homesteader's contract with the Canadian government called him back to the frontier and he was forced to continue the courtship by mail.[23]

On May 30, 1925, Patterson boarded the Canadian Pacific Railway's steamship, the Empress of Scotland, and returned to his cabin on the ridge. Letters to his boyhood friend Edwin Fenwick provide some details of

Marigold Portman on Gypsy, Fiddleford. February 24, 1928.

this next period of his life. They had each called the other by the nickname George since childhood. On July 28, 1925, Patterson wrote:

Dear George,

Some damned thing stuck a black muzzle in the open window about dawn the other morning & snarled but Bronzo [Patterson's other nickname] being very sleepy said Shoo! & apparently it navigated. Can't think what it was. I know it had to climb up so it may have been anything from a ground hog to a baby bear. Can't think what either could have been looking for....

His Excellency the Governor, Lord Byng of Vimy, passed within nine miles of here, on the Peace, some days ago. He didn't see me—the bush intervening. He was on his way to Aklavik & should be getting roasted & eaten alive on the Mackenzie within the Arctic circle by now....[24]

In the fall his news included a promise of a temporary abstinence from bad habits, notes from a hunting trip and comments on the province's silver anniversary.

I laid off all strong drink & all tobacco on the 16th September—resumption to be had on Christmas Day. There will be a massacre—I know it—because I owe wassail to many a thirsty trapper & intend to pay in full. Then I am spending New Year in Peace River with a McLeod & when the Grampions—or wherever the benighted tribe has its stomping ground—meet the Lammermuirs then we shall indubitably see something notable. Also I go in with two Norwegians....

Went out a week or so ago & hunted up a steer of mine on the range. The animal was remarkably wild & active so we pursued it in sleighs. I fired four times, each shot—.303 soft nosed—clean through the head as we travelled but only the last touched the spot. Damned nice beef. I have half outside now frozen, up in the poplar trees....

The province of Alberta celebrated its 20th birthday this year being created out of the North West Territories in 1905. So it built itself a walloping great house of parliament high above the Saskatchewan River in Edmonton, & now, instead of being governed by the Mounted Police from Regina, we run ourselves like a real country—only more cleverly, most politicians retiring rich.[25]

A few days later he reported on the federal election. As a lifelong Conservative, he took his duties very seriously.

We had a dominion election on October 29th [1925]. The riding of Peace River which is well larger than the British Isles returns one member to Ottawa....

Bronzo was scrutineer for the Conservative party in this township & also clerk of the poll—the storekeeper, Joe Bissett, being the registrar or something—I forget exactly what. Population was scarce as all those with no blasted barns, wells & fence posts to hold them are out after the fur. There was a rush of business about 11.0 a.m. when four of us voted & a second rush at about 3.0 p.m. when Mr. Benoit Laboucanne drove up with his dogs from Hay River & cast his vote—remind me to tell you about that sometime—total number of votes five—& we closed the poll about half past four having become bored with the thing. Legally it opens at eight & shuts at six but the clerk of the poll had six miles to go to the store & failed to see the sense of going there in the sub zero darkness. Also he shot a partridge by the Battle & it went down among some willows & was difficult to find, the election being consequently impeded.[26]

In spite of Patterson's work as a scrutineer for the Conservatives, the Liberals took the riding. "Our election was finely cooked—Indians (dead these twenty years) rose from their graves at Whitefish Lakes & voted—

residence by Lethe & Styx having apparently made them all of the Liberal persuasion."[27]

Fall turned into winter and once again Patterson spent Christmas with the menagerie of settlers on the frontier. Roy Scott had quit the homestead so the cabin on the ridge became Patterson's private residence. Much remained to do: logs were needed for the barn and posts for the corrals and fences. After packing a few supplies and his tarp and bedroll, Patterson headed into the bush. For building logs, he chose firekilled lumber—a decision that nearly cost him his life. He had set up camp in the midst of a dead Jackpine forest, sleeping and eating close to the work. One night a big wind blew through the dead wood and knocked down a sixty foot-high tree that crashed to the ground near his lean-to. Shards of broken branches screamed through the air and a large missile landed by the fire. He quickly moved camp the next morning, adding to his list of frontier rules: never make camp in an old burn.[28]

With a horse and sled, Patterson skidded the fenceposts and building logs home in the late winter and by spring, 1926, construction was well under way. Up went the barn, no mean feat without assistance, but by this time he was learning to do heavy tasks alone. The fences and corrals were less daunting, although they consumed many more hours as the days lengthened. That spring he also dug a well 42 feet deep and four feet square and cribbed it with lumber.[29] Other settlers had passed on this half section of land, fearing a lack of water, but Patterson's luck held and his well was shallow.

Good fortune seemed to follow the recent British immigrant, but luck also travels closely with good planning and intelligence. As the incident in the firekilled forest proved, one must always learn from near disaster. Another time, while riding The Urchin and packing a wood auger as well as carrying a dozen eggs in a small sack, Patterson mounted the saddle and caught his pants on the auger. His unpredictable mare immediately took advantage of the strange situation and began bucking and whirling. Luckily his pant leg tore and he flew through the air, landing face down on the eggs on a busy anthill. What a mess! This led him to write, "Think, especially when you are Alone, what the Consequences may be of any Action, however Simple."[30] He learned the lesson well and it became part of the strange mix of skills and wisdom that allowed him to survive a most unusual summer adventure the next year.

Planning for his 1927 northern adventure began that winter of 1926. Maps covered his crude table while coal-oil lamps and strategically placed candles held down the corners. His neighbours and friends encouraged him to avoid the big northern rivers totally, lest he perish. Still, the maps showed the Peace River that flowed within sight of his cabin draining into the Slave River and Great Slave Lake. From its western end, the Mackenzie River continued north and west until at Fort Simpson it almost doubled in size at its confluence with the mighty waters of the Liard. A unique river, the Liard rises in the Coast Range near the Pacific Ocean and punches its way through the massive Rocky Mountains on its way east and north to join the Mackenzie for its trek to the Beaufort Sea and the Arctic Ocean. Patterson reckoned that by putting a canoe into the nearby Peace River, he could float to the land of his dreams. Down the mighty Mackenzie he would paddle before turning northwest up the Liard. As he neared the mountains he would leave the charted territory on the map and turn right at a tributary whose name—the South Nahanni—held fear and terror and the promise of gold.

Meanwhile, until he could organize his northern escape, the homesteader improved his land and entertained himself. Letters to Edwin indicate he had invested spare cash in the Canadian Pacific Railway Company, only to receive immediately after a HBC offer of "a new issue of capital at special rates to existing shareholders." Anxious to maximize on an investment that was returning healthy dividends—20% in 1925, but it had been as high as 45% in 1922—he added what he could to his fur trade shares and lived from a rather light purse for the rest of the year.[31]

A March letter included a rather spirited rebuttal of Edwin's suggestion that he should settle and begin a writing career.

> I'm grieved to hear that you have a wireless. I think those things are of the Evil One & they certainly are Hell in the Home. Does yours function properly? What I mean is—has science made any recent strides in that direction or does the thing still inform you that a poah little girl at Blythe was severely scalded this afternoon by an overturning gurk plop, but has been removed with all possible speed, for proper treatment, to the infirmary at gurk plop?
>
> I prefer my news by way of The Morning Post, Punch & The Pink 'Un. By the way, one of the Winged Hats [Scandinavians] was deeply immersed in the Morning Post the other day & looking frightfully worried. He asked me whether the Lloyd Georgian land proposals, if they ever became law, would have any effect in this country. I told him, no. 'Vell' he said 'I am

a citizen not only of Canada but of the whole Empire now, & I am not so certain. But I will draw out my title deeds from the Bank & then if any doggone son of a moose comes to tell me that my land is not mine, then I vill shoot him dead.' That seemed to me sound sense.

Whoever told you that the Canadian duty is £9 on 250 cigarettes? I believe I pay about $5 on 200 of my South Africans & ordinarily smoke very little.

I have no atlas here—a state of affairs that must be remedied as I have never yet lived without one, & now I want to know where Curacao is. Is it in the Dutch East Indies or somewhere in the Caribbean? I see that the New Zealand line Rauhine etc.—call there.

As to getting married & writing books I don't know that I have any great aptitude for either. There was a time when I was convinced that the opposite sex had wings & an issue of at least one harp to— roughly—every three. And the more I see of them the more do I think that the contrary is the case & that we are the winged ones. So bang goes that ideal.

There are so many Jolly things to do in the world before getting tewed up with a lass or mewed up amongst ones books. Later on the latter may come of necessity.[32]

Two months later he foreshadowed his eventual decision to retire in Canada. "But if the country [England] is simply going to go to the devil then I think it is a wiser thing to base oneself in this country & make a home in that wonderland of waters around Victoria B.C."[33]

Since 1926 Mother had been pressuring her only son to make some life decisions. In response, he had defended his choice to stick with the homestead. "No, I don't intend to live here always. But I want to have this place for my own—partly as an investment & partly as a standby in case of adversity. When I have put in the time & the work on it, it passes to me outright & it would always be a home in the case of need. Or in after years I can sell it, when the country is opened up, & always get my money back on it & more, to say nothing of the new health & all the experience I have gained from it. During my two years in London I felt always rottener & rottener & in the end I think that life would have killed me. It was awful. Here—when I am hot & dusty & tired or half frozen & hungry, & when things are going awkwardly I can always find consolation in the thought of the City—not the George & Vulture—& how much worse off I might be.

"By the way, while I think of it, don't send me my £59 at midsummer. You must need it & I don't want it, as I don't suppose that I shall go to Calgary to the show this year now. I seem to have too much work to do, & perhaps we could go together some time. It is the best show of its kind in the West. I don't suppose I shall leave the Peace River now until October when I leave for home….

"Nobody walks briskly for exercise here—if they can dodge it. The native born will pursue his horse for an hour in the pasture rather than walk a mile to the store."[34]

By the time summer arrived, it was common knowledge in Little Prairie that Patterson had made up his mind to end his life on a voyage into the northern wilderness. Many tried to dissuade him. John Petersen was most adamant that he not go North and die in a canoe or in the jaws of a bear, encouraging him, instead, to stay home and help the other settlers make sense of the encroaching civilization. He told Patterson to find himself a pretty woman to marry, bring her back and set her up as the community postmistress. What with a few chickens and the mail to sort, she would be a very happy woman indeed.[35]

Patterson's answer was to leap on The Urchin and gallop off for Peace River. A train ride and a car trek later, he arrived in Calgary in time for the annual frolic called the Calgary Stampede. There he watched a bronc named Cyclone catapult his rider head over heels, headfirst into the ground. A letter to Mother fills in the details about the rest of his trip.

Braemar Lodge
Calgary, AB
Wednesday, July 7th, 1926
Dear Mother,

I got safely in to Peace River after two days ride under a terribly strong sun—well into the nineties. I don't feel this heat like I used to but Peace River down in that deep valley was simply an oven. Couldn't get a sleeper on the train so I slept in the day coach & met a party of men there—gold prospectors, store keepers & trappers—from Fort Grahame on the Finlay River. They were coming out for their yearly visit to Edmonton for supplies & I am going back with them about July 20. I shall take the train from Edmonton to Prince George in northern British Columbia & meet Jim Ferguson, a Scots trapper, there. From there we are to go over the Giscome Portage & load the canoes at the head of the Crooked River, & then go downstream to Macleod Lake & Fort Macleod

& from there down the Parsnip River to Finlay Forks where it meets the Finlay to form the Peace. They will go on up the Finlay to Fort Grahame but I shall leave them at Finlay Forks & find some way of getting down the Peace by the Ne Parle Pas Rapids, Hudson's Hope, Fort St. John & Dunvegan to Peace River & so back to the Battle River in time to get in my crop. You can find it all I think in that atlas by following up the Peace from Peace River. The journey will cost me almost nothing, except for blankets etc. & I have always wished to make it, & meeting as nice a man as Jim Ferguson I took the chance. I will try to keep a diary of the trip & as soon as I reach Peace River I will post it to you. It will be a great experience & in July little can be done & life becomes almost impossible owing to heat & mosquitoes.

I came in to Edmonton at midday on Saturday & got hold of my things & met Dennis [France] & we left in the car about eight that night & by driving until one a.m. reached some unknown place which proved to be Ponoka where the provincial lunatic asylum is. Sunday drove on to Lacombe & from there to Gull Lake & had lunch by the shore. In the afternoon we left Lacombe & reached Calgary about eleven p.m. getting two cots in a room on the seventh floor of the Palliser, as the town is packed, & we couldn't get these rooms till Monday. We stopped for coffee & eggs & strawberries on the way here from Lacombe at Red Deer & Didsbury. I loved the country & especially round Red Deer—it all seemed so soft & civilised after the north country. Somewhere between Innisfail & Olds we came out onto a long hogs back shortly before sunset & right against the sun & looking over a tremendous purple range country that lay below us in the shadow I saw the Rockies against the sky 150 [70] miles away, standing out of a mist that lay around their feet. The most amazing sense of space as on the left in to the east was the rolling prairie looking very cold & blue. Just off to Banff.[36]

Three days later, writing on official, blue, Banff Springs Hotel stationery adorned with an engraving of the hotel and the Bow River looking downstream, he informed Mother of the delights of the Rockies and the strange and unusual people he had met in the mountain playground.

This is my last night here. Dennis left for Edmonton at midday with sandwiches & a flagon of Chianti & a drive of 300 miles ahead of him as he must be back at work by eight tomorrow morning. Some friends of his are here—an Englishman, Gordon Matthews & his little Canadian wife—young, & awfully nice people from Edmonton. They have their car & tent & everything with them & as I have not to be at Giscome Portage for six days or so & don't want to spend five July days in Edmonton on the sweltering plains & in Exhibition week too, I am going on with the Matthews further into the mountains & over the divide into British Columbia. We have all had as much high life as we can stand & so tomorrow we revert to a state of nature & camp as we go beside the lakes & streams. We are going to Marble Canyon & Johnson's Canyon & shall camp one night within reach of Chateau Lake Louise—another C.P.R. palace—& shall put on our dinner jackets & motor in for the dance....

On a more civilized topic, he noted the hot and cool pools at the Banff Springs Hotel were open until 11 each evening and lit with romantic lanterns.

You would love this place despite the curiously garbed Americans who tear through—mostly under the impression that this is the Great North & the back of beyond. The four of us last night gave a party to thirteen Americans from New York. We had dinner alone & danced together & turned my room into a bar & Gordon mixed them an R.F.C. [Royal Flying Corps] cocktail—invented in France. I have <u>never</u> heard anything like the hellish uproar that issued from this peaceful room—& they were only talking with their penetrating Manhattan voices. I think the women's voices have no equal in Christendom—I stood a yard from Gordon & I had to shout at him to make myself heard. We stood together & bellowed criticisms & personal remarks about our guests to each other & no man could hear a word we said except ourselves. They were an amazing bunch—one millionaire, two company directors, one rancher, two nondescript youths, odd things that came & went & wives, sisters & daughters. We met them yesterday originally in the swimming pool. I think if we had seem them fully & wonderfully clothed we might have been more careful. But we did them proud & plied them with the most amazing mixtures while watching ourselves with care. We bathed before breakfast & not one American was on view till midday.

You & I must try to come here sometime—it is a wonderful place & so, I believe, is Lake Louise.

Love from

Raymond[37]

R. M. Patterson at Gull Lake, Alberta, July 1926.

Nowhere in his writings does Patterson mention that Gordon and Mollie Matthews were on their honeymoon when they were introduced by Dennis France. Gordon was born in England in 1897 and came from a military family with connections to the Bengal Lancers. The Great War found him in England, both parents dead, living with an aunt and attending Wellington school. Lying his way into the military as a 17-year-old, Matthews delivered dispatches on his own motorcycle in the early days of the war.

On the day he enlisted in 1914, fate intervened and created an interesting story. Matthews had bought a Longines watch that morning and had packed it into his gear for shipment to France. At the last minute he was taken off the ship, a vessel the Germans later sank. Somehow, his gear floated ashore, his watch still intact and still working. Longines bought his heroic timepiece from him, gave him another and used the story in an advertising campaign.

A year later Matthews enlisted with the Royal Flying Corps and trained as a navigator and observer. Flying as part of a combined British and Canadian squadron, he befriended legends including Conn Farrel, Billy

Barker, Punch Dickins and Wop May. Shot down twice, he received the Croix de Guerre from the French government—a reward for an event he discounted as a "little incident." "They had to decorate somebody so the French gave it to me."[38] In later life he received the Order of the British Empire for his contribution to World War II efforts in Canada. Although wounded six times, Matthews' only visible signs of wartime injury were a broken big toe, a fractured nose that resulted in a prominent Roman-looking profile and back problems associated with shrapnel wounds. As a result of these injuries, he received a Veteran's Pension until his death.

While on recuperation leave and a publicity tour for the British Armed Forces in 1919, Matthews found himself in New York City on Armistice Day. He crossed the border into Canada and at Montreal took his discharge with the rank of Acting Major. A few months later he took a job with the National Trust Company in Winnipeg. It sent him north in 1921 to Hudson Bay to settle the estate of a deceased free trader. There he fell in love with the Arctic and stayed on, learning to drive dog-sleds. Until 1924 he operated a string of four fur trade posts between Norway House and Hudson Bay. He moved to Edmonton in 1925.[39]

When Patterson met Matthews, he was a travelling salesman, representing Woods Eiderdown and the Plymouth Binder Twine companies. Patterson would later travel all over Alberta with Matthews. Patterson recalled these road trips: "We got into some very interesting places and the usual episodes of cars and roads in those days.

"I think what really sort of cemented our relationship was that we got thrown out of a picture-house, a movie-house at Strome. We went in there to see this movie and there was something funny going on and the thing that really moved us deeply was when a wife got into the old Ford car, disappeared into the garage. You heard the roar of the engine and the back of the car came out of the garage and she reversed and suddenly she threw it into forward gear and came straight out of the back end of the car…it was very, very amusing. It just hit the right spot. We laughed convulsively over this thing and that was fine. The next thing was a dreadful picture. It started with a deathbed scene. People were standing around this flaxen-haired little girl. Gordon and I were roaring with laughter. The manager said 'You can't do that here.' We said 'We're laughing at your movie, at your last movie.' It didn't matter. We got requested to leave, otherwise he'd stop the show."[40]

The other half of the Matthews pair was equally interesting. Mollie (nee Robertson) Matthews was from Boston Tea Party stock that came north during the American Revolution. Born in 1901 at St. Andrews, New Brunswick, she and her family moved west to Alberta in 1914 where her father was a civil servant. As the only daughter in a family with two brothers, Bob and William, she thrived on outdoor pursuits and was a great shot with a rifle. Intellectually talented too, she received one of the first commerce degrees awarded to a woman in Alberta in the 1920s. She taught in some of Alberta's one room schools, riding horseback to these isolated centres of instruction. Her son Dick later recalled that she "couldn't cook worth a damn" when she married Gordon, because her father would not allow her to learn, because he did "not want to be involved in the experiment."[41]

Gordon and Mollie made such an impression on Patterson they remained in contact for the rest of his life. Indeed, Matthews was very much on his mind the next summer as Patterson struggled up the South Nahanni. But first, Patterson had more adventures that summer of 1926. In letters to his chum Edwin he highlighted parts he'd left out when writing to Mother.

Battle River
Dear George,

Well, Sir, since I last wrote to you I have made, & safely returned from, an unexpected trip into Southern Alberta. I suggested the thing to Dennis early in the year & then forgot all about it, intending to stay in the Peace until I left for England. However, a hurried letter from Dennis set me pounding the Urchin down the trail on July 1st & I only returned last Wednesday night....

We took in the first three days of the Stampede & then pulled out of Calgary through the range country of the foothills to Banff in the Rockies.... I have done more & laughed more in this last month than for the last five years, but I want to tell you a few of the things that happened sometime. To maul on paper were a pity. At the end of his week Dennis left for Edmonton—on a Sunday....

I went on, camping, with an English fellow from Edmonton & his wife [Gordon and Mollie Matthews] in their car. We had our tent & blankets & meandered gently on up the Bow valley by way of Lake Louise & the Kicking Horse Pass into British Columbia as far as Emerald Lake, with side steps into the Kootenays & the Yoho Valley. Saw a waterfall called Takakkaw which is seven times as high as Niagara. Also marmots, bears, mule deer, elk & porcupines—the national parks being game sanctuaries & all guns sealed by the Mounties at the passes. Saw a bear bash in a bait can at Emerald [Lake], &, having cleaned up on the minnows, proceed next to bash in the canoe & the outfit generally, seeking always after the minnows. The American owner or lessee hit the trail for our car & gasped out his conviction that even the sanctity of game had its doggone limits.

Tired of the simple life & went back to Banff when life suddenly became violently complicated again for three days. Pulled out for Calgary & the plains with good resolutions on a Sunday, but met some friends in the cow city which is noted for its hospitality. Crawled northwards to Olds next morning & ran into the first rain of the trip & thanked God for it as it set the wheat right for harvest, cooled things down, & washed the air back to its normal glitter, it having become hazy with the smoke of the forest fires which were raging all the way from Idaho to Alaska. Four people were burned to death with their car on the Banff-Windermere road just a day after we were there.

From Olds we wallowed westwards, gloriously muddy, to Sundre & beyond into the foothills to the Ĥ◊J ranch. (I think I have the cuneiform right. Not "Mene, Mene" but "quarter circle H, diamond J.")

I got up first next morning—I had slept in my blankets on the floor not being desirous of fighting for bed room with a Cambridge lad called Kennard, just three weeks out. Crawled out of the ranch house, shoes in hand, into a morning I shall always remember—rain washed & sparkling with the sunrise & the cool air of the hills. I wandered away up the Big Red Deer River, which runs by the house, & back again, the tum clamouring for grub.

We were to drop our wife here for the Foothills Ranch, further into the hills, & then turn back en garcon to the prairies & Edmonton. Comrade Kennard was also going under the wing of Dickie Brown of the Foothills to see a little of Canadian ranching & find out whether he wished to set up in Canada or the Argentine. He was young, tall, frailish, had on grey flannel trousers, cowboots, I forget what kind of a shirt, a necktie wrongly tied & a gold wrist watch. He had bought a horse from the Ghost Ranch, by Cochrane, & had let the thing get away on him instead of keeping it corralled, & consequently was stuck at the Ĥ◊J with the above outfit on his back & a wonderful saddle, but no horse to fit under it.

I was sitting on the corral bars after breakfast watching Tony, one of D. B.'s cowboys, roping some horses, when Comrade K. asked me if I had a saddle horse. I said yes, one little one, & that one a long way away & probably in the pound by now. He asked me what the pound was so

I explained that institution to him, adding at the end "—originating, I believe, in England."

"A lovely country" he said. "Have you ever visited it?"

So you see how we are degenerating....

Of course Kennard had hardly opened his mouth the night before, while John Helmer, Tony, Matthews—this Englishman, who has spent some years in the Hudsons Bay north, from Norway House to the Barrens—& Bronzo had given tongue, over photos & maps, mainly about big horn sheep & the possibilities of a hunting trip in from the upper Red Deer. And I have no doubt that we were guessing, figuring & such like, to beat hell, as the saying goes.

There are trout in the river & I felt that I had found peace at the last on the Big Red Deer. The car stalled on a muddy hill—a mere trail. I corduroyed the trail with spruce boughs but with no effect so we backed down & left the sun to dry the hill for us. Comrade Matthews fished & caught a veritable monster. I navigated round to hunt up the survey marks, & Mrs Matthews went to sleep on a big, warm rock. A little black bear came out onto the stones of the far bank & leered horribly at us. I felt that it was clearly indicated that this pleasant place should be seized hastily by somebody so I broached the subject to Matthews & on our return to Edmonton we opened negotiations with the Hudson's Bay for 160 acres with a half mile river frontage etc. If we decide to buy we should be able to get it for a little under two quid an acre, but we hope to find time to look it over properly in the fall of this year. Don't mention this to anybody at all.

Later on the two of us pulled out for Olds & pints of beer & T-bone steaks & then for Red Deer. We wandered over the prairies for a few days & then came to Edmonton where we picked up Dennis. I took the first train to Peace River & so was only in Edmonton three days but things certainly hummed while it lasted. I don't think a western town is the right place for Dennis. I am damned certain it wouldn't be for me. Down east it is different. I have heard Calgary sneer at Toronto as Toronto the Good. But in the west the old fur trapping, gold running, railroad construction spirit is still alive in the cities in all classes. Pile up a big stake, come into the city, drink, dance, blow it in & get out broke back to your work again—I hope this attitude has a strong influence over every class. It's a sure thing that Toronto will have a deuce of a long wait before she can lay the brand of holiness on any city west of the lakes.

I covered the eighty odd miles out here in 24 hours with sleep & feeds & have set my house in order. The mosquitoes have gone and we are on the edge of the golden days now. Yesterday I rode out seven miles west & fished down James Creek to the Battle & down the Battle, catching two of some damned fish or other which tasted very good. I grilled them. They were a good size & one made my supper & the other my breakfast. It was a lovely day—sun & wind, like today, & I bathed in the Battle at lunch time & ate all the wild raspberries I could carry with safety. Started a red deer from a creek bottom & took a crack at it from the saddle with a heavy automatic—only one as I nearly got thrown for my pains. Presumably I missed the deer, but anyhow it was a jolly day. West of me there is nobody so I have all Canada to play the fool in. The weather has been good for the crops. Round Olds & in Central & Northern Alberta in most districts, crops will be splendid unless there is hail or bad weather. On Battle River grasshoppers have played hell. Cutting of my oats will start about Aug. 4th & I shall have to stook like a navvy....

I planted a small strip of fireguard with the garden stuff this spring. The grasshoppers took most, especially the sweet peas, & while I was away the wild flowers & weeds came in & choked other things—this ground has an abysmal fecundity—rabbit like in its production of life. But I am going out in a few minutes for lettuce & onions & it seems that snapdragon & mignonette can tell any pest to go to the devil. The whole thing was only an experiment.

Game laws up here are disregarded. I shall start on Aug. 12 to shoot prairie chicken for my own use. Nobody shoots moose, deer or any large animal for sport as what you shoot you are tacitly supposed to use & butchering alone in the bush on a hot day, or on any day, & packing the meat out fairly well wipes out the joy of shooting. But the meat is there for those who really need it & Battle River is exceptionally good for moose & deer. I took out a pistol yesterday not for deer but in hopes of catching a bear eating berries & getting in a good thoughtful shot—with a rest, & the oss andy.

Never think, Sir, of a home in British Columbia—however pleasant it may be as a land in which to keep holy day. Take it from me that sunny Alberta is good—a land, as they say in Calgary, where men are men & women are even worse than that.

If you could still gain contentment from such simple pleasures, then I shall be glad to clod with you through the frost to Steyning & to drink Mr Joyes' beer & belch & roar before his fire. I shall look forward to it as a December fixture.[42]

As of the fall of 1926, Patterson had won his bet with the Canadian government and the homestead was his, free and clear. Nothing else stood in the way of his plans to head north. Besides, the years were hurrying by and soon he would be thirty years old, almost past his prime. It was time to sow his last wild oats. Despite numerous warnings to avoid northern rivers, and despite knowing nothing about canoes, he began making preliminary plans for a three month expedition to The Falls of the Nahanni the next summer.[43]

While Patterson was planning his odyssey, three other naive Englishmen were voyaging north on their own adventure of a lifetime: one that was to take their lives.[44] Little did Patterson know how close he was to come to repeating their mistakes in the fall of 1927.

But first, Patterson had one more season to consider. Never one to suffer hardship when offered a pleasant alternative, he decided to escape the frigid Canadian winter in one of two places. Having done well on his investments, he considered a working holiday on a sheep station in Australia, a venture that would have also allowed him to return with fine Australian horses to breed for sale. Instead, he realized he "had to go home to England from Canada on some family business."[45] There, during the damp, dreary days of a smoggy winter, he nested deeply in a comfortable chair and read romantic books about the Canadian wilds. In his mind, he had already begun the quest for the treasures of the South Nahanni in the unmapped regions of the Northwest Territories.

Hard to Kill
1927

DYING in the North is not all that hard: many have lost their lives pursuing fortune or fame in a land they did not understand. As Patterson and his paddling partner Dennis France loaded their canoe for their summer's float on northern rivers, the last member of another British expedition was dying of starvation.

A year earlier, just as the waters began flowing in early 1926, John Hornby ("Hornby of Hudson Bay"), twenty-eight year-old Harold Adlard and Hornby's eighteen year-old cousin Edgar Vernon Christian threw a canoe into the same waters and headed north and east to the Thelon River Game Sanctuary. Hornby's arrogant confidence in his skills as a northern traveller was as appalling as it was legendary. He once boasted he could "outlive an Indian on the trail, and could live where an Indian would starve."[1]

Christian's letters and diaries give us a feel for that trip. On arriving by train at Waterways—today's Fort McMurray, they promptly departed downstream in a canoe. "The Athabasca is a fine big river with towering tar sand banks thickly wooded with spruce and poplar. In some places we passed clearings where oil wells had been sunk and gone smash. This was one thing that struck me to see the oil and tar on the banks and yet thousands of dollars being spent trying to extract oil in large quantities at commercial value all in vain."[2]

Bad weather hit as they approached Lake Athabasca. Stormbound for a few days, they hunkered in camp under heavy tarpaulins. Then it was on to Fort Chipewyan before heading down the Slave River to Fort Smith on the border with the Northwest Territories and on to Fort Resolution on the south shore of Great Slave Lake. At this point the group left the beaten track and headed northeast into the unknown.

Premonitions of disaster appear often in the diary, but Christian saw the bombastic aspects of Hornby's character as heroic attributes, not deadly flaws. "I have seen lots of trappers who have been on the trail with Jack and many won't go again because he is tough although they like [him] more than any man. I shall be with someone whose name runs through Canada with highest praise which makes me feel absolutely satisfied about the future."[3]

Hornby took only a minimum of necessities. Travelling light was not only a badge of honour; it was expedient for an expedition with far to go. He expected to live off the land. Trapping fur-bearing animals would make their heroic expedition a financial success.

By the end of June, 1926, Christian and his elders had reached the eastern end of Great Slave Lake. Here their story would diverge from Patterson's. After much hard work they arrived at the Thelon River Game Sanctuary where they intended to stay the winter. Running low on food early the next year, they rationed themselves to one small bannock for each fur-bearing animal they trapped. Hornby succumbed to starvation in April, 1927. Adlard died on May 4, leaving Christian, not quite nineteen, alone. He encased the corpses in canvas and Hudson's Bay blankets and stored them outside in the cold. In his last days he dug up scraps they had discarded earlier, cooked them and drank the thin soup and gnawed on bits of hide. The end of May brought another fierce snowstorm, four days of merciless howling, cold and flurries. Finally, on the first day of June the weather improved, but he felt very weak. "Sunshine is bright now. See if that does any good to me if I get out and bring in wood to make fire tonight. Make preparations now. Got out, too weak and all in now. Left things late." To his mother, he wrote in his last days: "Please don't Blame dear Jack." He then stuffed the letters and diaries into the stove, exhausted.

The stories of the two parties overlap on the last days of May and early June, 1927. When Edgar Christian was digging up fish bones and bits of hide, bright-eyed Patterson and France were travelling between Edmonton and Waterways on the Alberta & Great Waterways train. By the time the duo arrived at Lake Athabasca, the third member of the Hornby party was dead.

For more than a year the cabin sheltered Christian's remains. Prospectors stumbled onto the tragedy in the summer of 1928, finding Christian's corpse near the stove on which a bit of paper bore the barely legible note: "Who.... Look in Stove." Papers and a diary greeted the shocked but hardened northern travellers. *Unflinching: A Diary of Tragic Adventure* is the title Christian's father chose when he submitted it for publication in London in 1937. Today, all that remains are three mounds of earth marked with wooden crosses emblazed with the initials E. C., J. H. and H. A.[4]

The same hazards awaited the men who left Edmonton almost a year to the day after the doomed expedition. Patterson's story, however, would diverge in significant ways from that of Hornby's. The 1927 adventurers would minimize their risks by keeping closer to the beaten track, always within a few days' travel of an outpost of civilization. Patterson would not attempt to overwinter, or live off the land; he wisely recognized his own limited experience in this field. Above all, he would be careful to learn something from almost everyone he met.

Patterson was meticulous in his preparations. He spoke with the most reliable experts available at the time: others experienced in northern travel. The most important of these was his new friend Gordon Matthews. Although newly married and unable to join him on the summer trip, Matthews provided Patterson with a wealth of valuable information about northern life, based on his decade working for fur trade companies.

He also did what any educated person does before going into the wilds; he consulted all available published materials. While in England the previous winter, he had ordered maps from Harrod's, a famous London store. Over these he pored with a trained eye, absorbing as much information as the crude mapmakers could supply. The South Nahanni, of course, was not officially mapped, nor was the Liard River.[5] Later he would list Sir William Butler's *The Wild North Land*, Warburton Pike's *The Barren Grounds of Northern Canada* and Vilhjalmur Stefansson's *Hunters of the Great North* as sources of inspiration for his South Nahanni adventure.[6] But more than any other book it was Michael H. Mason's *The Arctic Forests* that had filled the dreary days of London's winter. The maps showed crude dotted lines, the imaginings of a cartographer, but with enough general information for him to pick out a circular route that included many sights without much backtracking. Of the Nahanni people it said, "They are a hardy, virile people, but have suffered much from white influence. They are hostile to strangers, and many white explorers have been done to death by them. This tribe was for many years under the complete domination of one woman, supposed to be partly of European descent."[7] That sounded interesting.

And then came the day of destiny while recuperating from the excision of his tonsils. Dr. Stott, his surgeon, said, "I strongly advise you to do no heavy work on your Canadian farm, at least for several months." That seemed fine to the patient and Patterson assured him, "As a matter of fact, I had rather thought of taking a canoe trip." "Splendid" said the doctor, "Gliding along, day after day, over the placid surfaces of one of your great rivers. The gentle splash of the paddle, the song of the wilderness in your ears...." That settled it. Patterson's adventure was medically prescribed.[8]

Besides, he really had nothing else to do that summer. The homestead was complete—he had done the minimum required to secure its title. Also, things were getting serious with Marigold Portman, the English blonde. His investments in the Hudson's Bay Company fur and trading empire as well as the great Canadian Pacific Railway Company were reaping unprecedented returns along with other British and Canadian speculations. What better time to seek the real thing itself—gold on the mythical source of northern wealth and fame. To this end he trained himself as an amateur prospector by reading Louis V. Pirsson's *Rocks and Rock Minerals.*

It is unlikely he could have amassed the contacts, financial resources and life skills necessary for the trip any sooner than 1927. Also, Dennis France had just quit his job with Revillons Freres, a rival fur trade company to the giant HBC, and had a free summer before heading back to England. He invited himself along for the trip as far as Fort Simpson, at which point he planned to return on the last steam-powered riverboat of the summer. Patterson reasoned, "...two can make light work which is hard for one, & there is danger in solitary travel from small accidents such as a sprained ankle or the slip of an axe. Also it is my show & my canoe & I shall steer the thing & if there is any rot Dennis can take his half of the grub & go back with the mail boat from Liard. Finally I think that it will do him a power of good & that away from his Edmonton friends & his cocktail parties (I am taking one bottle of brandy for medicinal purposes & nothing else) we shall probably get on very well."[9]

As it turned out, two neophytes on an expedition do not add up to one skilled wilderness adventurer, but that fact revealed itself slowly. Patterson had overlooked the potential hazards of his own green nature and his total lack of canoe skills. In the early 1950s he shook his head in amazement and wrote, "What I proposed to use in place of experience has often puzzled me." But he apparently believed the skills he had acquired in a punt on calm English rivers were enough to prepare him for the mighty northern rivers.[10] Once committed, the greenhorns threw caution to the wind. "We gave no thought to our lack of skill or to the hazards that might lie ahead, but with the full confidence of ignorance, carefully overloaded the canoe and shoved out into the river."[11]

They had one thing going for them. Patterson had met an English mining engineer named W. K. Cousins, a veteran of the Boer War and the Great War, who owned the Liard Coal Company and knew the Liard River well. He had counselled Patterson on the type of canoe to buy and what supplies to purchase. He had also offered to transport the pair on his own scows that would be laden with a Ford truck, horses, machinery and supplies bound for his coal mining venture on the Liard. His scheme counted on moving Liard River coal down the Mackenzie River to the Mackenzie Delta where, far from British Columbia coal mines, "a lump of coal at Aklavik…[was] worth its weight in platinum." Patterson and France could pitch in and help as stevedores on the scow in exchange for passage from Waterways to Fort Simpson. Patterson eagerly accepted the proposal: "…it will save me the crossing of the two great lakes & the wide Mackenzie River where the wind raises waves that are dangerous to a canoe, so that one must coast along the shores & lose time. We hope to travel twenty hours a day, making use of the short northern nights, & be at Simpson by June 8th or 9th."[12]

When the sun rose on June 10, 1927, however, Patterson and France were still 400 miles as the arrow flies from Fort Simpson, or about half way. Things had not gone according to plan. The pair had boarded the weekly Alberta & Great Waterways train in Edmonton on the last day of May and had arrived two days later at Waterways, the official End of Steel and the northernmost terminus of any Canadian railway. Cousins

Waterways, Alberta, June 1, 1927.

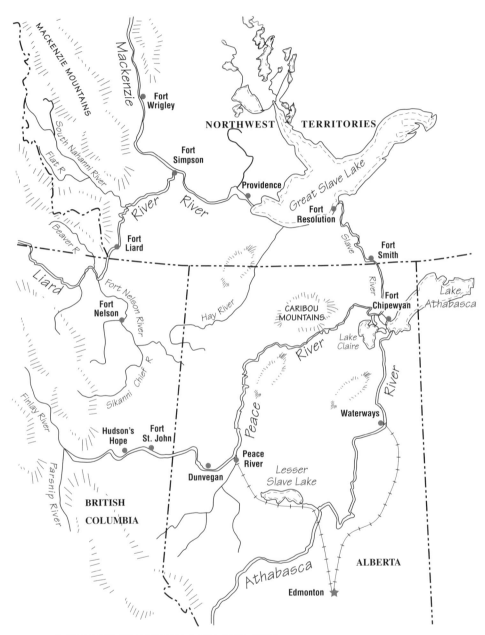

PATTERSON'S TRAVELS IN 1927 AND 1928

was nowhere to be seen, so they loaded the canoe, picked up canoe paddles for the first time in their lives and set off alone down the Athabasca River. Canoe historian Eric Morse describes this 200 mile stretch of river from Waterways to Lake Athabasca as "fast but dull." As any frequent user of the river could have told the pair, there was a shortcut from the Athabasca River across a minor portage into the Embarrass River. Named after the French term for debris, the Embarrass protected canoes from nasty squalls on Lake Athabasca by dumping its waters into the lake at Fort Chipewyan near the head of the Slave River.

Several attributes made Fort Chipewyan a special place in the days of the voyageurs. First, it was at the northwesterly limit of canoe travel from Methye Portage, which provided the link to the Churchill River and Hudson Bay, thus allowing voyageurs to make the round trip to the rendezvous point in one open-water season. Because the ice at this point breaks up a month earlier than the ice on the main body of the lake—usually about May 15 instead of June 15—it gave the fort a jump on lake shipping. Also, because a fur trade post had to feed a large staff, the floodplain wetlands insured plentiful supplies of game including moose, whitefish and waterfowl. And finally, because it serviced the drainage basins of the Mackenzie, Liard and Peace rivers, it was the logical transfer point for furs from the great northern rivers to the trade route south.[13]

Patterson and France knew none of this, however, and paddled past Embarrass Portage into the Athabasca Delta. On June 4 they camped "on a little green river" just off the Athabasca, and in the wind and rain baked bannock, dried out gear and prepared for a late day paddle if the wind died down. "A lovely morning now…" wrote Patterson in the first entry of his 1927 diary, "Bluebells & cranberry blossom. Song birds, fish & wildfowl & no mosquitoes. What a relief." Thus began a wonderfully intimate and detailed account of his little summer holiday in the north. Written as an extended letter to his mother in London, England, it later served as the basis for his 1954 masterpiece *The Dangerous River*.

A northern classic, Patterson's most famous book is first and foremost a tale of adventure. Like any good storyteller, the author used the facts as a basis upon which to build an entertaining account of the summer's expedition and his subsequent return trip to retrieve the gold. From the very first page he disavows any attempt to make the book a factual account, worse still, a textbook. "I am glad to say that we added little to the world's biggest curse—its stock of scientific knowledge."[14] Partly to protect his prospecting finds and also to grant himself the writer's prerogative of embellishing facts, he also warned, "It was the dying kick, in Canada, of the Age of Marvels, in which, if a cartographer found himself with an embarrassingly blank space on the map, he felt free to write there whatever had pleased him most out of a tangle of travellers' tales…. The Mackenzie Mountains in 1927 offered similar opportunities to the bold, inventive spirit."[15] With that statement, Patterson released himself from strict adherence to facts and proceeded to write a wonderful book about his adventures on the South Nahanni River in Canada's northern frontier.

As a result, this account of the 1927 trip will at times challenge Patterson's published version. Often the facts as he recorded them in his letters and diaries are every bit as fascinating as his published accounts. Indeed, they frequently reveal an immediacy that is fresh and invigorating. They are also a new source of information, a posthumous record about a most fascinating man.

For example, the summer's adventure nearly ended in early June. Barely a week after first paddling a canoe, Patterson and France were stormbound on an island within sight of Fort Chipewyan. From the mouth of the Athabasca River, they had set off across Lake Athabasca on glassy calm water. In the stern, Dennis was trying out the complicated steering strokes necessary to propel the canoe forward and control its direction at the same time, when, "In less than twenty minutes the east wind came up—fortunately behind us. The little canoe began to pitch in the waves like a ship at sea & I could see our island seven long miles away. Dennis paddled & steered well—at least as far as I could judge. I hadn't time to look—for two solid hours I sat & drove that canoe like a lunatic—we didn't speak at all for five miles. It was just a swing & dip of the paddle for all we were worth—you never know how much is in you until you are forced to it. The wind eased a little as we came near to our island & I saw that, although it was rocky & beautifully wooded, we should be forced to land on a lee shore— sand & possibly with a shoal. So we bided our time & tried to run past the rocky point of an island & make what we thought was the mainland. The wind rose again & we couldn't gain the point & were forced down the near shore of the island. Lunch was uppermost in my mind. It was now twelve & we had had nothing since a quarter to six & had been going all out for two hours. So we made for a little green beach under the cliffs but found that it was swampy & covered by the waves. We rested for five minutes & I said 'Let's turn here, in the smooth water & make for the little rocky island—tack in the lee of it, make for the

Mouse Island, Lake Athabasca, June 1927.

coast & creep in to Chipewyan Bay.' So we started, this time against the wind & waves. It was only a mile but I have never seen anything like it. I paddled like a son of a gun & Dennis did some notable steering. The canoe rose & dipped like a liner & I was soused with the spray. I think we put out our last ounce of strength. Half way I noticed a dead, fallen tree on the rocks of the island & I remember thinking how handy that would be to light a fire for tea when we got there. We just managed to make a little sheltered cove & flopped out on the rocks & began to laugh. Then we ate—properly…. This has been a great day—I feel that we have achieved a victory & foiled Lake Athabasca."[16]

Their victory was mostly luck. As inexperienced paddlers, they were fortunate to make the bit of rock they called Mouse Island. Had they capsized, death was a certainty. Even with life jackets—Patterson later said they were for tourists—the cold water would have killed them long before the waves would have pushed the canoe to shore.

For three days they recuperated on Mouse Island, with the canoe pulled up "In dock" on driftwood in a little bay. They dried out, did laundry, some baking and wrote. Always eloquent, especially when describing the landscape, Patterson noted, "T'is one of God's days that only seem to come in northern Alberta—the sun like a flame in a clear blue sky, not a trace of haze & all around the tumbling water & the lake gulls." Fort Chipewyan lay gleaming across the uncrossable waters, a small collection of white buildings on a rocky shore. On the island berries bloomed, promising fruit later in the season, strawberries and gooseberries to name but a few. "Below the waves are breaking & with me I have Jorrocks's *Jaunts & Jollities*. Could money buy more than this?"

Among the supplies in the overloaded canoe Patterson had tucked in a volume of witty stories by Robert Smith Surtees. Shortly before becoming the High Sheriff of Northumberland, Surtees had begun editing *New Sporting Magazine*, which included his own articles about Jorrocks until he gave up the work in 1836. Based on his keen observation of society and sporting life, these humorous articles transformed the obvious into the sublime as he insightfully insulted everyone, himself included, while rendering all speechless with laughter. In one tale, Jorrocks is convicted for trespassing by the length of his big toe. While swimming at Margate, Jorrocks loses his pantaloons to the tide. In "Mr. Jorrocks' Dinner Party," he is the first to lose control. "His legs deserted his body, and, after two or three lurches, down he went with a tremendous thump under the table. He called first for 'Batsay,' then for 'Binjimin,' and, game to the last, blurted out, 'Lift me up!—tie me in my chair!—fill my glass!'"[17] And so Patterson sat on the beach, chuckling as he read of the adventures of another tall, thin Brit, all the while drinking tea and eating bannock under a cloudless sky.

Early in the morning of the fourth day they crossed to Fort Chipewyan, bought a few things at the Bay and sent exposed films out by mail to Gordon

R. M. Patterson beside the *Muriel* loaded for the portage from Fitzgerald to Fort Smith, 1927.

Matthews in Edmonton to develop and forward to England. Then they headed off to make up for lost time. They found the Peace River flood keeping Lake Athabasca water from flowing north: "I really felt quite proud of it. It was doing this on this particular morning & creating dead calm water in this part of the lake, as it has done for centuries past." Patterson liked the idea that the Peace River water had recently flowed past his homestead far to the southwest. "Fires must be burning away up the river—it rushes in with a roar, swirls, white water & whirlpools as it strikes the other current & is bringing down tons of driftwood & great burnt trees—a great river." A stroke of luck visited them when they found the

R. M. Patterson at Slave River, 1927.

mouth of the Riviere des Rochers where Lake Athabasca drained north.

Their next objective, the Slave River, began at the point where the waters of the Riviere des Rochers and the Peace crashed together for the wild ride to Great Slave Lake. Travelling fast down this river, they made 25 miles before breaking for lunch on shore. Suddenly, around the bend came the HBC launch *Canadusa*, its captain insisting that Patterson and France add their gear to the top of the already heavily laden craft. The two adventurers were glad to rest their paddle-weary arms while the boat roared through the Demi Charge Rapids and into Fitzgerald at the upstream end of the last portage in Alberta. Across the 16 mile trail went the canoe and cargo to Fort Smith, the capital of the Northwest Territories at that time. Even large boats like the *Canadusa* made the overland journey, loaded on giant wagons with massive steel wheels. From the border town Patterson sent a wireless message home to Mother, the last until winter. Meanwhile, ravenous huskies devoured an eight pound sack of oatmeal they had left unattended in the canoe. Mosquitoes were vicious: "We had to use oil, face nets, bacon grease, smoke smudges, nets over our sleeping bags, gloves, thick clothes & tuck our trousers into our socks & moccasins...."

W. K. Cousins and Major Cornelius Foreman of The Liard Coal Company finally made an appearance and on Wednesday, June 15, the last of the Coal Company equipment arrived. "Cousins & I went to the office of the district agent—McDougall—King of the N.W.T.—an awfully nice man whom I had met on the train. He helped me a great deal with maps & information & asked us to supper at his house. Smith is a clean little place, standing in rocks, sand & pines overlooking the Slave River & the Rapid of the Drowned. Wireless men in khaki, black robed priests, mounted police in scarlet, Indians, breeds, trappers, prospectors, freighters in all colours, a little golf course amongst the pines, & a good restaurant run by Jean l'Allouette from Tadoussac in far off Quebec. The Hudson's Bay, stores, warehouses, mining recorder, a little hotel, great warehouses, scows building by the river, the river steamers waiting for the ice to break on the Great Slave & all set in the warm soft dust looking over a huge river...."[18]

Without much coaxing, Patterson and France accepted a ride on Cousins' scow, pushed by a launch named the *Muriel*. "In return I said I would work with them on the portage & cook for the four of us—Foreman having already given Cousins indigestion. Dennis is driving their car between Fitzgerald & Fort Smith & unloading freight & washing up."

Extended travel with unknown companions can cause tension, and by this time both Cousins and Patterson were having trouble with their partners. "…Cousins cursed Foreman hard this morning for his own good—I occupy the same position with regard to Dennis & periodically he hears home truths from me that he should have learnt & marked as a small boy. I told him that if there was any rot he could go to the devil & I would go on alone. I can look after myself & alone he would be useless. So I have the mastery in my show."

But Friday, June 24, found them stuck at Fort Smith because Great Slave Lake was still icebound. Worried about putting on weight owing to inactivity, Patterson hiked back to Fitzgerald to investigate the sights. "I walked out yesterday & fought through the bush to the edge of the Pelican Rapids where those ridiculous birds have a breeding place. Every spring they come back from the far south & there they stood on the rocks by the mile wide river looking just as idiotic as those in St James Park." Severely bored by the wait, he concluded, "I'm glad I saw only girls when I was at home—here I see only men & one must have a contrast."[19]

Sunday found him in better spirits, writing from the moving Coal Company vessel. After helping to celebrate Canada Day and competing in the

Major Cornelius Foreman, R. M. Patterson and W. K. Cousins at Fort Smith, 1927.

races at Fort Smith on the Friday, they had pushed off early Saturday and had made 60 miles before tying up for the night. "We have a collapsible table in the cabin for meals & there are two narrow seats on which Foreman & I sleep—Dennis being allotted the floor which we deemed just, as we have found him to be useless & at times annoying & unreliable. A little shopkeeper at heart—I made it quite plain to him, when I found out his real nature, that I had not the slightest intention of wet nursing him all over the N.W.T."

A 4 a.m. start got them well down into the delta of the Slave River. They had hoped to make the headwaters of the Mackenzie River the next day, but were delayed by a leak in the scow that had to be mended. Even after entering Great Slave Lake, they had trouble. "The pilot, Pierre la Hache, a French Canadian-Peau de Liévre Indian breed from Arctic Red River, stuck us once on a sandbank before we got into deep water but we were fortunately able to back off. We heard before he came on board, that he was able to talk neither French nor English nor even Cree, but only his own language—Kuchin, I believe—however, he can speak French & I can converse a little with him. We are accordingly vastly relieved, as an incomprehensible pilot might have us in difficulties very soon."[20]

At Fort Resolution on Great Slave Lake they offloaded freight. "Resolution was full of Dogribs & Yellowknives in for their treaty money & to sell their furs—quite a Mongol featured crew, quiet & dignified in comparison to the half breeds." Unwisely deciding to spend the calm night tied up in harbour, they set off just in time to get caught in a storm on the open water. Rough seas dumped Patterson off the bench that doubled as his bed. Then the engine quit and "Foreman, who was looking after the engine, had to choose this moment, of course, to be seasick, which pretty well ended his period of usefulness. However, we variously made shift, & chugged into Hay River very thankfully about five in the afternoon at the Hudson's Bay post."

A chance encounter at Hay River with De Melde, a friend from the Battle River area, introduced Patterson to yet another northern vocation, catching fish to sell to the Indians for dog food. "I was glad to meet him again & have a talk—he took me over to see his fishing camp & then amongst the Indians—Slaveys. I was introduced to the old chief & his son & saw things I had never seen before—birch bark canoes beautifully made, baskets of birch worked in colours, the insides of the tepees & all kinds of furs & work in silk, beads & buckskin." He also learned the steps and chorus to the Tea Dance and, best of all, danced with the chief's daughter. "I can't remember the Slavey for her name but it means 'Looks you straight in the Eyes.'" They gave him two 35-pound bull trout from the nets and four whitefish.

Patterson introduced himself to Dean Vale, the parson of the Church of England mission, who showed him around that denomination's only mission on the Mackenzie River system. It included a "farm, house, garden, hospital, church & school. They had about 40 children of every nation & tribe from Eskimos to Crees & it was very interesting." That evening Patterson and company departed Hay River with presents of rhubarb and radishes.

Shortly thereafter, an argument broke out over which channel to take on a map that meant nothing to the native pilot. "...The sight of about six people all arguing hard & talking at once, having in their hands every known instrument from opera glasses to prismatic compasses, merely scared & confused the old man. He seized my canoe & dropped it overboard to go & seek the last channel." Dennis volunteered to help and they returned hours later. "Dennis had about the first night's work of his life, as la Hache [the pilot] seems to have explored conscientiously about every channel from the lake to the Mackenzie & they didn't get back till 5:30—when we started immediately."

They had not gone far when the propeller shaft broke for the second time, so they tugged the outfit to shore with Patterson's canoe. "Indians came up in red & yellow birchbark canoes & watched us silently. Then they fished & when we stopped work at midnight they sold us their catch & slipped away downstream to their village round the bend."

Once again disaster struck at a most inopportune moment. "So we set off again & went well until we got into the swift water at Green Island when the rudder broke just as I was having a shave. We have broken pretty well everything that can be broken on a boat & I notice that they always smash when I wash or shave. Have decided to go unwashed for the future—like Samson.

"So we fell to again at the sweeps & swept very manfully—me with the shaving soap still on my face under a blazing sun. At last we brought her safe to Simpson—set high on a point where the great Liard comes with a brown muddy swirl from the mountains of B.C. & the Yukon into the clear, cold green of the Mackenzie. A clean, white painted little place overlooking a tremendous sweep of water on the two rivers—perhaps 15 miles up one reach of the Mackenzie & 10 miles down the northern reach & 2 up the Liard.

"We are awfully tired now—everything is repaired & I am writing at 11:30 p.m. The others are in bed & I can see through the mosquito netting & directly down the Mackenzie a wonderful flaming sunset. Outside the men are playing on a gramophone a foxtrot that Milly & I liked in 1921 & that was the favourite dance at that St. John's ball that ended my infancy & Oxford.

"I have changed my 18 ft canoe with the Hudson's Bay factor for a light 16 footer—told him I was a share holder & got a very good deal.‡ Tomorrow we tackle the Liard & its rapids & swift water. One hundred miles up is the mouth of the South Nahanni. Don't worry about me as there is no mail up there for me to write to you—of course if I see any way to get out a letter to you I will do so. I want to try to get far up where the gold is—it is very difficult but I shall do my best—you know

---

‡ Patterson's craft was a classic: a 16-foot Chestnut Prospector canoe fashioned of cedar and canvas. Only one step removed from its ancient birchbark cousin, the vibrant craft is an intricately designed combination of white cedar ribs attached to ash inwales, planked on the outer curve of the ribs with thin white cedar boards. A single piece of canvas supplies seaworthiness, stretched to conform to the shape of the canoe and then filled with waterproof compound, sanded and painted repeatedly to a final sheen. Patterson's Prospector was a solid grey colour.

Tracking up the rapids of the Liard in a large scow, 1927.

why I want it so. It is far up into the mountains & it may take me a long time—winter may come too soon."

This last letter to Mother contained pressed wild flowers from the shore where they repaired the rudder and included "wild roses, hare bellies, gentian, wild sweet peas, Indian paint brush, fireweed & many more."

At Fort Simpson Patterson parted company with France "the shopkeeper" who caught the next sternwheeler upstream to Alberta. They did not part on good terms, but better to have made the decision at that point in the venture than in a canyon on the South Nahanni. Rumour had it a Minnesota trapper named Faille was also headed for the River of Death, so perhaps they could help each other through the rough going.[21]

After a few days in Fort Simpson, and well over a month behind his original schedule, Patterson loaded his new canoe and supplies onto the Coal Company's scow, and with the launch *Muriel* pushing, they ascended the Liard River. The Liard was yellow-brown in colour, littered with trees and other debris from rivers that plummet down the eastern slopes of the Coast Range. "I just stood there…observing with awe the Liard flood, wondering what it was that I had run my head against this time and whether I could cope with it."[22] The *Muriel* laboured hard, pushing a scow, its captain taking advantage of every weak spot in the flow of the Mackenzie's major tributary. Mile after mile they struggled against the ceaseless current until they arrived at the Liard Rapids. Every bit of strength was necessary to tow the *Muriel* and her scow up that wall of water. All extra hands grunted along the shore in harness, pulling the heavy vessels upstream, while a man onboard steered and kept the hull afloat and off the rocks with a long pole. It took hours to navigate this final obstacle.

Above the rapid, Patterson loaded his provisions into his canoe and set off on his own adventure.

EARLIER, Patterson had visited the Imperial Oil Company Producing Department in Edmonton, looking for a Liard River map. Imperial, a subsidiary of Standard Oil of New Jersey, had prospected for oil in the Northwest Territories for many years and had a producing oilfield at Norman Wells down the Mackenzie.‡ Patterson's luck held: Geologists had let him copy R. G. McConnell's 1887 map of the Liard into his diary. It was proving its worth as he navigated the last fifty miles to the South Nahanni, his objective shown as a squiggle meandering off the map into unknown territory.

---

‡ For two years during World War II the Norman Wells oilfield supplied the Canadian-American Norman Oil Line (CANOL), which transported oil from the Mackenzie across the mountains to a refinery at Whitehorse. By the late 1980s a pipeline from that same field was pumping oil south into Alberta along the Mackenzie River.

Imperial's presence in the North made a powerful statement: transportation was quickly evolving from pre-industrial systems to the internal combustion engine. The Great War had witnessed the explosive growth of motorized vehicles and primitive airplanes, these wartime technological developments evolving into peaceful applications after 1918.

The February, 1921, edition of *The Beaver* included an article titled "The Wilderness is Shrinking" that was about an air-boat flying to Fort Norman in eight hours from Fort McMurray. Although regular air service did not begin until 1928, that early flight inaugurated airplane exploration and travel in the North. Another application for the internal combustion engine was the outboard motor, which became ubiquitous in the North by the end of the 1920s. Natives quickly abandoned birchbark canoes for their cedar and canvas descendants and powered them with Evinrude and Johnson "kickers"—the northern word for outboards. Fast on the heels of the noisy outboards came a series of wireless radio stations from Edmonton down the Athabasca and Mackenzie rivers to the Arctic Ocean. Fort McMurray, for example, came on line in early 1924.[23]

Before motors became common in the North, steam-powered vessels plied the Arctic waters. For example, when Patterson departed Edmonton for the North in the spring of 1927, he could have travelled on the HBC's Alberta and Arctic Transportation Department's rail and water system. Operating on the Athabasca, Slave and Mackenzie rivers, it served commercial and tourist traffic. A thirty-five day trip from Waterways to Aklavik on the Arctic Ocean cost $325. A ten day trip from Waterways to Fort Smith on the Northwest Territories border cost $60.00. By contrast, the Peace River to Hudson's Hope trip also took ten days and cost $45.00.[24]

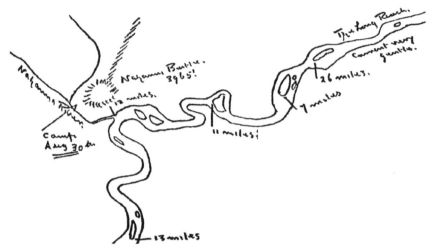

Patterson's hand-drawn map from his 1927 diary. The South Nahanni River
enters the Liard River at the left side of the map.

For the first few days Patterson staggered along under the constant
assault of howling wind and rain. Friday, the 22nd day of July found
him windbound just west of the Long Reach of the Liard, upstream of
the Lindbergs' cabins, and camped on the south bank near today's
Blackstone Landing.

Up before 3 a.m. on July 23, he set off quickly. "I have never seen so many
mosquitoes—I simply rolled up my bedding & mosquito net, oiled my face
& hands, took some dried apples, a drink of water and some cold beans,
put on my face net and fled. A lovely calm morning—the mountains looking very beautiful in their pale colouring. I went on until eight when I
stopped and made breakfast. The wind rose again promptly but after I had
fed and washed I decided to go on anyhow, so I started again—poling
mainly—past some islands, over many little riffles in a shallow, gravely
bottom. Very fortunate that I learned to punt on the Cherwell & the Isis.
Was caught suddenly by the wind about one & put on a lee shore—soft
mud. Floundered madly & bare footed & lugged the canoe by hand into the
shelter of a little point. Had lunch on the shingle & afterwards found the
wind worse—a gale. So I cooked a pot of rice & raisins & had a bath and
change of clothes and am still waiting—what a life. Nahanni can't be much
over 20 miles away—once in the smaller river I shall be safe from wind.

"The day is like a June day—all glitter & sunlight & blue shadows. The
mountains are deep blue, showing range after range now against the blue
sky. White clouds bowling across, throwing dark blue shadows on the

mountains slopes—the foothills—in shades of blue according to their distance, & the unending green of the forest.

"A young day—& me in khaki with a red handkerchief round my neck, sleeves rolled up, bare footed, often naked and hatless in the golden sunshine.

"The wind is easing so I shall load up ready to go on if I can."

Loading up was a simple enough chore, but not because he travelled light. Although an independent trader's cabin a few miles ahead at Nahanni Butte put up a feeble attempt to compete with the omnipresent HBC, Patterson carried nearly everything he could possibly need in the canoe with him, including a tin of canoe paint for repairs. A waterproof tarp protected perishable items from everything but a capsize, and ropes held the axe, rifle and other emergency items close at hand. An all-important roll of birchbark for starting fires filled the nose of the old classic.[25]

Although he had some idea of the provisions necessary for a summer without resupply, Patterson perhaps consulted an 1890's HBC Miner's Outfit list. Intended for a year on the trail, it listed the food, clothing and equipment necessary to keep body and soul together in the North. Provisions: evaporated apples and apricots, bacon, baking powder, pot barley, beef extract, candles, coffee, corn meal, flour, lime juice, matches, condensed milk, mustard, rolled oats, split peas, pepper, prunes, rice, salt, soap, baking soda, sugar, tea, tobacco, compressed vegetables and yeast cakes. Clothing: blankets, one each of cloth and fur caps, coats, dunnage bag, skin and wool gloves, snow goggles,

Tracking in swift water.

handkerchiefs, leather and wool mitts, mosquito netting, overalls, moleskin pants, ground sheet, flannel shirts, mackinaw shirts, wool socks, wool sweaters, towels and wool underwear. Footwear: laced and rubber boots, duffles, moccasins, long Arctic socks and snow shoes. Hardware: an auger and axe, brace and bits, camp kettles, chisel, pocket compass, tin cup, butcher's knife, knife and fork, files, fry pan, gold pan, hammer, hatchet, assorted nails, oakum, miner's pick and extra handles, pitch, tin plates, rope, hand and whip saws, gold scales, screw driver, miner's shovels and assorted spoons. In all, it totalled almost a ton of supplies.[26]

Although Patterson was headed into the bush for only a few months, his provisions and supplies probably weighed at least 400 pounds. Missing from this list was meat; he expected to bag game as he travelled.

Late July found Patterson camped on a huge sandbar called Swan Point, so large it even appears on the Sibbeston Lake topographic map at 1:250,000 scale. It offered a pleasant campsite with plentiful driftwood, a huge expanse of hot sand on which to dry out wet gear in the scorching sun, and a chance to pitch camp far away from trees and hungry insects.[27] Paddlers stop there today for the same reasons.

Patterson left early on Sunday morning, July 24. The wind had died during the night and the mosquito hordes had come out to feed. Hiding under his net he was safe, but at 6 a.m. he finally made a dash for the loaded canoe tied to a stake at the river's edge. "Took a hasty drink of water & a little cold rice & fled into the canoe & paddled until about nine. Had breakfast under a cutbank on a sandy ledge—sand in everything, also mosquitoes & smoke—not much wood—upset tea pail in fire & burnt my fingers—dropped the pail in the river & had to fish for it, being bitten the while. Left thankfully." Laurel and Hardy could not have done better.

Fifty years later he recalled mosquito doping options: "All we had then was either black your face or put on citronella oil which was almost as bad as...I mean, you got filthy with it. It mixed with sweat and ran down, tickly and smarted and got in our eyes."[28]

Often in discomfort he slogged upriver, poling most of the way, pulling on a rope or wading as the situation required. The day before the *MT Liard River* had passed him, pushing scows up the far side of the river. On this afternoon the air slowly reverberated with the increasingly insistent clamour of a kicker, and around the corner came a large freight canoe laden with dogs and captained by a man in garish red pants.

Patterson never lavished more praise on anyone than he did on the man he was about to meet, describing him as "the man who had taught me the ways of a canoe."[29] This lone wanderer was the other "lunatic" headed for the South Nahanni that summer. Fresh from a two-year stint trapping on the Beaver River at the Great Slave Lake, he, too, wanted to investigate the River of Death. Known far and wide for wearing such loud red wool pants that "a blind man couldn't miss him," Albert Faille—pronounced Faley—had waved at Patterson and the Coal Company party in early July at Wrigley Harbour at the Mackenzie River's source.[30]

Finally, they got to shake hands. Immediately after introductions, an unbroken litany began as they exchanged stories, passed on information and imparted the wisdom gained from experience, the latter mostly from the older woodsman to the summer paddler.[31] Patterson learned much from the trapper as they worked their way up the Liard and then the South Nahanni more or less together. Faille's destination was the Flat River where he hoped to build a cabin and overwinter.

Raised in Minnesota of Swiss descent, Faille was an outstanding woodsman. He lived alone in the bush most of his life, condescending to spend winters in Fort Simpson in a humble shack with outdoor plumbing only after reaching his eighth decade.[32]

Dick Turner, author of three books based on his five decades in the North, recalled meeting Faille in the early 1930s. Warned not to be shocked, he still found Faille a strange sight with his red wool pants, shoulder-length hair and matching red beard. "I saw Albert was talking before I shut the kickers off, and upon my word of honor he did not stop talking for two days and nights."[33] Faille's skill in a canoe was legendary, but Turner's most amazing story of the old trapper shows his astonishing ability to get the most out of his tools. Working upstream against a current that was stronger than the kicker, "Albert stood up, reached for one of the poles, held the steering handle between his knees, and used the pole to push the canoe forward. At the head of the riffle the drop was a bit too much for him. He calmly laid down the pole, set the steering handle carefully and stepped out into the water. Working his way to the bow he pulled the canoe up and over the drop, into calm water. Then with the kicker still humming along he stepped back into the canoe and continued on."[34]

Arriving at the small native village of Nahanni Butte at the mouth of the South Nahnni, Patterson and Faille bunked in Jack la Flair's trading post and waited out the rain. There, Faille tutored Patterson, six years his junior, in the fine points of upstream travel. Almost anyone could navigate the Liard, wide enough to be mistaken for a lake and moving about as swiftly, but travellers up the South Nahanni soon hit the confusing Splits, where channels coursed through countless islands, under giant piles of spring flood debris, even through the bush itself. Canyons awaited them too, legendary gorges cut through mountains where swift, brown torrents of meltwater flowed so quickly it made your head spin. Rapids, waterfalls, rock slides, monstrous bears and deadly Indians filled the rumours that made the Nahanni a perilous place. Many had already died in this inhospitable land.

As they watched the rain, Patterson absorbed countless details from the master paddler: how to load a canoe, how to track it efficiently, where to find weak spots in the current. He later wrote, "The Nahanni has probably never seen a finer canoeman, and to watch Faille search out the weak spot in a riffle and plant his canoe's nose exactly there, and neither to the right nor to the left by even a hand's breadth, is like watching a fine swordsman seeking for an opening, feeling out his adversary."[35]

Poling was another entrance requirement for anyone headed up the Nahanni, but in that subject the young Brit had already acquired a scholarly degree: "I had mastered that at Oxford, on summer Sundays upstream to Islip in search of beer and strawberries and cream. With the pole I could lay the nose of the canoe exactly where I wanted it—which proves, beyond any shadow of doubt, that a B.A.Oxon. is of value even on the South Nahanni."[36]

Poling is an unusual skill: one that defies logic. It is unsafe and foolish to stand in a canoe and lean over the edge, but that is exactly what the poler does. With a strong, thin tree cut 10 to 14 feet long, the canoeist stands, feet planted well apart near the stern of the fully loaded canoe, and pushes it upstream on quieter water near the bank. Given favourable conditions, it is the fastest way to climb a river. Tracking the canoe with a long rope from shore only works if the beach is unobstructed and the current is parallel to shore.

Faille neither poled nor tracked the lower stretches of the river. He fired up his 3.5 h.p. kicker on Tuesday, July 26, and left the deserted village— the natives all being away at Fort Simpson collecting treaty money. For ten miles he towed Patterson's canoe up sluggish waters to the infamous Splits, where began the practicum in navigation and upstream travel. Instead of running through steeply-treed banks, the river opens into a broad valley with dozens of channels, many cluttered with driftwood. "Very hard going in the Splits—up to my knees in fast water, hauling the canoe very often." He managed to catch up with Faille by noon the next day, only to fall behind again while ascending two tight bends.

Faille watched with interest at the foot of the Splits as Patterson tied a "bridle" onto the canoe for tracking. Fifty years later Patterson recalled, "He saw me that morning, and there was this fixed thing on this canoe like that, and he shook his head, and he said 'You'll be walking out of here talking to yourself in a couple of days time if you keep that on.'"[37] Although many trackers today swear by a bridle or yoke system—positioned to transfer the point of pull below the hull—Faille's system consisted of nothing more elaborate than an 80 foot-long rope, one end tied to the nose ring in the bow of the Chestnut, the other tied to the back seat.[38]

For the most part, Faille and Patterson travelled independently, partly out of preference, partly from necessity. The summer traveller went a bit slower without an outboard. The trapper stopped to hunt for fresh meat for his dogs. In this way Patterson and Faille leapfrogged all the way through the Splits.

Thursday was another early day for Patterson. Getting up at 4 a.m. was not unusual for him, and even with considerable dawdling, baking, making repairs and doing laundry, he was usually on the river by 8 a.m. Although the water had dropped from spring levels, he still found many channels unnavigable and had to backtrack and ascend others. Mid-afternoon called for a stop to sharpen his pole—a daily task as the "business end" tends to mushroom unless shod with a steel cap or collar. On he went, putting a rock in his place when he got out to pull the canoe along by the trackline.

Just then "...something caught my eye in the river, black & going hard down with the current. Thought it was a burnt stump at first—then a cow moose. Actually it was a black bear not seventy yards off. Never saw one swim before. It climbed out onto a shingle island—shook itself like a sheep dog, loped across, swam another branch of the river & disappeared in the bush.

"Bears & wolverine & wolves are plentiful here.... Heard a wolf yesterday. Two eagles swooped at me at lunch today but I got a knife in one hand & a blazing torch in the other & they sheered off." Not convinced that all the night sounds were harmless, he still slept with an automatic pistol under his pillow.

Cloud, wind and rain forced him to make camp early on Friday, July 29, but he was nearly through the Splits. Twisted Mountain was far behind, and the river ahead appeared to spill out from a solid wall of mountain. "It looks like hell—I wonder if I can get through it alone—I don't even know how long it is." Today, most paddlers look back on this scene and yearn to return to the deepest and most spectacular canyon on the South Nahanni, but for a man with only two months' canoeing experience, the cleft in the rock looked daunting. But first he made a brief stop to sip sulphur water. A bit farther on he stumbled on the hot springs that induce passersby to soak in the natural hot tub. In the meadows nearby he found evidence of native habitation and "a mass of wild raspberries, strawberries, black currants & red currants. I ate very hearty of fresh fruit." A place like nowhere else, it inspired him to write: "There was a slight blue haze in the hot sunshine & with that great gateway in front it seemed that 'a river came out of Eden.'" It was not the last time he likened a scene along the South Nahanni to the biblical garden.

Reality set in quickly as Patterson entered the Lower Canyon against the powerful current. It would take him two days to ascend Lower Canyon, a stretch that is passed through in only two hours when floating downstream. Sunday, July 31, dawned cool, but once the sun rose and shone into the gorge his old khaki shirt scorched under the harsh rays. All along the water edge, "I can see the gold gleaming in the black sand...—fine yellow gold that glitters as the waves wash it—too fine to pan. I lunched on an old gold claim—I happened to notice the claim stake—a hewed tree." Dozens of times Patterson would mention the tantalizing flakes of gold that captured his imagination and caused him to promise Mother a fortune. That day he nearly lost his entire outfit while tracking the canoe around a rock.

August 1 found him looking up at steep cliffs "getting more & more weird." Patterson and Faille vastly underestimated the height of Lower Canyon's walls, guessing them between 800 and 1000 feet. In places they soar more than 2000 feet overhead, a fact made all the more remarkable because the river predates the mountains. Patterson took a half day off, panning for gold and repairing his sore hands, cracked and made stiff by river silt. Then on he went that afternoon until he reached a fast stretch he could not ascend. He walked ahead to scout the route and decided to portage the gear and canoe. From a point he could see out of the canyon into an open valley, the infamous Dead Men's Valley where the headless corpses of the McLeod brothers were found in 1908.

That night, the noise of the river grated on Patterson's nerves, invading his sleep with a reminder of the hard work on the morrow. Time and again Patterson would complain about the constant noise of the swiftly moving river, "the sound of water that I have so often longed for on the prairie. Could do without it right now—should like a nice sluggish even running river—like the Cam or kindred ditch—that a fellow could make some headway against. However, everything worth having seems to be well guarded."

On August 2 Faille and Patterson reached Cache Rapid where they would need each other's help. The last navigational obstacle before entering Dead Men's Valley from Lower Canyon is a tricky ascent. Racing around the right side of an island, the full force of the Nahanni deflects off the cliff wall and caroms into the left bank. (Directions assume the observer is looking downstream.)

Lower Canyon of the South Nahanni, 1927.

They examined the challenge together. "What you do is get up high on this side," Faille probably directed, "and then you paddle like the dickens with the snoot of the canoe upstream and hope for the best." With luck they would catch that eddy at the bottom of the island, just upstream of the spot where the waves crash into the left bank. Off they went without incident, the four foot-high waves and fast current challenging the neophyte paddler. The psychological strain was extreme. The canoe and its contents were his only protection from death, but he suppressed thoughts of a capsize and did what had to be done. Once to the island, they worked their way up the inside corner in relatively placid water.

Less heavily loaded, Patterson escaped Lower Canyon first, pitched camp by a creek on river right and waited for Faille. That camp would become a favourite with the trapper who named it Bear Creek (today called Ram Creek). Black bears and Dall sheep frequent the area to this day, the bruins always hunting for tasty morsels of kid that scamper on the precipitous cliffs at the entrance to the Lower Canyon.

"I came, through the upper gateway of the canyon, to a lovely reach of calm water glittering in a burning sunlight. The walls went back & gave place to a wide valley with the forested mountains all round & streams of water clean as glass pouring in from clefts in the rock. The bush here is wonderful—generations of trees must have grown & died without fire. This must be the Eden—I may be the furtherest man up the river—so far as is known there is no white man or Indian ahead of me. Saw a thunderstorm coming up—the heat was intense. I made a rush for a spot sheltered by trees & just got a big fire lit, my tarp up & myself & things flung under it & the stuff in the canoe tarped up when down she came—came with a flash & a bang—whole water. Sand blew off the bars, smoke from a fire in the Yukon, lightning, thunder, river, rain, a gale, & the sun shone pale yellow over a mountain through it all—it looked first like hell. I sat under the tarp & fair cowered—torn between a desire not to get my rifle—loaded—wet & a wish to have it outside far away. Presently I took heart & wriggled out of my river things & into dry clothes—then I thought I would see how the chocolate was—untouched from Edmonton. Nothing wrong with it in the least. From that I went on to other things & by the time the rain was over, had made a very tolerable cold supper."

Also on August 2, "Haven't sneezed since leaving Edmonton—this has just occurred to me. I suppose a sudden return to the atmosphere of London could probably be fatal."

The next morning, Wednesday, August 3, Patterson let loose two long-range shots at a cow moose and her calf from under his mosquito net. Faille could have used the meat for the dogs, but his shots missed the mark. "It isn't everywhere you get moose shooting from your pillow." Shaved, bathed and well fed, he welcomed Faille into camp and told him about the moose. With the trapper off chasing the animal, Patterson repaired the canoe, touching up the patches with grey paint that would take a day to dry. "War declared on Germany 13 years ago today."

On Friday, August 5, they were off by nine and up through Dead Men's Valley into Second Canyon before nightfall. Today's paddlers often wonder why the canyons are numbered backward: Fourth starting at the Falls, then the matching pair called Third and Second and finally Lower or First Canyon. The first explorers, of course, did not fly into the headwaters and float out. They slogged up every reach of the river and named the canyons as they encountered them. Patterson understood the merits of upstream paddling. "You see a lot more of the river and you come away with a very clear memory of it, that I think would be impossible to obtain just coming downstream. You've dealt with every obstacle somehow or another and been there for a sufficient length of time to remember it as a feature."[39]

Saturday, August 6. "Up very early but owing to one thing after another cropping up didn't get away till ten to eight." After repairing a tear in the canoe canvas with pitch, he ascended into Third Canyon, stopping at a rock outcropping he named Library Rock. He napped in the nude, "in des habille" he called it, while his wet clothes dried in the sun. The afternoon went poorly. "The canoe wouldn't track properly & swung all over the place"—a sure sign of an improperly loaded canoe with perhaps too much weight in the bow. Poling, he nearly fell overboard several times. Paddling was almost as futile, the blade hitting rocks on every stroke in the shallow water. Finally, he crumpled on shore and ate chocolate, raspberries and red currants. Food has amazing restorative powers.

Porridge, milk and raspberries laid the foundation for a good breakfast the next morning. Sunday chores included a shave and a hair wash, sharpening the axe and the knives and baking bannocks. More canoe repairs took until the afternoon. "In the meantime I shall take another stroll into the raspberry patch. 'Opes I shalln't be ill,' as Mr. Jorrocks says."

A bit down in spirits, he plodded through Third Canyon, wondering when it would open into the Flat River valley. "After a long tough track & pull up a very steep rapid I came to a most wonderful place, where the

Albert Faille passing through The Gate below Pulpit Rock, 1927.

Nahanni cuts clean through a mountain. The water beneath is calm & like glass—on the left a sheer precipice, & on the right the same but broken by a huge mass of rock that stands out like a pulpit. The rocks are tawny & red with iron, the water is green, above & beyond is the forest & over all hung a pale blue smoke haze. The whole thing was like a great gateway through which I glided silently, midget like. I have seen many beautiful places in my lifetime, but never anything of this kind."

The Gate and Pulpit Rock take their names from this Patterson quote that is so evocative of the way the river slips, almost without current, through its self-made slice in the rock to form a rare cut-off antecedent meander.

Patterson snapped two pictures, then passed upstream into a canyon flanked by steep walls. Red screes plummeted to shoreline and little beaches of black sand twinkled with omnipresent "river gold." Faille's footprints and those of his dogs covered the sand. Patterson packed it in for the day after only six hours—eight or nine being his usual quota. "This poling, hard paddling, tracking & wading knee deep in swift water over rough, sharp & slippery rocks is very tiring. I find it more so now that the river is almost continuously fast, with few calm stretches."

Later in life he admitted to a potentially serious accident in this part of Third Canyon. When asked if he would recommend solo travel, he replied, "Not really. I think we had some very good luck. I had a fall when tracking somewhere above The Gate, and it was before I was too experienced in tracking. I didn't let my canoe far enough out into the stream in those days and I caught a certain rush at the head of an eddy. The rocks were a little slippery with rain and it pulled me off my feet."[40]

He ran into the trapper the next day, Monday, August 8, reading about Father Lacombe, a French Canadian Oblate missionary who helped bring Catholicism to the west. "Discouraged" is how Patterson found him, faced with a box canyon that seemed invincible. The current was stronger than Faille's kicker, there was no poling bottom, and the sheer walls were too steep to climb. After a hearty meal they tackled the job together and portaged to a beach above the rapid. "I cut a trail down to the beach—it may be used in later years in some great gold rush up here." It took many trips to carry their food, trapping and prospecting supplies and equipment. Finally, only the canoes remained. "Look here," Faille probably said, "I think we can just make it if we go hard." Off Faille went, ferrying to the far shore and upriver, then crossing back to the little sandy bay. He made it all look easy. Both arms waving, he encouraged Patterson across. "I felt doubtful but took a hold on myself & put to sea. For about 90 seconds there seemed to be water in all directions racing past me & then I landed at the foot of the cliff & tracked up through the swirls & crossed to the new camp."

Faille brought up his second canoe and they repacked, ready for the morning. Fifty years later Patterson recounted the trick for not losing a load during the night: "Always moor to a tree if you possibly can or to a very solid rock, passing your line round where it can't slip off the rock. If for some reason, you decided to camp on a great shingle or gravel bar where there's no tree within reach and no stranded tree above you, then I always used to beach the canoe solidly and slide it up on a log.... The thing I did make a point of doing under those conditions was to hitch the canoe solidly to my sleeping bag. A few friendly tugs on the sleeping bag would wake me and I'd do something about it because it might be a perfectly fine night there but if there's been a cloudburst up in those glaciated mountains above the Falls, then you might get one of these phenomenally big rises."[41]

Faille's Norwegian Logging Cake—an egg, milk and flour mixture—tasted fine the next morning. Patterson added bacon and honey to the meal as well as a fresh fruit salad of raspberries, cranberries and hips and haws from the plentiful rosebushes. A precious can of cream topped the feast. That day Patterson saw gold, "in larger quantities than ever." Dreams of wealth and glory were gradually swelling his head. Gold in abundance lay ahead and in his imagination he was already spending it. From his sleeping roll on a bed of thick moss he watched the day end in a glorious sunset of gold shot through with purple. "In years to come this will be a great playground...."

Wednesday, August 10, started off well but deteriorated. Patterson was on the river by 7:30 a.m. after completing a round of camp chores that included bandaging an injured ankle. On into the valley of the Flat River he went, passing one of Faille's two canoes. No doubt the trapper had his hands full in this current with even one canoe. Then came another set of splits, just as the Flat comes into the South Nahanni, which itself is just flowing out of Fourth Canyon. "Most difficult & most tiring," he noted after ten long hours of wading in numbing-cold water. Damn, he had wanted to see Faille, leave behind some gear and make a quick dash for the Falls. Instead he fired off a shot to indicate his passing and pushed on past a great campsite at a reasonable supper hour. Instead, he camped upriver at a miserable spot with the bugs. "All I can say is—what an unspeakable afternoon."

Evening grub made his spirits rise. "Saw a curious bird floating on the water—large, whitish head, red brown body & dark brown or black tipped wings & tail." That night the almost full moon rose and set low in the southern sky shortly after sunset at 9:30. As a result, the aurora borealis illuminated the sky, thrilling the Londoner with his first view of the ghostly apparitions that summer. Dancing across the heavens were multicoloured shards, chandeliers and "rainbow-coloured fire."

Figure-of-Eight Rapid, the canoe headed upstream.

The next day was yet "another day of strife." The morning weather suckered Patterson with an intimation of rain, so he dawdled, waiting for the downpour. Instead, the sun broke out hot and the sky cleared just as he finished building a waterproof camp in the woods. Back on the river, he worked hard to make headway against the current in canyons of many colours. Battling "very sharp rocks...I circumnavigated a fearful boil by a masterpiece of strategy & came at the top to an old camping place." There, he bathed and shaved and made fresh bannocks. By this time he was allowing himself a half day of rest every four days. The "fearful boil" he avoided that day is still hard to miss. Called Wrigley's, it awaits the unsuspecting paddler at the bottom of an island, just downstream of the mouth of Wrigley Creek.

On August 12 Patterson encountered the most unusual rapid on the South Nahanni—a confused spot where the river runs headlong into a cliff and bounces off into two huge eddies, one upstream, the other downstream. Faille named it "Figure-of-Eight Rapid" when he saw it a few weeks later.

"I came about ten to a bay, beyond which the walls went on again with a swift current between them. At the far end I could hear the roar & see the boiling, white water of a bad rapid, so I beached the canoe & went ahead through the bush to a little point from which I could look down on the rapid. The worst so far—a most curious place...." Six foot-high waves separated the whirlpools, the upper one circulating clockwise, the lower, counterclockwise. Where they met they plowed into the swift main current, creating a wild cacophony of rooster-tails that danced about in a seemingly unpredictable pattern. Patterson watched, perplexed. Whatever happened, he vowed to avoid that cliff face where he suspected the waves would surely crush the canoe like kindling.

At the little bay below the rapid he unloaded his gear, took a bite of chocolate and committed himself to the river. He left behind the little diary in case everything went wrong. Upstream he paddled, on river left. "I worked my way up the far side [within a hundred feet of the point] & beyond that I could not get, paddle as hard as I might. So after 5 tries I turned & shot back to the bay."

"Persistence is one thing and plain obstinacy is another," he wrote twenty-five years later in *The Dangerous River*.[42] Shouldering his pack, he cleared a trail through the lightly-forested bush along the top of the cliff to the sand of the upper bay. "Over that trail I portaged every damn thing I have." It took half a dozen trips or more to move the gear—his tarp alone weighed more than the standard tent, sleeping pad and bag of today's paddler.

Then it was time to portage the canoe. Although only 16 feet long, the waterlogged cedar and canvas canoe weighed in excess of 100 pounds. To the uninitiated, flinging a canoe onto one's shoulders is a Herculean task. With proper technique, however, even a heavy canoe slides up with relative ease. Patterson's diary reveals a less than smooth first attempt: "The struggle to get the canoe up onto my head was intense—the tracks on the sands of the bay look as if a circus had been to town. I had never done it before—there is a trick to lifting it that I had been told & had forgotten, so I had to find it out, with much cursing, for myself."

Patterson plodded on the next day, enjoying himself immensely, but getting awfully tired. At one spot he portaged half the gear and waded the lightened canoe up "...a canyon of red & yellow rocks & loose stones, sharp as knives, which played hell with the canoe & the soles of my old running shoes."

Farther up the canyon "...was a mass of white water—I was almost disheartened but the Nahanni is a fine river for building character—it develops in one an appalling obstinacy." Ferrying from side to side to take advantage of slacker water, he learned the meaning of fear. Once, waves grabbed the canoe, sucking it into the maw of white water between the crests as he bashed away with the paddle, furiously trying to overcome the incredible current; "…shipping water & swearing hard as the white tops curled over the canoe."

The thunder of the Falls was constant by this point. For days a slight rumble had shaken the earth but now the Falls seemed just around the corner. Few people had seen them, and the only photograph taken to date had been lost when a canoe tipped in a rapid. If only he could reach the Falls and snap a few precious exposures he would have something unique to show the world. That and gold nuggets, if he could find the source of the fine flour gold that tantalized on every beach.

Meat wandered into camp that night. "I shot a cow moose this evening. I was bailing out the canoe just after crossing the last swells to my camping place when I heard a grunting in the water, & I saw in front of me a cow moose & her calf swimming to shore. They landed a little way down & as the calf seemed well able to take care of himself I shot the cow. She fell & in her struggle rolled over the bank & died in the water. Before I could get to her she was swept away by the current & I saw my rump steak vanishing down the rapids—a meal for the wolves & a wicked waste of meat & game. I wish now I had taken their photograph instead—it would have made a beautiful picture."

R. M. Patterson portaging canoe, 1927.

Cries from the orphaned calf awoke him several times early the next morning. Bleating sorrowfully, it eventually swam down river to an uncertain future. As time passed, Patterson tried to forget this incident. In the Foreword to *The Dangerous River,* he claimed a near-perfect record as far as game waste: "...nothing was shot uselessly with the exception of one mountain sheep that was swept away down the rapids." Late in Part 2 of the same book he tells a hilarious story of a cow and calf moose that wrecked his camp, supper and pots and pans before making their escape. The winner-take-all attitude he displayed in his early years in Canada probably became embarrassing and prevented him from telling the more factual account. Besides, as he matured he rewrote the past to reflect the kind of person he would have liked to have been that summer of 1927.

The sad incident with the calf comes immediately before a puzzling entry: "Sunday is always a tough day for me." Patterson never explained why. Years later his wife and daughter suggested he was probably lonely on the Sabbath. Although his family was Presbyterian, it was more likely the social aspect of Sundays that he missed. His grandfather's home, where he lived as a child, was always busy with "a lot of comings and goings." Similarly, his "home away from home" at the Fenwicks "was such a cheerful household, and they did go on picnics and walks on the moors. They must also have spent time in the big gardens, and generally enjoyed each other's company."[43] That lonely moose tugged at his emotions.

That Sunday, August 14, went from bad to worse. He pushed on "Battered and bruised" up the rough Fourth Canyon. "I had to risk myself & my worldly goods once this morning in the rough water & twice I saw my home & bed & board swing madly on the end of the trackline in a riffle. The falls are supposed to be at latitude 62° & it would be a pity to lose all for the sake of a five mile scramble. Also dangerous in this lonely country."

That afternoon, around a point he saw a beach with trees and the chance of a nice camp. "I was so cheered that I slipped back into the eddy & laughed like an idiot. Then I tackled the crossing. The canoe leapt & pitched worse than on Lake Athabasca & twice white water came clean over the side. I got down on my knees & fairly dug into the water & just got her over—30 yards further down & I should have been under a cliff, heading for a bad rapid."

Then followed more sheer canyon walls with "curious battlements & pinnacles" and waves to frighten the most experienced voyageur. Tired and depressed, he wandered upstream on foot, seeking an easier way.

There was none, so at 5 p.m. he jammed the canoe fast between two rocks and scrambled out of the canyon. Cranberries greeted him at the cliff top, as well as a birch log with saw cuts. "Who could have been here with a saw?" he wondered aloud as he looked about. Then something stopped him in his tracks; the horns and head of a Dall ram sticking up above a knoll. Reaching for his pistol—the rifle was in the canoe—he slid back and slowly moved around the knoll until fifty yards from his target. The first bullet made no impression. Neither did the second, nor the third. Had he missed? Then the sheep was gone. "Now what?" he thought as he scrambled over the rocks and scree. But the ram lay dead under a tree, three bullets lodged firmly between its eyes.

Back to the canoe he plummeted, to return with a bag, knives, sharpening stone and axe, and the camera to record the event. As he dressed out the

Ovis dalli sheep's head.

head he marvelled how a casual Sunday afternoon hike had bagged him a trophy head, with a 9 millimetre Luger pistol, no less. Luck was on his side again. The ram had probably never seen a bandy-legged human before, "dusty, unshaved, an old red handkerchief round my neck & an old khaki shirt, ripped to tatters."

Only a few months before, firmly planted in a deep chair with good books all around, he had daydreamed of many heroic adventures. "When I had my tonsils out that book I had in the home said that the possession of the head of a bighorn sheep placed a man in the first rank among hunters—I very much wonder." It now seemed like the easiest thing in the world.

Not so the goal ahead: reaching The Falls of the Nahanni. Indecision weighed strongly upon him that evening, so he decided to rest, do camp chores, bake and make repairs to the canoe and himself. The next reach seemed impossible but it might look better in the morning.

Patterson procrastinated the next day, in the morning skinning the ram head and stretching the hide. Salted and mounted on a paddle blade, the cape was an apparition. He then took his weekly bath and shave while boiling up a good mutton stew to eat with cooked raspberries. Canoe repairs consumed the whole afternoon. "Feet & legs about as badly hacked

also." After this he sorted gear for an overland hike to the Falls. He budg-
eted three days and two nights through rough country. Scrambling
through gullies and over hummocks would consume precious energy so
he rejected the blanket and counted on a fire to warm him throughout the
short summer night.

The plans slowly dissolved the next day, August 16, as he continued to
prepare for the hike. Nine o'clock came and went, then noon, then mid-
afternoon. Attempts to make a good food cache failed. Finally he realized
it was impossible. Even chocolate failed to improve his mood. Disappointed, he lay down. The vibration of the Falls through the ground, the
roar down the canyon and the mist in the air: they all taunted him. He
had given up. Why?

"Reasons—I can't leave my camp if I can't make my food safe from the
animals. I am not at all sure that I can get my canoe across but would try
if I had to do it. Having got across there may be another 5 miles of this
swift water & sharp rocks & I have only one canoe, one pair of shoes &
one pair of feet to go nearly 1000 miles with before winter catches me.
Also—& particularly—I wish to look up the Flat River & at least one of its
creeks before I finally turn for the Liard as, although there is gold in the
water here, I feel convinced that a certain amount comes from the Flat &
its creeks, & gold comes before falls much as I want to see them. Also, I
want to get that skull back to Faille on the Flat as he has a large tub in
which I can boil the rest of the meat off & sterilise it."

It took him decades to admit failure. Twenty-five years later he fabri-
cated a heroic story for *The Dangerous River*. According to that tale, con-
quering all, he had rounded the last bend to see the magnificent Falls of
the Nahanni, alone. Unfortunately, his camera was at Faille's cache—so
the tale went—so he had no picture to prove his success. On he had
paddled, drawing closer and closer, until a riptide that pulled him toward the Falls had endangered his life. Only a superhuman effort had
saved the day. A climb up both sides of the cascade had revealed prehistoric fossils. An overnight stay had ended the dramatic reward for a
job well done.[44]

That's how the record stood in 1954. Patterson's comfort with the mid-
August failure apparently increased with time. In *The Buffalo Head*, published in 1961, Patterson made no mention of the fictional visit to the
Falls. Instead, he gave Faille credit for helping him arrive there as a result
of their combined efforts later that summer. Finally, in 1989 his widow
presented his papers to the British Columbia Archives and Records Serv-

ice in Victoria, British Columbia. The diaries, written as extended letters home to Mother, tell the true story of that first attempt.

On August 16 he decided to make a quick trip back to the Flat River to share his tales with Faille. There he would clean up the trophy, then return to Alberta. The next two days went quickly and without incident. On the 17th he paddled through big waves alone for the first time. Although he found it thrilling, he made a note to ask Faille a few questions about technique. A quick lunch at the top of the portage trail at Figure-of-Eight Rapid fortified him and by supper he was in a cozy camp in the little bay at the downstream end of the portage. "There was less of a circus this time when I upended the canoe & got it on my head & altogether I am becoming a successful voyageur in the oldest way that Canada has known." He was still kicking himself for not making the Falls: "…if only I had had more time—or less weight with me."

On the 18th he reached the mouth of the Flat River, covering in one hour what took him more than a day on the way up. Looking for Faille, he fired his rifle and hollered a bit, then plodded up the South Nahanni tributary. There Patterson found Faille's camp. A cabin was under construction and dogs leapt to greet the weary traveller, but of Faille himself there was no sign. Patterson settled down to eat a hearty lunch of mutton and barley stew, bannock and cheese, washed down with tea and chased by chocolate for desert. The ram's head would have to overwinter with

Faille's shack on the Flat River, 1927.

Faille, as Patterson had no hunting license, but the trapper had offered to bring out anything he managed to bag the next spring. Faille had also said something about running down to the Splits to pick up a load of supplies at the cache when Patterson went out. But where was Faille? Just as Patterson finished his bath and shave, the trapper returned with news of a caribou kill a mile upstream.

The next day Patterson agreed to lend Faille the pick and prospecting pan, and in return the trapper agreed to set aside a nice set of marten and mink pelts for Patterson's mother. Questions went back and forth as the friends deepened their ties. Faille had been trapping since age fourteen. An old Scots had taught him to read and write in the Minnesota north woods. He loved reading, had visited England and France and knew lots about the world. On into the night they talked. But try as he might, Patterson could not convince Faille of some basic truths: the diary describes the old trapper as a man who "will argue at any time & prove— that the Earth is not round & that there is an undiscovered hot continent hidden away in the South Pacific."

Puzzling over two strange blazes that Patterson found on trees at the mouth of the river, the two men shrugged their shoulders and chanted their now-familiar refrain, "To hell with it, whatever it is—we can deal with it."[45]

At some point Patterson admitted his failure to reach the Falls but Faille cheered him up. He also wanted to see the Falls and survey the creeks en route for gold and fur, so he said something like: "You just go up that Flat—see if you can find that gold. Then you come down here in four days and we go up to the Falls together." That sounded great, though the colours were already turning. Patterson packed a few light things and threw the rest into the cache. If he found gold up the Flat he would come back another year, stay over, prospect until he found the source of the wealth, and then head for Fort Simpson and stake the claims.

On Saturday, August 20, the summer paddler headed off and by nightfall was ten miles up the Flat. The lightly loaded canoe poled, paddled and tracked easily. It seemed every other fleck of sand was river gold, glittering with a radiance greater than anywhere else on his trip. The Flat appeared to be the source, somewhere up toward the Yukon border. "I found gold all along this afternoon—if I find much more I shall in any case, try to get Gordon & come in very early next year and track it down—there is a fortune somewhere, both here & on the Nahanni. Let it be mine." He would share with Gordon Matthews, of course, the skilled trapper with sled-dog experience. Daydreams flooded his mind as he sat eating caribou at camp that night. Perhaps he would make a quick trip home in the winter, visit Mother, offer an engagement ring to that special girl. Then make a return trip up the Flat with a strong outboard motor and well-outfitted canoes. It was a lot to juggle but his investments were doing well. "What do you think?" he wrote Mother, "Have I enough money to ask a girl to marry me even without the gold & would a girl wait a year for me? I know which girl I like best now & I don't suppose she will remain single for ever…. I should like to have a home some day & not always to be a bachelor, much as I love this life in the mountain west." If she would just wait another year, he could find the gold and then settle down to a pleasant life somewhere in the foothills of the Rockies….

By the firelight he wrote much more. Nearby, a trout jumped and a great black bear stumbled out of the bush and crossed the river. Then the stars came out and filled the night with their twinkling, just as the gold had glittered in the sand that afternoon. Finally, the aurora appeared, dancing across the sky in long, quivering spokes. It curled into a Question Mark, then later filled the sky with "weird blobs & patches" until it extinguished the starlight with its haunting glow.

The next day, another Sunday, passed quickly. Gold was everywhere. "If we can trace down the source of this yellow stuff I'll give you Edenhall" he wrote Mother, promising her the famous Musgrove castle in Cumberland, England. His widowed mother had no need for Raymond's gold; she was living comfortably in a luxurious London flat after her marriage to Sir John Scott. Nevertheless, her only son still wanted to win her a castle.

Monday, August 22, was turn back day. On up the Flat he went until he came to a tributary, probably Caribou Creek. After determining there was almost no gold in that valley, he returned to the Flat and on a whim decided to make a dash back to Faille's camp that same afternoon. Barefoot in the canoe, he sat still as the crystal clear water floated him downstream. The rocks and pebbles on the riverbed flew by at a furious pace in the fast stretches between deep pools of calm green water. "I was perfectly happy—few people know what that means—some never are. The perfect day—the sense of power & speed—the gliding swiftly past the cliffs in the still reaches, & then the roar of the water ahead—the canoe gains speed, flies down a hill of water into the waves, through the foam & out into the calm below—it is a splendid way to travel."

He reached camp in under five hours after travelling twenty miles or more. Darkness was falling when he ran the last rapid, a thrilling commitment that sometimes results in a sudden jolt when the canoe high-centres on a shallow rock. Faille welcomed him with a well-deserved supper of deliciously tender caribou stew.

On Tuesday they were up with the sun to work on the cabin. By the end of the day the little cabin was done. With candles and the best china and linen—candles anyway—they warmed the house with a great supper. Bed was a welcome relief.

The next morning, August 24, they set out for The Falls of the Nahanni in Faille's big canoe. Thick smoke from forest fires to the west obscured the view at Murder Creek (today's Clearwater Creek). Ash fell like snow and their throats grew sore and raspy and their eyes red.

At Figure-of-Eight Rapid[46] they scouted the boils from the portage trail. Faille "went and sat down on the point on the right bank where the current is thrown across the River and splits at this point into two whirlpools. He sat there for quite a long time looking at it and then he said, 'Well, that's the funniest piece of water I ever did see.'"[47] They decided to portage the gear and try the rapid with an empty canoe. A first attempt expelled them into the lower eddy, pummelled by waves. On the second try waves pushed them against the wall, pinning the canoe and threatening to swamp them. Faille's clear head prevailed and he hollered something like "Grab that wall, quick." So Patterson dropped his paddle and yanked on the rocks. Slowly the canoe scraped along the cliff, then squirted free into the upper whirlpool.

Blasting upriver at incredible speed, they were to cover the twenty miles between the Flat and the Falls in only two days. That first evening a weary Patterson rolled out his tarp right after supper and climbed into his sleeping bag. "Faille is talking hard all this time—as a man talks who won't have much chance of talking for another six months except to himself."

On August 25 the smoke cleared as they slogged "up through the cañons with much swearing & damning" until they reached Patterson's turn back camp, where they lunched. Cold and wet, they built a blazing fire and recuperated. Back in the water, they crossed to river left and continued upstream, Patterson tracking, Faille steering. "We heard the roar of the falls simultaneously & shouted. I was first round the bend & saw them first—I hauled on the trackline & pulled Faille into view. They were within less than half a mile of my last camp—their thunder had been choked off

Faille at The Falls of the Nahanni, August 25, 1927.

from me by the deep twisting cañon & the mists that I had seen in the early mornings were their spray floated down the valley. A sight worth travelling to see—counting the cataract above the drop must be 200 ft. or over & they are split in the middle by a great tower of rock."

In fact, the drop is 392 feet. Split by a massive pyramid of rock—to-day named Mason's Rock after famed Canadian filmmaker and paddler Bill Mason—the Falls inspire from every angle. On a sunny day, an elegant rainbow crosses the chasm below the raging torrent.

Over a trail they trekked, feasting on blueberries, now and then poking their noses out of the woods to see the Falls from many vantage points. Above the precipice, the wa-

The Falls from the trail. This rock is today informally named after Bill Mason.

103

ter kicked up frantic roostertails before catapulting into the canyon. Wood that appeared match-stick sized on the beach below was actually huge pieces of driftwood, stripped in Sluice Box Rapids above the Falls. For half a mile, this vicious rapid crashed over rock ledges, leapt over stone abutments and poured through fissures only water can carve through bedrock. Upstream of the rapids, the Nahanni looked peaceful. "Like a great lake" it seemed, stretching on into the sunset almost as far as the eye could see. "Took photos & back to camp for supper—it rained a little at night & the spray drifted over us."

Two images survive from that memorable day, both from river left below the Falls. One shows just the Falls. In the other, Faille stands on a rock in the river, legs apart, hat cocked at a jaunty angle.

Fenley Hunter, who was to arrive at the Falls the next summer, would name them after his daughter Virginia. Not once in all his writings does Patterson call them "Virginia Falls." The Falls of the Nahanni was the name he and Faille used their first summer on the river and it stuck in their minds for life. Besides, The Falls of the Nahanni has a wonderful ring to it, full of possession, mystery and majesty.

The quick trip back to Faille's cabin on the Flat went without incident. One can imagine the two paddlers howling with glee as they bashed through the waves of Fourth Canyon without the benefit of spray decks. Two days of hard labour up to the Falls were undone in a couple of hours. They "shot through the Figure-of-Eight-Rapids in one mighty surge" and lunched at Faille's cabin.[48] There they cooked and prepared for a quick run down the river the next day. As summer turned to fall, Patterson was growing anxious. He still had many hundreds of miles to travel on northern rivers, an unpleasant task once ice begins to form along the banks. Would his tardy schedule haunt him later that fall?

On Saturday, August 27, superlatives fill his diary. "Early mists gave way to the most lovely morning of all—never have I seen such colouring of greens & grays, sunshine & soft clouds as in the upper cañon." They flew down the river and lunched "at the great gateway" where Patterson took a mystical photo of Faille floating through the gorge, his large 18-foot canoe appearing as but a twig on the placid surface below Pulpit Rock.

Through the afternoon and evening they paddled, into the Upper Splits at the top end of Dead Men's Valley. The next morning everything glistened with dew and frost from the cool, damp night. "I got up, dressed, pulled a few dry spruce twigs for kindling, slipped on a sharp snag with my moccasined foot & fell down the mossy bank into the stones below—crashing my hand.... I lay there & groaned & swore until I felt better—the dogs cheerfully wagging their tails the while." A call to Faille rescued the day and after a breakfast that rivalled the feast of the the night before, they set off for Lower Canyon.

Through Lower Canyon they raced, hurrying to reach the hot springs. Now called Kraus' Hotsprings after Gus and Mary Kraus who lived there from 1940 to 1971, this natural upwelling of sulphur-laden 102° Fahrenheit water has soothed tired muscles for centuries. "The Indians had come there to bathe for generations past & had cut many of the trees & all the brush for fires, so that there was a beautiful meadow of wild hay round about. The moose seem to come there & there were fresh bear tracks by the stream. I saw a humming bird amongst the flowers."

On they paddled into the Splits, arriving at Faille's cache near the contorted face of Twisted Mountain late that night. "Had supper in the dark & talked a long time" as the rain splattered their tarps. Finally, a downpour arrived and they fell asleep on their last night together.

On August 29, Patterson's last day on the South Nahanni, Faille clicked off a snapshot of his apprentice and friend. In it Patterson stands proud and tall, sweater sleeves rolled up, silk scarf knotted at his neck. Round, wire-rimmed glasses perched on a prominent nose grace a face topped with short hair. A contented grin fills the corners of his mouth. At his waist, pants that fitted well in May are baggy, cinched tight with a belt and secured again with a gunbelt that bristles with shells for the pistol in the leather holster at his right hip. The left arm, elbow cocked to the side, bears no sign of a watch. This image shows Patterson as he really was by the end of his trip, so in tune with the daily rhythms of life on the river that an artificial timepiece was superfluous. Specific times of day do appear throughout the entire diary, so his watch was apparently close at hand in order to allow him to make precise observations.

"I had an early lunch & left at one for South Nahanni Post—we said Good bye & for a long time I saw Faille & the dogs standing on a point of rock until I rounded the bend."

It took Patterson six hours to reach Nahanni Butte, a marathon of paddling that still tricks voyageurs to this day. When almost at the rounded mountain, the river makes an abrupt turn southwest, adding an extra ten inconvenient miles as it makes a lazy attempt to cut cross-country to the Pacific Ocean before meandering halfheartedly back to the Butte. During the night, Patterson awoke to find a bear traipsing through the cooking area and stepping in the washbowl and frying pan. The clang of the bolt loading a shell into the rifle chamber scared it off and Patterson fell back to sleep.

PATTERSON wrote almost 15,000 words or half the text of the 1927 diary after leaving Nahanni Butte. For many readers of *The Dangerous River*, this story is unknown because recent editions leave out the chapter titled The Trail South. Yet this half of the story includes the most amazing feats of courage and resourcefulness and a tangle with destiny. It was the trail south that earned him the title "Hard to kill."

August 30 to September 6, 1927—Nahanni Butte to Fort Liard
"Put to sea in thick mist at 8:25" the diary records for August 30. In a downpour he turned up the Liard River and made about 26 miles before calling it a day. On the 31st, friends Arthur George and his wife invited him into their trapping cabin to warm up and dry out. Their beans, bannock and cheese fuelled him until he arrived at Bill Eppler and Joe Mulholland's cabin 18 miles farther south. There, Patterson and Eppler read *Saturday Evening Post*s while Mulholland shot mice. "One quick move" he warned, "and you will be sharing a grave with a mouse." A leaky roof forced them to tarp up the inside of the small cabin. Even so, they "had rain in one half of the shack & fair weather in the other. Kept the stove roaring to dry the water as it fell." Patterson put off his departure while the deluge continued. "Later we argued long on the merits of king & president. Every 3 hours or so we had dinner, to vary the monotony."

Bidding his bachelor hosts adieu, he slogged on toward the post. "The wind was fair so I ripped up a grain sack & put up a mast & sail which helped a good deal but made me lose my temper a lot." Then a willow branch ambushed him, snatched the glasses from his face and catapulted them into the river. An extra pair saved the day. "Temper got worse & by supper time I was incoherent absolutely but supper, a warm fire & bed made me whistle a little."

Seven days of almost continuous rain made for tiresome travel. "The frost doesn't bother me but I hate the rain like any cat." He expected snow in his camp any morning, dustings of it evident on the hills about the river. Finally, on September 6, Fort Liard came into view. As was his custom, Patterson made up hot water and bathed, shaved and dressed in clean clothes before presenting himself in civilized company. Months before he had sent a sack of provisions and winter clothing on ahead with the Liard Coal Company scow. His thoughtful care package to himself included 25 lbs. of flour, 6 lbs. of sugar, 2 lbs. of raisins, 1 lb. of tea, 1 lb. of baking powder, 1 mosquito net, 1 can of canoe paint, mitts, woollen mitts, insoles, tie and pin, an exposure meter, padlock and keys, receipts, a tobacco pouch, soap, maps and moccasin rubbers.

Most intriguing were his comments regarding letters awaiting him at the fort. "They had letters for me & so had the Bay & the old priest at the mission—Père Bouet—all dated in May before you knew I was coming up here. I was awfully glad to get them." Apparently, Patterson did not inform Mother until late May that he was heading into the wilderness for a summer jaunt. The remainder of the page is neatly cut from the diary and a few lines on the back of the page erased, then blanked out with dark ink. The mail also included letters from Gordon Matthews, from boyhood chum Edwin Fenwick—"remember, we are now middle aged & take care"—and from two women: prospective fiancée Marigold Portman and enticing American Rafaelle Kennedy.

Relaxing in a comfy chair, watching the world pass outside the window of the trading post, Patterson passed judgement on the natives, "A degenerate, low, Mongol type, these Indians of the north…. I am glad they are dying out—they make way for the white man." In spite of his impression of the locals, Patterson of the Ghostly Nahanni was a big hit at Fort Liard. Numerous offers of meals exceeded even his appetite during his one-day stay. Gifts of butter, honey, milk, beans, apples and bread eased his need for groceries when he shopped at the Hudson's Bay Company post. One thoughtful Northerner even presented him with a sack of doughnuts.

September 7 to 11, 1927—Fort Liard to Nelson Forks

Upriver travel on the Liard was old hat to Patterson by this point, and in good weather he covered the fifty miles in four days. Tricky bits of rapids challenged him, but none of it equalled the South Nahanni. On September 7 a great harvest moon rose just before sunset, evoking romantic memories of a woman back home. On another day he found an old powderhorn, the strap rotted away. Could some old voyageur have dropped it here in the 1700s?

Camped across the river from the post at Nelson Forks, he bathed, shaved and "treated myself to my one remaining new toothbrush." A couple of days before he had met Mr. Thomas, a trapper with a cabin on the Liard. The hardened woodsman had warned the unusual looking Patterson that he still had many days to go, twice the number the Brit had actually taken. "My friend Mr. Thomas was mad—not I. This is written on the north west bank of the Liard, opposite the mouth of the Fort Nelson River up which I have to go about 200 miles. Thomas probably underestimated my travelling powers—I may not be good for much in this life but I can move, & in addition I get as obstinate as three mules & a Scotsman under these conditions. Wish you could see me—brown, wiry & tattered. Thomas would notice my glasses & probably set me down as a travelling poet & correspondingly incapable."

Patterson delivered mail to the post and graciously accepted a lunch of moose meat, fresh bread and honey. The HBC stood him the meal as he decided he "might as well have a little out of the company besides dividends." Dividends paid a healthy 20% that year so lunch was just the icing on a most tasty cake.

September 12 to 18, 1927—Nelson Forks to Fort Nelson

Travel on the Fort Nelson River was easy. And except for an occasional afternoon squall, the days were hot. "About four o'clock came down a sudden deluge—I proceeded unmoved, being now in B.C. where it has as much right to rain as in the Lake District." However, afternoon sundogs and great flocks of geese and cranes winging south warned of coming snows. Nights were growing colder and frost covered the canoe each morning. To warm himself, he ate a good breakfast built on a firm foundation of porridge that he set out each night before retiring.

Long days of monotonous travel provided a chance to think and to write Mother. "I am anxious to know what you think of my plans to take one of the Christmas special excursions home from the West. I believe that on the Flat River is the gold, & if Gordon will come I can get at it. But if we go it will mean a full year in there & I shall not see you or Marigold. Is it right & possible to get engaged & then go away into the mountains? I believe if a girl was fond of one she would wait a year—it might mean horses & a car & all that make life good to live—all excellent this—the open life, that no money can buy. I wonder if she likes me."

The river quickened. In spots it was too shallow for paddling, the bottom too mushy for poling and the banks too overgrown to let him track along the shore. A "foolish, blustering wind was blowing which, though it helped me in some places, bothered me in others & made me fume & swear. A wind ruffles the water & makes it all look alike so that one can't spot the shallows & swift water. Also it makes a light canoe very difficult to steer as it can whirl it about like a cork. A wind seems to me sometimes such a silly, pointless, swaggering thing...." Without noticing it, he badly strained muscles in his back and suffered the rest of the way to the fur trade post.

Nearing Fort Nelson he rounded a bend and spied a grey HBC scow tied to the far shore. Corporal and Mrs. Barber of the British Columbia Police were on board, along with Bay employees and other passengers. Repairs to their damaged rudder were underway, so they invited Patterson on board and plied him with "venison, pastry & lemon pie & tea." In return, he delivered the first mail of the year to the news-starved party. Mrs. Barber, from England, gobbled up the high-society news. "She was grieved at Cyril Maude's leaving of the stage & Charles Hawtney's death."

On Saturday, the 17th, Patterson wrote: "Shaved & tined my hair—like Jezebel—ready for my arrival at Nelson." He stayed that night in his last river camp of the year. He noted he preferred eating his "own good grub & sleeping in the cool, clean woods on a perfect night to being invited to eat & sleep in a stuffy shack—which one can't very well refuse."

September 19 to 27, 1927—Fort Nelson to Fort Nelson

Errors in judgement and an incorrect assumption nearly cost Patterson his life in the final days of September. Despite the late date, he left alone on a cross-country hike from Fort Nelson to Fort St. John. Owing to his poor understanding of native ways, he counted on buying food from them at a post along the way. As a result, his diary reads rather like the last entries of the doomed Hornby expedition.

Monday, September 19. "Hit trail for Sikanni [Chief] Post. With pack of 45 lb. Camped at edge of muskeg damned tired & had to dig well in moss for water. Shot Partridge."

Tuesday, September 20. "Camped in poplar bush on hill clean done to the World. No water."

Wednesday, September 21. "Camped by stream—not so tired—getting used to it but not much grub. Met bear on trail last night. Shot Partridge & squirrel with revolver & stewed up berries & hips & haws—it all helps. Hope to meet Chehtaneta & his Indians tomorrow at Fish Lake & get meat. Trail hard to find in places—not much idea where I am or how far

I have gone—it was 90 miles to the Post from Fort Nelson. Going to bed. Raining. I'll tell you the details when I get out of this mess."

Thursday, September 22. "Rained & misted all day except a little at midday. Camp in the forest in the hills somewhere. Reached Fish Lake—no Indians—trails forking all over the place—hope I am on the right one as I have only enough grub for two days left now. Saw no partridges, & spent 3 hours this afternoon trying to make sure of the right trail from the Lake to the Post. Have done my best & must stand by it now. Rain makes things miserable & mist makes it hard to get an idea of direction."[49] With neither map nor compass he was navigating by dead reckoning.

Friday, September 23. "Worst day since Mar. 21, 1918." That was the day he was captured by the Prussians in the Great War. Snowed continuously, obscuring trails. Turned back to Fish Lake when his day ended at an abandoned Indian hunting cabin.

Saturday, September 24. After bad luck, some good—a chinook wind blew in, melted the snow and helped him find the trail back to Fish Lake. Broke into three locked cabins to scavenge food. Found only candles and a bit of tea. "Nothing for it now but to pull out early in the morning back for Nelson—65 miles on half a pound of cheese, 3 1/2 biscuits, tea & a little sugar, 1/2 lb. of pemmican, 1/2 lb. of raisins, 1 1/2 candles. The last of the rice & bacon I shall have for breakfast."

Worst Day Camp on the shoulder of Fish Lake Mountain, September 23, 1927.

Patterson was becoming concerned. "…The snow is the trouble—one needs more food, the walking is bad & in places I am liable to lose the trail…. Count on me to do my best—I will say a strong prayer & if the cold land gets me you know you have all my love—& give my love to Marigold. I dreamt, last night out in the snow, that she & I were arm in arm trying to come down stairs three steps at a time—I explaining that this was the way Powell & I used to do it at Rossall."

"Isn't this shocking luck? & carelessness—I was told the way was easy to find & that Indians were at the Lake." If only he could have found the right trail, Sikanni Chief Post was only twenty-five miles away.

To save weight, he stashed the tarp, camera and a few other nonessentials "at the tip of a young tamarack on the trail one mile this side of Fish Lake." He kept his blanket. Without food he had to stay warm. Even so, hypothermia began to cloud his thoughts. "I have shaved & combed my hair & eaten a little—now I am going to sleep—I hardly feel anxious because I know you love me & it seems a protection somehow."

Sunday, September 25. After almost ten hours on the trail, he warmed himself by a fire, and after a pitiful supper, cleaned his teeth. "Both knees raw with wet cords rubbing on them."

Monday, September 26. Another long day on the trail, but this time with a partner—a big bush wolf. "I have heard that those animals can tell when a man is up against it." A partridge put its head in the way of a pistol shot and its heart and liver became a noon snack. He roasted the rest of the bird on a willow branch over the supper fire, tearing it apart with his fingers and teeth. "I have two thirds of a biscuit, 1 ounce of cheese, a little pemmican, tea, a twist of sugar & a handful of raisins left."

Fort Nelson was only a day away, so he promised Mother they would eat lobster salad together soon. "When the first storm of the winter caught me grubless in the cold foothills of Fish Lake, light & laughter & pretty things looked a long way away to me. This Chinook & that partridge have almost put me within reach of the tails & my stove pipe hat again."

Tuesday, September 27. Patterson stumbled through muskeg for three hours before snacking on meat, biscuit and cheese crumbs. Weakness was a constant companion. "One's footsteps become less accurate & you trip where, with full strength, you step over. Logs get in your way, you curse swamps & mud holes childishly, willows whip back at you & you slash back at them with the axe in a rage & all nature seems to fight you. It always does in this country but, well fed, you can dare it & beat it."

Trudging along, cold, exhausted and starving, he had lots of time to think. In this, his first self-made contest with nature, he was coming up short. Why? Wanting to prove himself an independent man, he had left Fort Nelson without a guide, adequate food or supplies, counting on unlimited good luck. This was not entirely careless. Travelling on foot, he was limited to a forty-five pound backpack. Wanting to carry as much food as possible, he had winnowed his kit so severely he even had to leave the compass behind. But his biggest mistake was caused by his ignorance of the ways of the Sikannis. He had counted on buying food from them at Fish Lake. Luckily, the fresh snow had saved his life by obscuring the trail to Sikanni Chief Post. Otherwise, he would have pressed on and found the post also vacant. Although he usually gleaned valuable information from everyone he met, his superior attitude toward the natives had almost cost him his life. He was learning an important lesson.

This experience also began teaching him the deeper meaning in Jack London's books: that nature is not a brutal enemy to be conquered but can be a life-giving force that rewards the teachable spirit; that people prove themselves when they exchange their adversarial approach to life for one that takes advantage of opportunities and graciously welcomes setbacks as gifts. Gradually, as he matured into this attitude, a myth arose that everything he touched turned to gold in spite of a record that included many failed ventures.

It began raining heavily just as he reached the bank across the river from Fort Nelson. In fading daylight he lit a soggy match to sodden wood, slowly coaxed a flame to life and added horse manure to produce smoke. Then waving his trademark red handkerchief tied on the end of a stick, he fired off two rounds with his pistol to hail the fort. Within the hour he was changed, warm and the centre of attention in the HBC house, eating and talking at the same time. "Four moose steaks with fried potatoes, corn & Worcester sauce, two bowls of cornflakes & tinned cream, toast, butter, brandy, pineapples & tea. Opes I shalln't be sick." He talked and talked as the people of the post listened, laughed and cheered him on. "My weariness fell off & a vein of humour fell on me & between mouthfuls I told a few stories of the trip against myself that made these men here roar."

Midnight found Patterson sitting in bemused wonder in the warm Bay house, watching a scene of great contrast to the soggy world outside: Sikannis dancing to tunes from a radio station in Atlantic City. That night the diary recorded two smiling observations, "I wasn't sick & that bush wolf was an optimist." And "Not so bad—hard to kill."

September 29 to October 3, 1927—at Fort Nelson

For the time being he rested and devised new travel plans. As he waited to join a pack train headed for Fort St. John, northern hospitality appeased his ravenous appetite. The Barbers of the British Columbia Police hosted him several times, stuffing his thin frame with fine British fare: Yorkshire pudding, scones and afternoon tea as well as the last three fingers of the corporal's best brandy. Trapper Sutherland, his native wife and their beautiful daughter not only bought his wreck of a canoe, they fed him sumptuous breakfasts of pancakes, bacon, butter and golden syrup, chased down with strong coffee. Elsewhere the food varied in quality. Over-ripe moose at the Bay house seemed past redemption to everyone except Patterson who devoured it and convinced others to partake. Food poisoning resulted. "We were all violently disturbed along of a stew of moose, rice & vegetables which had gone a little sour."

Veterans of the Athabasca, Slave, Mackenzie, South Nahanni, Liard and Fort Nelson rivers, Patterson's two sets of clothes were in tatters, so he replaced them with new wool garments from the Bay. While there, he checked over the HBC books for the Fontas post, putting his banking experience to good use and finding "several mistakes which helped things along."

He bounced back from lack of food quickly enough, but his leg muscles took longer to heal. Both ankles suffered from "snowshoe sickness" caused by excessively tight moccasins and cold wet feet stomping through muskeg. In addition, a badly twisted ankle effectively hobbled him for most of the week. Each day he had to dress his sore knees and bad ankle with medicinal compounds.

Finally he was ready to leave. Archie Gardiner, one-quarter native, was going out on horseback to Sikanni Chief Post and agreed to take Patterson along for five dollars a day. That would get him half way and perhaps by then his legs would be ready for a hike to Fort St. John.

While recuperating, he caught up on letter writing. "No need for you to give my love to Marigold," he wrote Mother on September 29, "not this tide—one more storm weathered. Isn't life fun?"

October 3 to 15, 1927—Fort Nelson to Fort St. John

Patterson was still quite stiff, but determined to get to Edmonton. "I am still a bit crocked but am off today if I have to have a ladder to get into the saddle." At the last minute Corporal Barber decided to join the pack train. On the trail they ate well and camped each night in fully outfitted sleeping bags on beds of evergreen boughs by a cozy fire. A bit of animal trouble

Chusnáneta, the Sikanni Chief, Corporal Barber, Archie Gardiner and Belle Feuille
at the Sikanni Chief River crossing, 1927.

along the way caused some inconvenience when a horse or dog strayed
during the night. But most days they covered 30 miles. Along the way they
often met Sikannis. What a difference a few weeks had made. These natives
had food to spare—moose, deer and other wild game—and smiled broadly
as Patterson took their pictures. At Holdup Creek he took a snapshot of an
Indian baby's grave suspended high between two poplar trees.

Archie turned out to be a wealth of information. He was a grandson of
General Gardiner, the son of a mounted policeman and related in some
way to Earl Haig. According to him, the proper Indian pronunciation for
the Nahanni tribe was Ná-ániké—"The people who speak like ducks."
Barber managed to cut a finger and thumb to the bone while cooking so
Patterson became chief cook and bottlewasher for the remainder of the
trip, "Archie being hopeless."

At Sikanni Chief Post, Barber and Patterson hired horses from Angus
Beatton for the remainder of the ride to Fort St. John. There, luck smiled
on the traveller yet again and on October 15 he was writing up his diary
by lantern light aboard Harry Weaver's scow. For a mere thirteen dollars
he had booked passage with Weaver to Peace River from where he would
pick up the weekly train to Edmonton. Even though he was in a rush to
get home, Patterson, ever the adventurer, jumped at the chance to see this
upper stretch of the Peace.

October 16 to October 21, 1927—Fort St. John to Edmonton

For six days Patterson travelled the Peace River from Fort St. John up to Hudson's Hope and then back down to the town of Peace River. The scow stopped often, depositing people and supplies at homesteads and little settlements. At Cache Creek the settlers met Mr. Humphreys, a provincial surveyor of British Columbia, and General Sutton, a retired Englishman from Victoria and something of an engineer. Together with an entourage, they were surveying the route for a railway through the mountains from the west that would connect with the line from Edmonton.

"This morning we were up early & unloaded our freight on the beach & were having breakfast when Sutton's gang appeared—Sutton, Humphreys, a man journalist, a girl journalist, the Bay manager from Hudson's Hope, a practical prospector & four men to look after them— all correctly attired for the far west in fringed buckskin jackets, red scarves, khaki breaches & field boots. The lady journalist in purple & white wool with tassels here & there & a monstrous pair of fleece lined, buckskin thigh boots. I talked with the prospector who had heard I was from the Nahanni & was at me immediately—said good day to the General & took stock of the outfit—garbed as I was in moccasins, stained cords & a shirt torn up the back—all that is left to me. The funny part is that in all probability we shall all be staying at the Macdonald in a weeks time—& probably I shall be the best dressed of all."

Aboard Harry Weaver's scow on the Peace River, 1927.

At Cache Creek they took on 150 sacks of wheat. By the time they reached Rolla Landing their cargo included skis, vegetables, furniture, wheat as well as a cow named Buttercup and her calf. All told, they had enough on board to start a colony. On they raced into the night. When darkness overtook them on October 20, they navigated by searchlight until 10:30 p.m. Chilled by the cool night air, Patterson made coffee and porridge for the riverboat captain and himself.

An early start the next day landed them in Dunvegan before eight. There, Buttercup and her offspring struggled up the bank after their owner. Then the boat floated through the morning mists, drifting, while the men ate a moose steak and onion breakfast as Weaver played melodies on his violin, a daily "after breakfast habit." They arrived at Peace River by mid-afternoon of the next day, in good time for Patterson to get a haircut and shampoo, tip a beer glass or two at the bar and still make the 7:30 p.m. weekly train to Edmonton.

That night he enjoyed a thorough cleansing followed by a refreshing sleep on the Matthews' verandah. He did not suffer his usual Lord's Day gloom on Sunday the 23rd. A breakfast of milk, eggs and honey preceded a sumptuous lunch at the famous Macdonald Hotel. That afternoon the men examined maps, planning the trip north in the spring of 1928 "to run down that gold." It was decided that after a quick trip home to England to settle a few important business and family matters, Patterson would return in early 1928 and begin provisioning for a year in the North. His last entries in the 1927 diary record his impression of his summer adventure.

"I am the better for the trail I have made—in every way. A little stronger & heavier, more obstinate, quicker to think & act alone & able to do without things & to drive myself on against my own will.

"I know the way into the gold rivers—& I have seen very great beauties in a wonderful mountain world."

Gold and Fur
1928 and 1929

A YEAR to the day after leaving Edmonton for the Nahanni in 1927, Patterson was on the river again. An overcast dawn came before 4:00 a.m. on May 31, 1928, revealing two soggy men and five bad-tempered dogs camped in the Splits. Finally, a weak sun appeared. Raymond Patterson and Gordon Matthews sorted gear to leave in a cache at the bottom of the flooded waste-land. "Rather a mosquito evening," wrote Patterson in his diary.

He had returned with an overriding goal: find gold, trap furs and re-turn to civilization after the last full winter of the 1920s as a hero. Wealth for Mother, a comfortable financial underpinning for a marriage to the most beautiful blonde in the world, and a place in history as the man who started the gold rush on the Flat River were all in his plan.

The venture had unfolded since October 22, 1927, when the train had deposited Patterson in Edmonton and he had bunked with Gordon and Mollie Matthews. Cramped for far too long in the city, Matthews had immediately signed on with the return expedition and begun prepara-tions, buying and training more dogs for winter travel and arranging for his wife Mollie during his absence. Provisioning would take months; there were hundreds of items to purchase, repack and prepare.

Patterson, as planned, took the steamship to England. There he regaled friends and relatives with stories, reassured Mother and placed a spar-kling engagement ring on Marigold Portman's left hand. Then he was off back to Canada in early February.

The ship was delayed two days en route by fog. In New York harbour "a Jamaica banana boat bumped into us as we lay at anchor & damaged herself." On the Hudson River, the ship narrowly missed a string of barges. Patterson was most annoyed. "I left New York the same day at 6:30 in the evening & very thankful to get out of it—I detest the place."

The train deposited him the next day in Toronto, where he was welcomed by his Canadian relatives. He lunched with Aunt Nellie and Annette, and played badminton at their club before joining them for tea at their home. Marigold's picture was "much admired." Two aunts were already planning to attend the wedding and young Annette agreed to act as a bridesmaid. Uncle George arrived for dinner and delivered him to the evening train bound for Winnipeg.

The interminable miles across the top of Lake Superior made Patterson anxious for the new adventure. Prudently, he bought life insurance in Winnipeg: premiums on a $10,000 policy with Canada Life Assurance cost about £50 or $250 Canadian. On his uncle's advice he sold Lake of the Woods shares and bought thirty in International Nickel. He also bought 120 speculative Sherrit Gordon mining shares. Uncle George also suggested International Paper, but Patterson was running out of cash—he had to cable Mother for an extra £100, an unprecedented request.

Mail from Marigold beat him to Edmonton where he again bunked with the Matthews. The plan required Patterson and Matthews to move gear with sleds pulled by hefty German shepherds. Though still midwinter, the snow was almost gone from the Alberta capital. Edmontonians, therefore, were not entirely pleased when they took the dogs on regular training runs on the icebound North Saskatchewan River right under the newly constructed legislature buildings.

Alberta changed Patterson's habits. Though the ring of a bell brought a maid in England, in Canada he had to fend for himself. "It seems funny to be monkeying round a cook stove again, but we are having all our meals at home as we need all our money just now."

Counting pennies became a way of life. The expedition cost each man about $500 for provisions, train fares, canoes, team and sleigh rentals as well as trapping licences. From the hardware store they ordered an outboard engine, No. 2 and No. 3 traps and many other items. Patterson's guns and ammunition came from England. The canoes came direct from the Chestnut Company factory in New Brunswick.

Meanwhile, news from the North entertained. Major Cornelius Foreman told stories of taking the Coal Company's small boat, the *Muriel*, down the Liard and back up the Mackenzie. It nearly capsized at Beaver Dam rapids: running backward, the canoe they were towing swamped and their clothes got washed away. Seasickness hit during a storm on the Mackenzie below Providence and while retching overboard, half their outfit fell into the river. Three times they avoided drowning on Great

Slave Lake. "He agreed with me that if we all had our last summer's experiences & yarns down in one book it would be the funniest thing on earth, but we also decided that the book would be suppressed by the Canadian Government & we should be thrown out of Canada for giving the northland an evil name."

Before leaving Edmonton, Patterson sent Mother a copy of a book called *Moccasin Telegraph*, a novel about the Nahanni. The author had cobbled together the myths for an interesting read. Patterson also disclosed that fur prices had doubled in the last year.[1]

On March 8, 1928, the Edmonton, Dunvegan and British Columbia Railway train chugged out of Edmonton with Patterson and Matthews aboard. The idea was to travel from Edmonton to Spirit River by train, then sled overland to the Sikanni Chief River via Fort St. John, paddle downstream into the Liard and arrive at the mouth of the South Nahanni by early June. They planned to complete the circle in early 1929 by travelling down the Liard and up the Mackenzie, Slave and Athabasca rivers to Waterways. From there Patterson would make a quick dash to England for his wedding.

Getting the outfit to the train had been a logistical nightmare. The baggage car became a kennel for dogs and pups. Although they had tickets for seats in the passenger car, Patterson and Matthews stayed with their outfit and mutts for the day and the night it took to reach Spirit River. There, the local policeman arranged for them to board their dogs in a vacant gristmill after they promised to leave at first light. The howling dogs kept the town awake all night. Finally, the dog team left Spirit River pulling the toboggan, the rest of the outfit following on a wagon pulled by a team of quiet horses. Everything went well until the dogs scared a team off the trail, causing it to dump its load of grain. Stopping places along the trail to Fort St. John accommodated them grudgingly.

On March 17 they transferred their outfit to Clay Martin's sleighs at Finch's store in Fort St. John. Two sleighs made the trip to Sikanni Chief River, one with the outfit and the other with food for the horses on the return trip. The dogs pulled the toboggan. Inside the canvas carryall Mamselle and her puppies howled in the makeshift nursery.

After a journey hindered by chinooks melting the snow, they reached Holdup Creek on March 18. "Suggested scouring out the copper tea pail but [Matthews] said it was an antique, made at York Factory in the eighteenth century & had never yet been cleaned. Thought of all the bearded voyageurs who had drunk tea from it & decided not to clean it."

Gordon Matthews and Clay Martin on the Fort Nelson Trail, March 1928.

With the snow gone, they had to hitch all four horses to each sleigh and drag them one at a time toward the tributaries of the Fort Nelson River. They finally reached the confluence of the Sikanni Chief River and Conroy Creek on March 27. The tiny settlement there was full of fur traders, busy cutting lumber with whipsaws to build scows and boats.

Needing a peaceful place to await the spring breakup, Patterson and Matthews moved their ton and a half of gear downstream over the frozen ice to a point of land between Kenai Creek and the Sikanni Chief River. "...on the whole, and as usual, everybody was quite glad to see us go."[2] The weather stayed warm most of April. Ducks of all descriptions landing in the pond provided pleasant alternatives to gamey moose and deer. The partners sorted and repacked gear. Matthews took the dogs for runs on the frozen creeks and rivers. Patterson read books, wrote letters and worked large spreads of canvas into canoe sails. Regular knock down, drag-out fights between sled-dogs Spud and Poilu kept boredom to a minimum. Mamselle sometimes joined in, leaving her nursing pups to fend for themselves.[3]

Finally, ice began breaking up on the Sikanni Chief. Patterson and Matthews quickly tried to load the supplies into the two canoes, but without success. So Patterson built a triangular raft, one he hoped would handle better in the current when tied alongside the smaller canoe. Then off they went down the river, Matthews captaining the large, motorized freight canoe, the dogs riding on top and the puppies howling from a wooden crate.

Matthews shot a Canada goose and put it into the pot with a stew of duck, venison, barley, beans and condiments. But it caused trouble; although goose grease makes good waterproofing on footwear, it is nearly impossible to digest. But navigating an unknown river, they ignored the increasing pain in their guts. Finally, they headed for a shore, and moaning and cursing, collapsed. Occasionally they awoke and fed the noxious stew to the dogs who loved it. Two days later they had recovered enough to make a rice pudding and a pot of tea.[4]

On reaching Fort Nelson River, they made the penultimate cultural stop at Fort Nelson. Just short of the post, they cleaned up, shaved and dressed to kill. But what was that strong smell? Bottles of rum and brandy carefully wrapped in their town clothes had broken and they arrived smelling like a distillery. The fort welcomed them and provided new homes for the pups. The policeman bought Spud, a fierce mutt that treed the constable. Needing another canoe, the gold-seekers purchased a battered 18-foot freight canoe from the HBC post. When asked about their plans, Matthews muttered "Going in to study the flora and fauna." Within a few hours the locals were saying, "Didn't rightly catch what he said, but looks like no doubt there's a couple of squaws mixed up in it somewhere!"[5]

On May 24 they reached the confluence of the South Nahanni and the Liard rivers. The easy downstream travel was over. On arriving at Jack la Flair's trading post at Nahanni Butte, they learned the fur catch had been poor and Faille was still somewhere upriver. Goldminers Jack Starke and Steve Stevens were spreading a rumour that Patterson was a geologist and had found gold on the Flat. Starke and Stevens were headed to Fort Simpson for supplies and were coming back for the gold. The race was on.

Gordon Matthews and R. M. Patterson
at Fort Liard, May 1928.

Patterson and Matthews left Nahanni Butte and motored into the sunset late on Saturday, May 26. They were on the river at 5:15 the next morning, the four horsepower Johnson outboard easily pushing the three canoes up the placid river. In less than five hours they hit the tumultuous water in the Splits and the marathon began. The next month was interminable as Patterson slogged through the Splits countless times, almost single-handedly ferrying supplies through the mosquito-infested wetlands. Faille had proved in August of 1927 that a canoe and outboard could handle the river. But conditions were different in 1928. Patterson and Matthews had arrived just in time for the spring runoff, and their outboard was giving them trouble. Closer examination revealed a nut was missing and the bracket was fractured. As they cobbled together repairs in deluging rain, "Gordon began to realise the fearful desolation of the Splits that had been impressed upon me the year before." Twisted Mountain beckoned, offering a safe place to stow part of the gear, but though they could see it, it took several days of travel on the flooded river to reach Faille's old cache.

Tuesday, May 29, began under cloudy skies. They set off at seven but the kicker soon died. Patterson jumped out to hold the outfit but the current won and swept them back down the river. Finally, they abandoned the engine and decided to cache a thousand pounds of gear up a tree. "So we shall travel as the Lord intended men to travel in the north west—by pole, trackline & paddle & such strength as we have—& the devil take me if ever I fool with an engine again in a wild country."

On Wednesday, Patterson built his first cache on the stumps of four trees cut off ten feet in the air and ringed with tin to protect against mice and bears.

June was a frustrating month. Matthews was unskilled in a canoe and took slowly to poling, almost losing his canoe and its contents numerous times. Once Patterson had to chase downstream to rescue the canoe when it got away from him. However, immediately after Patterson questions his partner's abilities in his diary, he mentions his own near-brushes with catastrophe. At times his waders filled with water or the river washed him backward downstream after hours of hard work. Another time, while clearing brush along the bank, the big building axe flew from his hand into the river. Desperate, he tied a rope to a tree and holding on to it, dove repeatedly into the frigid floodwaters, but failed to find the precious axe. Almost hypothermic, he warmed himself by a bonfire.

On June 1, Matthews offered to stay behind while Patterson took a trial load upstream. By June 6 Patterson had dragged the first load of gear halfway through the Splits. As a reward he hiked up Twisted Mountain and with his Zeiss 8 power monocular spied Starke and Stevens struggling upstream with a motorized outfit. "Life didn't seem to be all jam & honey for them, hauling in their scow." They joined forces the next day and together the three men worked up to the hot springs. They were full of news: Faille had survived the winter, trapping had been poor, two of Faille's dogs had drowned and many of his traps had disappeared.

Patterson spent the next ten days learning another way not to ascend a flooded river, finally deciding that Starke and Stevens were "not canoe men & artists with the delicate paddle, such as Faille." But they were experienced gold-seekers. Starke, in his fifties, was a Scot, and known as the "Black Pirate" for his dark clothing, black hat and pipe. He had been in the gold rush of '98. Stevens was probably younger than Patterson, tall, lean and a champion boxer. After each successful venture they would return to Edmonton and live high until down to their grubstake.[6]

With block and tackle, this unusual trio winched the heavily laden scow upriver, pulling from deadmen sunk into the gravel. "Simply bull work" Patterson called it. Each day they cut back the brush along the bank, then two men pulled the tracking rope while the motor ran flat out and the other man steered the scow. They averaged about two miles a day through the Splits, three on a good day. Lost or jammed propellers often forced one of them to dive into the numbing water to effect repairs.

While struggling upstream they wore headnets, long-sleeved shirts and leather gloves as protection against the bugs. On June 10 Patterson wrote, "The two mosquito months of the year sap ones energy & wear one down thin & lean. They pester, torture, suck blood & give no rest—many a white man, since Canada's history began, must have fallen & died in the northern bush, clean worn out by their attacks or else driven raving mad."

Patterson built a cache at the hot springs on Sunday, June 17, and raised 340 pounds of gear onto the triangular platform. "1 sack of dog harness—1 sack 50 lbs. whole wheat—1 bale 40 lbs. rolled oats—1 box candles—my top boots, rubber boots, shoes & 1 moccasin rubber. On the ground below are the stove & two sacks of traps." He bathed and "changed into clean summer clothes & so came as near to godliness as this country will allow." Starke and Stevens decided to rest at the hot springs and allow the water to drop.

On Tuesday, June 19, Patterson dropped down to the Twisted Mountain cache in two hours, reloaded and travelled five hours upstream before calling it a day. Two days later he arrived at Starke and Stevens' for a beaver tail breakfast. He cached his gear, left at 10:00 a.m. and arrived in time for supper at Matthews' camp. Matthews showed up shortly, the kicker working again. Rumour had it a fellow named Astley was prospecting for coal up Jackfish River. Cousins' lumber mill had burned down the day after Patterson and Matthews had left Fort Liard and Father Gouet's scow had been wrecked on a drift pile, but the cows swam to shore. And Faille had passed by, headed out with "a sack of gold." That evening, Matthews used the rejuvenated motor to push the small canoe upstream inside the 19 footer. Patterson followed with the rest of the outfit.

The water rose steadily for the next three days, up more than 18 inches, so on Sunday, June 24, they stayed put in camp. Faille arrived the next day and entertained them with more news. He'd been struggling upstream with a ton of supplies from Simpson for a month. A winter on the Flat River convinced him it was no good for fur. While he was away on the trapline, a wolverine had demolished his cabin, devoured his food and ruined the pelts. He had nearly starved. And when a caribou wandered into camp, he had missed a broadside shot. A few weeks earlier he had slipped and fallen, in the process dislodging the sights and injuring his back. He'd sent Patterson's Dall ram head from Simpson to the Bank of Montreal in Edmonton. The bag of gold he took to Simpson turned out to be "fool's gold." But, maybe there was gold above the Falls! So he fired up his kicker and disappeared upriver. No one saw him again until 1930, most presuming him dead.

On June 26 Patterson and Matthews headed upstream with the last load. "After much bedevilment the vibration finally & irretrievably smashed the repairs to the engine—so thank God we at last know where we are." After a month in the Splits, Patterson's pole snapped, causing him to write on the 28th, "I have taken this year from Marigold & everything seems to be turning against us so that we can achieve nothing. The luck must turn soon."

They finally built another cache just across from Jackfish Mountain on Friday, June 29, and there abandoned the large wreck of a canoe—"our unspeakable Noah's Ark." Decades later Patterson described it as "a shockingly battered antique with its canvas hide flapping loosely over its cedar frame, the sort of thing that a sane man would hesitate to use on a quiet lake, let alone on the Nahanni."[7] Patterson also fixed a paddle he broke "over Quiz' head" when the dog shifted in the canoe. That night he wrote,

R. M. Patterson and Gordon Matthews at the hot springs, 1928, looking tired.

"Now I am safe under the net with the mosquitoes roaring outside. For once we have done in a day all that we set out to do."

July 1 was another discouraging day. "Sunday always seems to be with me what Corporal Barber would call 'one sweet scented son of a female dog.'" Still stuck in the Splits, with a partner not quite up to the task, the expedition was unravelling in a cloud of mosquitoes. The useless dogs ate huge amounts of meat—Mrs. Blimp, Mrs. Doin's and Mrs. Wallop-her-tail-then were some of Patterson's names for the mutts. Competition for the gold had arrived and even though Starke and Stevens had become friends, between them and Faille, the Nahanni was no longer Patterson's private paradise. On the bright side, a nice breeze was keeping the bugs at bay, and the end of the Splits was almost in sight. Besides, Matthews was "such a pleasant companion & we get on so well."

Stressful times can strain friendships, but Patterson and Matthews were adjusting well and dividing the work according to their abilities. Matthews would eventually prove himself in Dead Men's Valley as a skilled hunter, trapper, fisherman, trail maker and cabin builder. Wisely, they also spent time apart, alleviating the cabin-fever that infects all relationships.

Purposefully, the friends set out early on Monday, July 2, and struggled to within one day of the hot springs. Another hard day landed them at the cache just below the springs. They were short of meat, Patterson writing, "when I get hold of a moose or bear there's going to be a memorable eating." Meanwhile, an unending supply of "vast quantities of porridge" kept them alive.

On Wednesday they relaxed in the hot springs; just the day before Patterson had sliced into his ankle with an axe. Later, lying in their bedrolls by the fire, they reconsidered their plans. Without the engine, a base camp up the Flat River was out of reach, leaving Dead Men's Valley as the only alternative. Matthews would build the cabin and scout out traplines for the winter, while Patterson would run up the Flat with the small canoe to find the source of the gold. For the time being, Patterson would bring up the last load from the cache.

Patterson returned to Jackfish Mountain on July 5, a twenty-five mile trip accomplished in less than four hours and cached the ornery canoe, motor and fuel. Up at four the next morning and on the river by six, he fought the current and mosquitoes for almost twelve hours. He shot and killed a moose at Twisted Mountain, but the current snatched it away— a crushing waste. On he struggled through the meandering Splits, frustrated by the fact that the hot springs were only nine miles away "by flight of crow, but about three times as far if that crow had had to swim behind my canoe."[8]‡

---

‡ Most Nahanni adventurers avoid upstream travel but in the fall of 1985 a brave Nahanni guide, Neil Hartling, and five friends—Scott Fisher, Mary Coutts, Ian Hosler, Brad Summers and Debbie Large—ascended the rivers from Blackstone Landing to Virginia Falls in a large, voyageur-style canoe loaded with camping gear and food.

The party soon realized they could not paddle the heavily loaded canoe upstream, even on the placid Liard River. So five people plodded along the shore, pulling the canoe with a 200 foot-long polypropylene rope while the sixth person steered. The overworked waders jealously waited their turn to ride while the person steering froze. Day after cold day they worked from before dawn until after dark, a tight schedule allowing only thirty minutes for lunch and two other fifteen minute breaks. Water froze in pails as they camped under the big canoe. On the river, the canoe was stacked with so much gear there was "hardly room for the people to see—they had to peer around the sides of it," recalls Hartling.

Moving up through the Splits was the hardest and the rope got stuck often on driftwood. "It seemed like, at least every hundred yards, someone would have to walk back and unhook it from a snag of some sort. It was terrorizing on our morale." The going got easier in the canyons. But each slave on this trip wore out at least one pair of shoes.

At Figure-of-Eight Rapid they portaged the gear and paddled the empty canoe upstream along the rock wall with the current in the whirlpool. Then Ian Hosler, sitting in the stern, set up a front ferry across the big waves and they all paddled hard. Recalls

By Saturday, July 7, Patterson was back at the hot springs, absolutely spent from two gruelling days on the river. Unable to sleep in the tent, he set up his usual sleeping outfit: a tarp and mosquito net. Then he bathed, changed into clean clothes and took target practise with a rifle and a telescopic sight he had purchased in England. A new invention to Patterson, it gave a bang to the eye socket "that made my head fairly sing." Meanwhile, a busy Matthews had gleaned an axe head, two chisels, a prospector's shovel and the *Fourth Canadian Reader* from the abandoned cabins at the hot springs. With the Splits behind them, Patterson and Matthews were ready for their luck to change.

It took ten days to reach Dead Men's Valley. At the first bend they met Lafferty's Riffle. Starke and Stevens had been stuck there with their scow, waiting eight days for the water to drop. Patterson and Matthews gave them a tin of engine grease, and in exchange took an axe, salt, dried moose meat and a magazine, then moved on to Last Man Camp in time for supper.

On Tuesday, July 10, rising flood waters convinced them to stay put. A blazing sun on Wednesday encouraged them four miles up the canyon. Rain fell and waters rose on Thursday but they soldiered on, sometimes sliding high along rock ledges while tracking the canoes at the end of 200 feet of rope. "The sun had broken through & lit up the canyon walls to gold, with the shadows a lovely blue—& overhead a deep blue sky with white clouds driving across before a strong wind. It might have been a May sky in England." On Friday Patterson wrote, "It's high time we had a little good

---

Hartling, "I heard this cry from Ian Hosler…a shriek of impending doom, and I turned around and the look on his face was of horror, and his eyes were fixed on the bottom of the canoe. I looked at the bottom of the canoe and in the centre, in my mind anyhow, it was almost touching the centre thwart." Without gear in the hull, the fibreglass buckled and wowed menacingly, but held.

Finally, after twelve days, they reached Virginia Falls. The hardest tracking was in the Painted Canyon, immediately below the Falls "where it was difficult to make your way along the walls, going upstream."

Downstream travel was relatively straightforward in low water. Without spray covers, they took the rapids wide, slow and conservatively. Because the purpose of the trip was to see "if there was a place for the big canoes on the Nahanni," by travelling upstream first, they had a chance to examine the hazards along the way. Eventually, they concluded large canoes would work well. Immediately after the trip, Neil began building large sectional canoes to fit into the various bush planes that fly to the Nahanni.

luck," bemoaning the poor progress to date. It was raining again with a high wind that soaked everything. "About supper time the water began to rise prodigiously, & we had to set to work & shift the tent & our gear to a higher spot, as the canoes threatened to float in at the door."

Waiting out the high water, Patterson hiked up a side valley to the plateau above the river. He saw no animals, but took copper and galena samples. On Sunday he used the little aneroid barometer Mother had given him to measure the cliffs of Lower Canyon.[9] Faille guessed them to be 1000 feet high and Patterson a more conservative 800. "I was amazed to find that in this clear, mountain air we had been hopelessly underestimating our heights. The main canyon walls just here are a good 1500 feet, & the topmost cliffs that rise almost sheer above the Nahanni are an easy 3000 feet or more above the river." On he climbed until he reached a round grassy hill, 4500 feet higher than camp. It was like looking at a map. "I could see the country beyond the Liard—lazy in the sunshine, Nahanni Butte fifty miles away, the Long Walls, the Twisted Mountain, the whole range of the Mackenzie Mountains & a mass of mountains away towards the Yukon border." As the day cooled, he scampered back to camp, arriving weary and hungry. His day's efforts resulted in a map maker naming the side valley Patterson Creek.

On a sunny Monday, July 16, with the river dropping, they worked hard, "but met with illimitable damnation under a cliff & around a pile of boulders where the water, still high, swirled dangerously." On Tuesday Starke and Stevens arrived. United, they fought upstream on Wednesday, eating supper at the worst rapid—the one Faille and Patterson had named Cache Rapid after caches they had built on the island. It guarded the top end of Lower Canyon into Dead Men's Valley. To get there, Patterson and Matthews had portaged everything over a nasty point of rock, "So it was not till after eight that we landed in the little sandy bay at the foot of the Cache Rapid—very tired & with tempers raw."

Matthews and Stevens nearly killed Patterson at Cache Rapid on Thursday the 19th. While gnawing on "very tough dried moose meat," Stevens spied a sheep on the far side of the river. "That's a good 400 yards—better let George get his telescope sight," said Matthews, referring to Patterson by his northern nickname. Twice the big rifle roared, each time punching Patterson's eye with the scope, and the ram fell dead. Matthews and Stevens offered to help Patterson ferry across to the island. Accustomed to pulling a scow, Stevens "was using more brute strength & less cunning & patience than a canoe demands." Suddenly, Patterson found himself in the middle of the fiercest part of the current as the canoe sped across and dove into an angry eddy behind a rock at midstream, "about six inches from the most evil of all that tearing water." Back and forth upstream they worked until above the standing waves. Then, the two men on shore leapt into the canoe and all paddled like maniacs for the island. From there they were forced to wade a snye up to their waists to retrieve the sheep. Back on the island, they camped and warmed by a fire "put on dry clothes & warmed our innards with mountain mutton & strong tea. He was a yearling ram, & never was meat so tender or so well tasting—practically lamb."

The next day Patterson and Matthews moved their first load into Dead Men's Valley. Windbound for two days at Ram Creek, they dried themselves out in the sunshine, cooked mutton steaks and Faille's famous Logging Cake, and washed it down with strong tea. While they waited in vain for Starke and Stevens to appear, they repaired their badly beaten canoes and climbed Little Butte, measuring it at 550 feet with the aneroid. They each shot a sheep, but the current swept Patterson's into the canyon.

On Monday, July 23, they began the upstream search for a place to build a cabin. They arrived at Prairie Creek under a cloudless sky and drank from its clear waters, then continued into the Upper Splits. On Tuesday morning Matthews missed shooting a black bear "with excuse as the bear was a snapshot on the run & I had not even time to get my rifle." After lunch they explored above the mouth of the Meilleur River, looking in vain for a site with building timber. At the gates to Second Canyon they quit and returned to Prairie Creek. "We might as well build at that little creek coming in on the right," Patterson probably suggested to Matthews. "Faille and I camped there on the way out last fall. I camped under that big spruce and watched the northern lights dance on the mountains. That's the place for us."

During a "very excellent supper" of oatmeal with raisins, a moose came out on a gravel bar at mid river. Down went the plates, up went the rifles and two slugs dropped the animal. After supper and a leisurely smoke they went to retrieve the meat. But the moose stood and "tried to tackle" Matthews so Patterson quickly put a bullet into its heart. On Wednesday, July 25, they moved to their new home at the beach across from Prairie Creek. Matthews took three dogs while Patterson took Poilu and "all the moose meat—a gory, ghastly load, piled high & not over safe in wind—my canoe looked like a butcher's shop."

Dogs and Gordon Matthews packing meat, 1928.

Gordon Matthews with owl, 1928.

Game galore showed itself: in the next two days they saw eleven moose and a grey wolf. The timber was as good as could be had in that windy valley and Prairie Creek was full of fish. In this paradise Matthews dried moose meat while Patterson built a large cache, eleven feet up from the ground. Then Starke and Stevens arrived and moved in for the night. Lower Canyon had nearly demolished the scow and they were down to their last propeller.

On Monday, July 30, Patterson and Matthews headed down to the hot springs for another load. They almost tipped the empty canoe on a rock in mid river; both ogling the canyons and neither paying attention to navigation. Then they took in water at Lafferty's Riffle—Patterson called it Galoom "because his waves lashing a narrow channel against the foot of the precipice, & when I first saw them in the summer dusk last year they seemed to be yelling 'Galoom, galoom, galoom.'" That night Matthews made a cozy fire by the old cabins while Patterson picked three quarts of raspberries and served them with cream and sugar, "—a most civilised meal." On July 31 Patterson dropped down to the cache just below the hot springs and returned to camp. Then Matthews loaded the canoe while Patterson did laundry and made raspberry pancakes. Gooseberries, strawberries and red currants they ate raw, stewed, cooked in porridge and baked into bannocks.

The heavens opened on Wednesday, August 1, and the river rose again. Thursday was cold, windy and miserable, "A cheerless day," but despite the rain they pressed on up the canyon. Friday was better, but it could have snowed for all the good it did them. Patterson could not move, struck down by "that old rheumatism of mine." He'd foolishly left the hot springs just as he felt another attack coming on and so lay incapacitated all day Friday, Saturday and Sunday. Perhaps the cause was "so many raspberries." Matthews was "most patient" and provided breakfast in bed on both Saturday and Sunday. Patterson was philosophical about his ailment: "It puzzles me why so many strong, fit men are content to work in banks & offices when, physically speaking, they might tackle these wild places without let or hindrance—while those who make these journeys are often hampered by some weakness such as this of mine."

On Saturday an airplane buzzed the canyon, an all too frequent nuisance for Nahanni visitors today. On Sunday another airplane flew over and a strange canoe arrived. "My God!" exclaimed Gordon, "A plane over Deadmen's Valley only three weeks ago—and now this! There's at least one white man in the party—possibly two. I'll tell you what it is: this blasted country's getting overrun. We might just as well have built our winter cabin in Picadilly Circus!"[10] Out of a collapsible canoe stepped Fenley Hunter of Flushing, New York, and George Ball and Albert Dease of Dease Lake.

These ambitious summer trippers hoped to reach the Nahanni headwaters, portage over to the Gravel River (today's Natla-Keele), descend it to the Mackenzie and follow it down to Fort McPherson. Then ascend the Rat and Bell rivers, cross over the divide and head down the Porcupine River to Fort Yukon—all before winter! Patterson was skeptical, but he humoured Hunter who had medicine and offered to post letters to

Albert Dease and George Ball, August 1928.

Gordon Matthews and Fenley Hunter, August 1928.

Mother and Marigold. And he had news: the airplane was from the Upper Liard Post, flu was killing off natives along the Liard and Mackenzie rivers, and most important, prospectors Sherwood and Poole Field were en route to look for gold up the Flat River. Patterson's resolve was strengthened; he had to find the gold soon.

On Monday, August 6, Patterson "stepped out of bed & into the canoe" and steered, poled and bailed while Matthews pulled on the trackline. They ascended Lower Canyon on Tuesday and Wednesday, arriving at Cache Rapid without incident. On Wednesday, Patterson hacked the legs off his tattered khaki trousers to make shorts. "Hence my legs much sunburned & likely to be more so as time goes on."

Thursday evening found them in camp at Ram Creek, glad to be alive. While ascending Cache Rapid, the dogs lurched and water poured into the canoe. Matthews jumped for shore with the trackline and impaled himself on a rock that served as an anchor. "Nose in the air & tail completely under water," the canoe filled as Patterson threw gear ashore and somehow managed to beach the foundering craft. Plenty of strong, hot coffee and porridge revived them and they "went at it again with awful caution" and just made it. "Most dangerous" noted Patterson, using the adjective for the seventh time in his 1928-29 diary.

Hunter's party was also camped at Ram Creek, and it is here where Hunter's and Patterson's diaries overlap. Wrote Hunter: "This was a big day in the sticks: lots of shooting but no meat. I never saw the like of it—in other words, lots of game for one day but no marksmen."[11] Patterson mused, "They had seen six black bears, three sheep & one moose—& had failed to bag a single animal!"

On Friday Patterson corrected Hunter's working maps, naming places that appear on official maps today. Credited to Faille and Patterson from 1927 were Cache Rapid and Twisted Mountain. Today's Ram Creek was Faille's Bear Creek and Hunter's Sheep Creek. Hunter gave Patterson's name to the side creek he ascended from Lower Canyon to the plateau, prompting Patterson to write Mother, "poor creek—it's so beautiful a valley to meet with such a fate." Patterson's Lake was the name Starke suggested for the calm stretch of deep water above Lower Canyon, perhaps for the many game birds dropped by the man with the black eye. In turn, Patterson named the small waterway above the cabin site, Wheatsheaf Creek, after an English pub.

Later, Hunter would give the name Hell's Gate to Figure-of-Eight Rapid and on August 19 would rename The Falls of the Nahanni after his daughter Virginia. Three days later his description of the raging mill stream above the Falls as "a sluice box with 3 large rocks in the middle" would become the source of today's Sluice Box Rapids.

Albert Dease at the lip of The Falls of the Nahanni, August 1928.

Fenley Hunter was a Fellow of the Royal Geographical Society and the man who later nominated Patterson for the Society. He had already published an account of his 1923 exploits in the Frances River and Lake region of the Northwest Territories. His diary, "A Trip to the Western Arctic—1928," offers another view of a month on the dangerous river.‡

Dropped off by the Northern Trader's scow at Nahanni Butte after an upstream ride from Fort Simpson, they picked up gasoline and oil from a stash. It took four hours to get the motor started on their canoe on July 29, a most frustrating delay as they were getting by on four hours of sleep a night in order to maximize travel time. The motor delayed them seven hours the next day, so they only made it to the foot of the Splits.

August 2 was a camp day, spent collecting insects for Dr. MacDonough, drying sleeping bags and catching up on sleep. They had hoped to prospect and hunt farther upstream but were bored in the Splits. Two days later they reached the hot springs near a cabin and some caches. At 4:45 p.m. a "hydroplane" passed overhead, circled and went south to avoid a storm.

After taking a reading of 95.9° Fahrenheit at the hot springs on August 5, they met Patterson and Matthews in Lower Canyon. Hunter gave them food and took three letters to mail, noting, "Nice Englishmen and I enjoyed chatting with them for 2 hours." They pushed on through the canyon. "Patterson and Matthews say that on top of the north side of the canyon is a real prairie which is flat and treeless—we will have a look later on." Progress was slow. On August 6 Hunter named their bivouac Hurricane Camp owing to winds. The next day he commented, "The South

---

‡ A copy of Hunter's 1928 diary resides in the National Archives of Canada and tells quite a story. He and guides Albert Dease and George Ball travelled in a collapsible 20-foot canoe with an outboard motor down the Peace River from Peace River Crossing to Lake Athabasca, and from there to Fort Simpson. Then they headed up the Liard to the South Nahanni, spending July 26 to August 27 on its waters. On returning to Fort Simpson in early September—their food cache at Nahanni Butte had been raided—they boarded the season's last northbound steamer and arrived in Fort McPherson on the HBC *Distributor* September 13. "I traded that double skinned kayak at McPherson to old John Firth for $44.00 worth of grub which hoisted us over La Pierre trail barring the last couple of days as George, Albert (God rest his soul) and a couple of Loucheaux ate a lot. I got so tired I could not eat, at least, one night I had to take a sleep for myself before I could eat. That was really bad."[12] They humped the 2.5 horsepower kicker overland into the Yukon. "...it was about 1800 feet where I crossed the Divide between McPherson and the head of the Bell River. It is about 100 miles across there and we were lucky to find a 7 ft. 6 in. beaver canoe—plenty tippy, at the head of the Bell...."[13] On September 21 they descended the Bell and Porcupine rivers in the 12-foot canoe that they exchanged for an 18-foot Chestnut at Salmon Cache. With ice freezing to their craft, they arrived at Fort Yukon, having covered 3000 miles in ninety days.[14]

Fenley Hunter at The Falls of the Nahanni, August 22, 1928.

Nahanni River is unknown because she is almost impregnable." The last three miles took them all day and required motoring, poling, tracking and portaging. At one time they barely squeezed the canoe between two large rocks. Finally out of the canyon, they moved into the camp at Ram Creek with Patterson, Matthews, Starke and Stevens.

Bad luck hunting ended on August 10 when the party shot a bear. After a few days' rest at Ram Creek, they set off on August 15 for the Falls. Patterson had already left for the Flat River but they caught up to him in his camp at The Gate on August 17, visited and pressed on.

Motor troubles continued, but at 4:30 p.m. on August 19 they reached the Figure-of-Eight Rapid. There they portaged the gear and Hunter mapped the feature. The next day they repaired the canoe and carefully powered it upstream through the waves to Birthday Camp. Hunter wrote excitedly, "We will soon be to the Falls which I shall name after Sis [nickname for his daughter]—'Virginia Falls.'"

Under the mistaken assumption he was the first white man to reach the Falls, Hunter wrote on August 21, "Man is queer to want to make his campfire where no one else has left ashes and to see what no on else has seen. He may do all that for a price, which we have paid in full since leaving the mouth of the South Nahanni on July 29th." The next day they measured the Falls "with the D.B. Aneroid and the Abney Level" and took pictures. They patched ten more holes in the canoe and hoped it would last until Simpson.

An early start on August 24 put them at the Wheatsheaf Creek cabin for supper. "I found Matthews here with the cabin half built and we helped him shift some top logs. I got some good bugs for our collection so we spent the night. It is great to have a mental companion. The fire has gone out so I must stop." They stayed on another day, shot three rams, caught fish and made repairs to the motor. "Matthews who is an old Royal Air Force man put in an entire new set of parts which we hope are going to work. It has been a 7 hour job so far." Meanwhile, the dogs helped pack meat back to camp from a good hunt. "After supper I had a good talk with Matthews on geography in all its ramifications. It is about midnight now and I am writing this by candlelight in Matthews's little tent. We go down the river tomorrow, or bust." Naturally, after this ultimatum the motor delayed them two more days but finally, Matthews' genius saved the aging kicker. They set off on August 28 and arrived at Fort Simpson a few days later.[15]

A determined Patterson used the weekend of August 11 to prepare for a month on the Flat River. He also wrote a letter to Mother for Hunter to post in Simpson, in which he described Hunter as "an American traveller and sportsman…travels simply for pleasure—having previously packed off his wife and family to Europe—and loves this life."

This last letter home in 1928 mentioned his plans: he was off for the Flat the next day, and would explore further than in the summer of 1927 with lots of food, snowshoes and winter clothing in case of early snow. "If I strike any gold up there, we shall try to get back to it—either over the ice in the winter with our dogs or by canoe in the lower water in May." A late northern spring might delay him until August 1929 he warned Mother, so he requested that she ask "Marigold if she will have a September wedding day. I'm so sorry that it can't be June—I had hoped for that, but unless something most unusual happens we shall be stuck in here behind the canyon until the second boat leaves Simpson in July. And September is a lovely month. I would do anything to be home in June—do please help and make my peace for me."

He also asked for two packages to be forwarded from England. The first was to be mostly treats, including "a copy of Facey Ronford's Hounds by Surtees in the little red edition." He also wanted 300 Connaught Virginia cigarettes and 200 Rhodesian Virginia cigarettes from John Woods, and from Harrods a sealed tin of a "jolly good box of chocolates." He gave instructions for it to be sent all duty paid and registered to protect against theft. It had to arrive in Edmonton in time to catch the "arctic dog mail" in late November—"Marigold knows." Matthews was planning a mail run to Simpson in January while Patterson tended the traps so these late Christmas presents would arrive at a most needy time of the year.

The other parcel was for clothing. From Robinson & Cleavers he wanted a pair of light grey flannel trousers, two light-coloured khaki Viyella shirts, two pairs grey socks, two thin short-sleeved vests and two pairs Aertex knee pants, all registered and duty paid to Fort Simpson so that he could return to Edmonton "like a Christian…I'm awfully sorry to bother you but this Nahanni country simply rends clothes and we shall emerge as scarecrows."

Patterson also mentioned that Faille had taken out his 1927 ram head and sent it through the Northern Trading Company to Edmonton. He asked Mother to have it mounted by Rowland Ward in Piccadilly on a black shield with the following inscription:

R.M.P.
Falls of the Nahanni
Aug. 14, 1927

In spite of all the changes to plans since leaving London early in the year, the letter retained a positive, excited tone. He and Matthews were getting along well and he concluded: "Take care of yourself and I'll do the same— I do hope this journey turns out well."[16]

Patterson left Matthews and the Hunter party at Wheatsheaf Creek on Monday, August 13. He made good time upriver, travelling quickly through Second Canyon in glorious August sunshine, his canoe light on the trackline. On Wednesday, August 15, he wrote, "I find that about $8\frac{1}{2}$ hrs. is my limit for this upstream work. Longer than that &, if I have been travelling hard & steadily, I become played out & might as well camp as hobble onwards." The next day, despite torrential rain, he determined to reach The Gate before resting. "A dangerous place, I was cold through & my hands had no feeling left in them." A riffle defeated him. "Feeling very much badgered & alone & wishing I was at home in England," he built a small fire under a ledge, changed clothes, and ate a hot supper "sitting literally on top of the fire." The mist rolled back to reveal snow on nearby mountains. Refreshed, he portaged the canoe over a gravel bar and camped in the little bay below The Gate.

On Friday, August 17, he hiked to the top of The Gate, measured it with his aneroid, took pictures and dropped rocks into the abyss. It took them nine seconds to hit the water. While he was eating blueberries, a "mystery plane" flew over twice. A call from below beckoned him to camp and there he lunched with Hunter's party who were rushing to the Falls. Later he scouted the creek that comes in above The Gate, decided it drained a large territory and caught a trout from it for supper.

He reached the Flat on Monday, August 20, and crossed the tricky line where the South Nahanni and Flat rivers converge. "One drive of the paddle & she [the canoe] passed from the olive green of the Nahanni into the still emerald of the Flat with a swirl & a surge that made her take in water." An hour later he read the note on Faille's cabin door: "A. Faille left here for the Fals July 8." Patterson retrieved the axe, pick and gold pan he had left the summer before and camped two miles upstream.

While he was brushing suds onto his face for a shave the next morning, a movement caught his eye. Crashing through the woods about 300 yards away came a moose. Down went the soap and brush, and picking up the rifle, he made a quick sprint to within range at 200 yards. Three of four shots hit the target and the steaks on the hoof fell dead. Leaning his rifle against a log, Patterson finished shaving, ate breakfast, then cut up the moose. Fresh kidneys and liver adorned the lunch plate "& thank the Lord for it all." He made a stew with some of the meat and smoked and dried the rest on spruce boughs in the hot sun.

The Flat River canyon, 1928.

On Thursday the 23rd he caught up with Starke and Stevens at Caribou Creek, where, with the river dropping and almost out of gasoline, they had decided to build a cabin. After a visit Patterson pushed on. Blueberries and cranberries filled a pail in the bow of the canoe—a wonderfully handy snack. Supper was a dream: "There are few steaks to equal the tenderloin of one's own moose when one is hungry."

Friday was another gorgeous day but the only gold he saw was in the fall colours. Still, game tracks littered every beach and fished jumped in the pools between the riffles. "It seems that in these fall months one need not starve in Eden." To the west Patterson could see the jagged teeth of a mountain range where the McLeod brothers of Dead Men's Valley fame were rumoured to have found their gold. The day ended with a "gorgeous ripple sunset—red, green & gold—reflected on the calm water with the black points of the tall spruce standing into it—the Canada one sees in pictures."

Weariness overcame the gold seeker on Saturday, August 25, so he rested, in the morning exploring a side creek and finding Stanier's little falls. From its pool he pulled three trout that he fried up with moose for lunch. "Evening now & I am shaved, bathed & cleaned & in my right mind." Lying in bed, he was haunted by the "everlasting noise of water."

After two days of hard going he reached Irvine Creek on Monday evening. That night a large trout spat out the hook just as it reached the shore so Patterson beat at it with his alder fishing pole. Mildly irritated, the fish swam away as the pole broke in two.

Tuesday, August 28, marked his farthest west, about four miles upstream of Irvine Creek. "At last—this far & no further. The river got worse after leaving Irvine Creek—simply one long, damned boulder rapid & for three hours I fought with it—soaked to the waist. One might as well try to take a canoe up a trout stream at home." So Patterson made a base camp, lounged in the sun and laughed himself to sleep reading Jorrocks' antics.

On Wednesday he rested and ate a good breakfast. "Not everybody has eaten six different kinds of fruit at once—cold rice cooked with apples & cranberries, & over that poured cold stewed red currants, black currants, raspberries & gooseberries. A most pleasant eating." Then he was off with a light pack and the aneroid for a hike into the hills. From a height of 1700 feet he surveyed the land. As he suspected, the steep canyon of the Flat was nearby, now called the Cascade-of-the-Thirteen-Steps. And Borden Creek—Gold Creek—was another eight miles up the river.

On Thursday he built a quick cache. Weather permitting, he planned to "start away tomorrow—I only trust it won't be like my last adventure on foot, last September, from Fort Nelson into the Fish Lake hills." Memories of that close call with starvation stayed with him for life, a reminder of the narrow margin between healthy adventure and disaster. He was also glad to escape the river noise, "there are voices & weird sounds in a rapid."

By noon on the second day Patterson had to admit defeat. Borden Creek and its gold were impossible to reach through the tangle of trees, dead fall, moss and muskeg. "I could carry my load no further through the bush. It was beyond my strength, consisting of: rifle, pistol (& cartridges), shovel, pick & gold pan, food, tea pail, frying pan etc., axe, bedding, camera & the odd things that are necessary." At one point he even notched footholds into the side of the bank with his axe, and suspended 500 feet above the river, risked life and limb with every step. Finally he turned back and made an alternate plan to retreat to Irvine Creek and seek gold up that tributary. "The canyon of the Flat is bad—rapids that are almost falls & tremendous boulders. The country behind is a hard one to get into—no wonder it keeps its gold. It's difficult to see how to tackle it—if only I could have my four free Canadian years over again I'd try it."

On Monday, September 3, he paddled down to Irvine Creek in four-and-a-half hours, running all the rapids. "It's a splendid feeling—the sight ahead of a slope of dancing, white water—the sudden rush into the noisy waves—the sharp swing to avoid a rock & then the shooting out into the calm waters of the pool below." That evening a monstrous trout "a thing the size of Leviathin himself" took his last Indiana Spinner.

After lunch on Tuesday he panned for gold on Irvine Creek, but found none. Frustrated, he gave up on the gold and decided he "had better get back to Gordon & do some honest work & make some money." Three hours in the canoe on a perfect fall afternoon cheered him up a bit. A young moose offered itself up late in the afternoon but Patterson passed it up—it was too late in the day and a rapid ahead promised to make it tough to shoot both the moose and the tricky water. On Wednesday he saw a caribou and told himself, "But for the Devil's interference, there goes my supper." Shooting a running caribou from a moving canoe was tricky, but by six that evening he was sharing caribou steak with Starke and Stevens.

Patterson left Caribou Creek after lunch on Thursday, Starke and Stevens promising to visit in the spring and travel out together to Simpson and Edmonton in June or July, or whenever the Mackenzie opened for navigation. The next day, September 7, he left the Flat and by Saturday noon had reached the cabin at Wheatsheaf Creek.

Was the trip a success? Although he had found no gold, the Flat River trip had another payoff. Hunter had encouraged Patterson to keep a detailed account of the trip and submit it as an official exploration record to the government of Canada or to the Geographical Society in London, England.[17] As a result, Patterson self-published an eight-page booklet titled *The Flat River Country North West Territories of Canada* in 1933. With text, a map and photographs, he described this major Nahanni tributary and its tributaries for the very first time: its navigational hazards, the

Wheatsheaf Creek cabin interior, 1928-29.

cabins along its banks and their inhabitants, the natives that frequented the area, the game—or lack thereof, the mineral and timber resources and the weather: "As to climate, Faille described the winter of 1927-8 as 'dammed cold,' but, as most of his supplies had been eaten or destroyed by the wolverine, this may be a biased opinion due to lack of internal warmth." In contrast, Patterson wrote, "My own experience of the Flat River has been in August and September of both 1927 and 1928, and in those months I can imagine no more perfect climate in the world."[18] He also stated that the trail from Frances Lake into the Flat River, though often used in the past, was no longer travelled. As for trapping, Starke and Stevens had concluded it was "a good meat country but a poor fur country," an analysis proved by Faille. Fenley Hunter would mention this booklet when he nominated Patterson for membership in the Royal Geographical Society in 1932.

Back at the cabin, Patterson got to work. "Being naturally indolent," he said twenty-five years later, "and so having a horror of working with anything but the sharpest of tools, I set to on the first morning with a file and a stone and sharpened to a razor edge the crosscut and all the axes." The crosscut saw was a toothed monstrosity—Peace River settlers called it the Homesteader's Fiddle—that he used to cut planks to fashion the door, window shutters, table, shelves and other cabin details. In one week the cabin was finished. Dug a foot into the ground, the inside measured fourteen by thirteen feet. The door, with a wooden bolt, faced south. The roof was of a single layer of spruce poles covered with sods. Photos show few luxuries in a utilitarian interior. Clothing and hides hung on pegs and a few shelves held books and supplies. A cello-glass window let in a bit of light and outside a pair of heavy shutters protected against the marauding wolverine when the trappers were away from home.[19]

For variety, they hiked around Dead Men's Valley scouting animal trails for game—a task that was to preoccupy them all that fall. On September 20 a little black bear provided twenty pounds of "good white bear grease" for the cold winter days to come. One of the dogs gulped Patterson's shaving brush that same day.

Visitors arrived on Tuesday, September 18. Four men had come down the Flat River in two canoes: leaky-sectioned behemoths. Dropped off by plane on August 4, the prospectors had noticed a mysterious boot impression in the sand that was Patterson's. A Wrigley and a McLeod were among the men in this party, the latter a relative of the headless brothers. Suspicion hung over the visit like a dark cloud, each group wondering what the other knew about the Flat River gold. "I would give a great deal to know what they found & how near I came to them…," wrote Patterson. "However, if a gold rush starts we are well on the way & can rush with the rest." Although invited to stay the night, the men pushed on, saying they planned to stay at the upper hot springs at Dry Canyon. This was news to Patterson and he vowed to find the springs soon.

A hard frost arrived on Thursday, September 20, and the Nahanni ran clear, without the usual cloudy glacial sediment.[20] Out hunting, Patterson shot three sheep at Prairie Creek: two ewes and a ram. His rifle jammed repeatedly, but luckily he was after sheep and not a wounded bear or a hormonal moose. Lighting smoke smudges to protect against predators, he dropped some of the finest morsels into his pack "& took half the biggest sheep on my shoulders & packed him down to my canoe by the Nahanni, much as my forbears have packed English sheep back across the Border after a raid into Northumberland."

On Sunday, September 23, Patterson celebrated the first anniversary of not starving to death by discovering "a new & most excellent way of baking bannock" by crisply frying the outside and then baking it in the oven. He pronounced it "eminently eatable." He moved into the cabin the next day and tested the new table and chairs with his first indoor supper. In the next few days he built a bedframe, made a broom out of birch wood and added to the huge wood pile necessary to heat the cabin throughout the coming winter.

The first snow fell on Saturday, September 29. Moose tracks were everywhere, but they saw no actual animals. Partridges, trout, ducks and other small game helped put food on the table, but did little to fill the larder against winter, prompting Patterson to write, "Indeed, our luck is clean out just now." On October 5, Patterson took a quick trip to Dry Canyon Creek to find the mysterious upper hot springs, but finally had to admit the prospectors had successfully pulled his leg. Then on October 6, Matthews shot a coyote, the first fur of the year. Patterson's sore back and legs returned the next day. "Damn—why can't these things be reserved for stay-at-home folk?" he complained as the lumbago pestered him regularly for the next month.

On October 13, Matthews set off to the south and returned late, "very wet & weary,"with news that he'd shot three moose at the salt lick. Because a chinook had melted the snow, they had to backpack more than 1000 pounds of meat to the cabin, and quickly, in order to prevent the wolves from devouring their winter fare. The dogs helped, carrying meat in panniers. On one trip, stumbling along under a heavy pack, Patterson met a snorting bull moose. Dropping his load, he scrambled up a small spruce that swayed under his weight and somehow shot the animal from his insecure perch. On October 15 Patterson noted, "Packing meat on ones back that distance is exhausting, bloody, in both senses of the word—& everlasting."

WINTER arrived on Sunday, October 27. "The sun came up with a roar of light into a frozen, shining world, the snows squeaked underfoot, one's nose stung in the clear air & the moose steaks I had cut overnight were frozen like bricks." The sled and dogs finally proved their worth in hauling the meat from the kill. A few days later Patterson noticed a small white head peeking at him from the woodpile, so he shot a squirrel and a whiskey jack for the ermine to eat. They never regarded it as a pet and later added it to their catch of fur. When the river froze solidly on the 31st, they pulled the canoes up into the woods.

With the onset of winter they mustered an arsenal against its ravages. Most important, of course, was food. As the season progressed, fat became important, so the rotund little bears always attracted their attention. Cutting deadfall for the woodpile, hunting and walking the long traplines kept them warm. In their winter clothing they looked like twins

Gordon Matthews in winter gear.

most days: khaki shirts, dark-blue wool mackinaw stag jackets with double shoulders and red silk scarves. On colder days they added sweaters, khaki "bib" overalls to cut the wind, woollen hats and balaclava helmets, fur hats with ear flaps, parkas, brown woollen gloves, mitts and over mitts. Their feet stayed warm in bumble boots or woollen felt packs covered by moose hide moccasins and overboots.[21]

In spite of these defences against the cold, Patterson's lumbago flared up regularly, confining him to bed. Immobilized on November 1, he wrote, "South Africa, the South Seas or Australia for me the next time— I've wooed the frozen north & she has treated me very ill." When Matthews returned from the trapline on Monday, November 5, they set off Chinese rockets and other firecrackers, "...brought originally to impress the Indians, but now not needed, since the once dreaded Nahannis are down to a small & miserable remnant, gathered round the posts on the Liard."

On November 8 a wolf dragged away a large No. 3 trap. Patterson regretted the loss but also sympathized. "Don't like to think of the poor beast in misery & unable to hunt—too much like my own case these last weeks. And Faille lost ten wolves in the same way last winter." Unable to walk, he made fur stretchers, skinned furs, boiled traps with bark from the aspen poplar to rid them of human scent,[22] mended clothing and footwear, and cleaned the chimney with a canoe pole and an old sock. On November 10 he wrote, "In a day spent in camp there's little to write about, & that little would only be monstrous in the telling."

Poilu and Quiz disappeared on Wednesday, November 14. With wolves about the dogs were not safe. Matthews found each of them in a No. 3 trap, Poilu limping home, dragging his and Quiz, unable to move, "yelling his soul out for any wandering wolf to hear." After releasing the pair, Matthews taught them a lesson with a willow switch.

Chinooks were frequent throughout November and December, melting away the snow and making trapping difficult. With no snow to show animal tracks or to cover the traps, it was a waste of time to set them. On Wednesday, November 21, a disgusted Patterson returned from the trapline after discovering the American-made Victor traps were not springing when animals stepped in them. "Consequently, I returned home in no even temper." He fiddled with them for hours that evening, filing and oiling them, attempting to repair the instruments of death. Back over the trapline he went, resetting the questionable traps, hoping for the best. But the next month was still not good. So the trappers branched out, setting traps in every tributary that ran into their valley, but with the same meagre results. On November 29 Patterson wrote, "Feel decidedly blue today—I gave up so much for this trip & yet it seems that the luck & weather are always against us."

As the days shortened in December they began using an alarm clock to help them get on the trapline in the hours before dawn. On December 3 Patterson shot a blue grouse with his rifle but nothing was left "to bring home & the wretched grouse [was] scattered all over the map." One bird was not a big loss, but the four they were keeping for Christmas blew down from the cache and mysteriously "disappeared down some dog's throat." Perhaps their luck would turn in the New Year.

On December 14 they scouted Lower Canyon. On finding Cache Rapid silent under solid ice, Matthews decided to head for Simpson with the dog team on the 19th. They designated the 17th as Christmas Eve and had a party. Pancakes with butter, sugar and maple syrup seemed very rich after a diet of moose meat, Patterson managing to eat only four and a half while Matthews choked down five. "If only we could have our twenty-one-year-old appetites back again." The

Gordon Matthews and dog team in Lower Canyon.

next day their Christmas Day feast included partridges and grouse, two each, trimmed with cranberries, followed by "a lusty dessert." Quiz the dog caught and ate a partridge. "The more strength to any dog who can rustle his own feed." After breakfast Patterson finished off letters and cables and saw Matthews off to civilization.

Three days later the solitary resident of Death Valley returned home to find Matthews and the dogs relaxing in the warm cabin. Open water in Lower Canyon had forced them to return for the small canoe. The next day was the real Christmas Eve, Patterson's "fourth to be spent in strange places away from home." They made sled runners for the canoe from a curved birch tree, and after loading the dogsled into the canoe, Patterson photographed the unusual outfit as it set off once more for the canyon. Feeling low, he promised himself a fine Christmas present when he got back to England, "a piece of old German glass, such as I have long coveted." Christmas Day was spent mending moccasins. The remainder of the

The hide of The Wolverine.

year was as exciting: doing monotonous chores and setting traps that almost always came up empty. December 31 dawned clear and cold, the coldest so far, but he could not check the temperature—the thermometer had blown up on December 1 when they had warmed it in the oven.[23] "Dead still outside & the coldest night we have had. There is frost round the door, the hot air steams as it goes out of the shack & the smoke is rising thickly from the chimney."

January, 1929, was a disappointing month. Not only did fur avoid the traps, much more seriously for Patterson, the game disappeared. The first catch of the year was the most miserable beast of the North. On January 4 Patterson found a snarling ball of furious fur, "lashing & plunging on the chain." Eight times he shot it with his 9 mm Luger pistol and seven times it came right back for more. Skinning the wolverine was almost impossible, but eventually he threw the carcass into the cache as insurance against starvation.

Wheatsheaf Creek cabin in the snow. The temperature is 44° below zero Fahrenheit.

Snow began to fall, and on January 8 there was finally enough to pull out the snowshoes. Patterson checked traps up toward McLeod Creek and arrived home with a small weasel, feeling "a little stiff in the re-awakened snowshoe muscles." The snow continued to fall in blankets, obliterating all animal tracks.

The diary for Sunday, January 13, records two serious facts: Patterson's footgear was worn out and he was down to the last piece of moose meat. The traps had stayed empty for ten days. Nothing could mask the fact he was forced to eat wolverine stew. "…all through the day, from matins to evensong, I 'remembered the wolverine' with all the rustic simplicity and zest of a village choir." Hiking along, "with clear, melodious trumpet note, I remembered the wolverine…."[24]

The temperature fell to about fifty below zero on January 21, the little patches of open water "steaming hard in the cold air & spreading a raw mist over the floor of the valley." Reduced to eating boiled wolverine, he anxiously awaited Matthews' return. On the 24th he wrote the understatement of the month, "If Gordon doesn't show up soon there's going to be a shortage of grub in this outfit." Two days later he shot a partridge, on the 29th he packed, and on Wednesday the 30th he left Death Valley on an emergency trip to Fort Simpson.

There the diary ends.

147

The last words in the little book are alarming: "Probably start tomorrow & if my leg doesn't turn bad & if I can get through the canyon I'll probably get there in four days or so—barring weather and accidents." In preparation he precooked food at the cabin and froze it on aluminum plates.[25]

Although experienced in snowshoeing (he had bought his first pair five years earlier in trade "for an English knife with a handle that was fashioned in the shape of a thistle."[26]), Patterson was still recovering from lumbago, was low on food and was fighting through deep snow with a heavy pack on his back. Sometimes the snowshoes skidded on river ice, stressing his ankles, knees, hips and back. Any accidental misstep could prove disastrous.

But luck was with him and he arrived safely at Jack la Flair's trading post at Nahanni Butte.[27] There he bought a few supplies and stitched up a pair of overmitts for himself.[28] He then set off downriver, stopping briefly at Ole and Anna Lindberg's cabin on the Long Reach of the Liard. They fed him and lent him a little toboggan fifteen inches wide and six feet long to carry his pack. It made snowshoeing so much easier.[29]

Even so, the going was tough. In 1951, while editing his letters home from Rossall, he described his skill at sleeping almost anywhere by linking a boarding school bivouac in August 1915 with this emergency trip out of the South Nahanni in 1929. "That ability to rest and sleep under any sort of conditions saved me many a night's misery in later years, on

Jack la Flair's trading post at Nahanni Butte.

hunting trips in the North. A peak to that sort of thing was reached in February 1929 in the North West Territories when I snowshoed alone for 200 miles down the frozen Liard River to Fort Simpson on the Mackenzie, travelling light.

"The weather was cold and the nights ranged from 30º below zero to over 60º below—but I slept, rolled in my one blanket by the fire, on a bed of spruce boughs under my tarpaulin lean-to; dry moccasins loosely on my feet, my parka thrown over my fur hat—waking every two hours of the six hours of sleep to reach out and roll another big log into the fire.

"Coldest of all was the hour before the dawn when one sat before the fire eating bacon and oatmeal and drinking tea, waiting for the first faint light of the short northern day, when the trees would take shape again out of the shadows and you could see again that wind-drifted wrinkle in the snow—the river trail."[30]

Patterson could have stayed with la Flair or with the Lindbergs, but he was determined to get to Fort Simpson—a decision that nearly cost him his life. Inevitably, the accident came at the end of the day when he was weary and inattentive. An invisible hand from below the snow grabbed a snowshoe, jerked it sideways, and tossed him into the snow with an injured knee.[31] The accident completely immobilized him and only the kindness of a passing Slave Indian saved him from certain death.[32] A few days later he was recuperating in Fort Simpson, thawing out his face and tending to his sore ankles and knees.

Matthews' trip had also turned into a bit of an epic: he had fallen into the river twice, each time nearly drowning himself and the dogs. Heavy snow had delayed his return to the cabin and then Patterson had showed up with swollen legs.[33] So they decided to stay a few more days in Fort Simpson, resting and re-supplying. The days sped by as the Nahanni hermits visited with hotel owner Andy Whittington—an ex-Klondiker, Indian Agent Flynn Harris, blacksmith Hall of the HBC, and Inspector and Mrs. Moorehead of the RCMP. They also picked up the Christmas mail, sent out letters and caught up on the news brought by the regular mail plane that landed every few weeks at the community. Always, their ears were peeled for the sound of dogfights and many times they scrambled to separate their wolf-like charges from the fray. In between, they lounged in Andy's hotel and ate civilized meals, all for a dollar per meal regardless of how much you ate, and with a bed thrown into the bargain.[34]

When February turned into March, Patterson and Matthews felt pressure to return to the trapline. An elaborate and unspoken cat and mouse game ensued as the men in Simpson waited with carefully masked impatience for someone else to set trail for other dogsleds to follow. Finally, a few sleds left together, each taking turns breaking trail up the frozen Liard River. After a brief stop at la Flair's post, Patterson and Matthews scampered through the Splits and Lower Canyon in three days and moved back into the cabin on Wheatsheaf Creek. Along the way, they opened the Christmas mail, read to each other from books they had borrowed from the Simpson library, ate of the tasty treats from home and smoked excellent Ramon Allones cigars.[35]

In the next two months they collected most of the winter's fur catch. The cabin was really only large enough for one person at a time so they rotated trips on the trapline, one staying in lean-to camps while the other used the cabin. Fur trapping chores consumed almost every waking hour and when questions arose, they consulted a fur trade publication released by the Dominion government with a foreword by Sir Clifford Sifton.[36]

Slowly the stacks of fur rose. Many would be sold in May to the fur buyer in Simpson. One hundred and twenty of the finest Patterson set aside as an act of "atonement for snoring at the opera."[37] More than forty-five years later he said, "They were all big and some were very big because I was engaged to be married at the time and I kept out a lot of them, the best of them, and brought them back to England and gave them to my wife who had them made up. I thought it would make a nice little collar for her. Well, it made a thing about that wide, and so it could hang down to here and she could go like that with it [thrown around her neck like a long scarf] and she was absolutely swathed in them."[38]

Time flew by and soon the snow was gone and the river was starting to melt. Slush made bush travel impossible, so they prepared to leave their little log cabin as soon as possible after Patterson's birthday on May 13. On the afternoon of the 12th, Matthews began hollering at Patterson from the river. "Throw on all the coffee," he yelled as the dogs went wild and raced for the little landing on the Nahanni. Though Second Canyon looked blocked with ice, Starke and Stevens had somehow navigated their massive scow through a narrow opening and were about to arrive at the cabin. Stevens' birthday was May 11 so the respective partners pulled out all stops and hosted a combined birthday party. The dregs of Wheatsheaf Creek cabin coffee and sugar went into the pot to make Coffee Royals with the last few ounces of rum from the Flat River cabin. Together they sang Christmas carols, added another beaver to the pot and bragged of the damage they would do to food and drink at the Butte and at Simpson.[39]

Patterson, anxious to get married, badgered the others to get going to Fort Simpson. Finally, Starke gave in with a grumble, "Oh, for heaven's sake let's get him out of here and down to Simpson Island and then we can all camp there in misery instead of up here in comfort."[40] So Patterson set off in the small canoe, choosing campsites for the men who followed in the lumbering scow. Arriving at Fort Simpson, they fulfilled Starke's prophecy and waited by the banks of the sluggish Mackenzie River for the ice to descend from Great Slave Lake and allow the floatplane to begin its flights along the great arctic river.

Patterson and Matthews had done amazingly well as trappers. Weasels and marten were selling well in May 1929—about $24 each—and that part of the catch alone brought them $1,980.[41] A master of bargaining, Matthews sold their outfit—canoes, traps, tents, tarps and related trapping and prospecting gear—for more than it had cost them sixteen months earlier.[42] "Patterson of the Golden Touch" was shocked, however, to read that his mining shares had not risen in value. Later in Edmonton he would discover they had been split three for one, tripling his investment.[43] Totalling in excess of $10,000 at a time when a man made a dollar a day, these earnings provided Patterson with the nest egg necessary to marry his sweetheart.

As May turned into June, Patterson was still impatiently pacing the shore, waiting for the ice to descend from the Upper Mackenzie. Then late one night, a few ice cakes slid by in the light of the midnight sun.

Jack "The Black Pirate" Starke steering the scow on the way out from the Nahanni, 1929.

Soon the far side of the Mackenzie was white, "sedately moving galleons of the ice as they swept on into the north-west, breaking the mirror of the golden clouds, a phantom armada sailing into the sunset." When the ice passed, the clear green Mackenzie ran parallel to the flooding brown Liard as they surged past the community on Simpson Island.

A few days later Patterson stepped out of a canoe and climbed into the mail plane piloted by Punch Dickins.‡ As the floats gently left the Mackenzie River on takeoff, Patterson looked to the west with a new appreciation of the dangerous South Nahanni and its mysterious Death Valley. "That was the Butte, the gateway to Deadmen's Valley and to Faille's Country, and on it I kept my eyes fixed until it sank once more beneath the horizon."[44] Soon he would be back in Canada "with two incompatible possessions—a brand new wife, and a love of wandering and the wilderness."

Thus ended Patterson's second of four adventures on the South Nahanni River. When he returned in the 1950s he carefully heeded warnings to prepare himself for the emotional slump that often comes when returning to an exciting place of youth. "I knew that no machine-powered trip in the safe company of men could ever give again the wonder of those early years, almost a quarter of a century past, when I had first come poling and tracking my canoe through the canyons, all eyes for what might lie round the next bend, heading into a blank on the map, as did 'untutored men of early ages, to whom everything unknown was marvellous.' You can only do that once. Never again will there be the same thrill, the same sense of achievement, of single-handed victory over obstacles."[45]

---

‡ C. H. "Punch" Dickins won the Distinguished Flying Cross as a fighter pilot ace in World War I. In 1928 he won the McKee Trophy, the "Nobel prize of Canadian aviation," for a 4000 mile exploratory flight over the Barren Lands and around Baker Lake and Great Slave Lake in a Fokker seaplane. In 1929 he became the first pilot to cross the Arctic Circle in the western Arctic, landing at the mouth of the Mackenzie River on July 1, 1929. On a second trip north he continued on to the HBC post at Fort Good Hope on the Mackenzie River and returned to Edmonton with a plane full of baled furs, the first export of marketable goods from the North by plane. In all, he logged in excess of 800,000 air miles in the North between 1927 and 1939.[46]

In January, 1928, Punch began delivering mail for the Canadian government on one of a handful of experimental mail routes, his being from Waterways to Fort Simpson. By 1929 there were sixteen regular mail routes in the Canadian West and North. Incorporated on December 10, 1926, Western Canada Airways Limited of Winnipeg operated Route #10 from Waterways in Alberta to Aklavik on the Arctic Ocean—a 1500 mile route.[47] On the blue fuselage were the white letters G-CASM. The Versailles Peace Conference of 1919 required all civilian planes to show prominent call letters and under that convention the letter G was assigned to the British Commonwealth and CA to Canada. The remaining letters identified it as part of the Western Canada Airways fleet.[48]

The Buffalo Head Years
1929 to 1946

TWENTY-SIX year-old Marigold Portman awaited Patterson when he returned to London. She had not won his affections without competition; Rafaelle Kennedy, "a young American girl," had seriously distracted Patterson in the mid-1920s. Arriving in London with her mother, Rafaelle claimed the British mistook her for someone "certain to be hunting a husband, with a title of course, and to have plenty of dollars." She was seeking a husband, of course, but she was without the wealth her expensive raiment suggested. Rafaelle found the British to be very elegant: the women in their gowns, tiaras and jewels; the men in their white tie and tails. She fell first for Raymond, home on a visit from his Alberta homestead and looking tanned and healthy. "He was off to the tall timbers of Canada, and wanted me to go with him. I think I might have done so had I been more adventurous," she recalled years later, "so I lost a good man…."

But Patterson was not necessarily hers to lose. Instead, he chose Marigold, who Rafaelle described as "a lovely English blonde…full of laughter…the right wife for him." Intrigued with him even on his wedding day, the American attended the wedding at the chapel in Ennismore Gardens even though she wasn't on the guest list. After catching his eye, she bolted "like streaked lightning right out the door that his bride had just entered!"[1]

Raymond and Marigold exchanged vows on July 4, 1929, and then enjoyed a travelling honeymoon in the north of England and the Canadian west. In the small village called Blanchland in Northumberland near Hadrian's Wall they stayed in the Lord Crewe Arms Hotel—originally constructed as an abbey in the 11th century. A few days later they drove to nearby Wolsingham where they visited Patterson's boyhood chum Edwin and stayed at the Fenwicks' country estate—a huge, two storey,

R. M. Patterson and Marigold Patterson on
their honeymoon, August, 1929.

multi-winged 1880's country house called Forester's Lodge. The holiday continued in Jasper, Alberta, and ended in Victoria, British Columbia, where they looked unsuccessfully for a home. By the fall they were house-hunting in southern Alberta. Marigold's mother considered Raymond "a fool for leaving England," but the bride found the adventure exciting. Raymond was deeply in love and willing to settle down a bit if necessary. But as much as he liked the good life of the city, he yearned for a life on the edge. Most people lived in herds like pack animals, he thought. If he could just find the right property, he could, perhaps, juggle these competing desires. Because the homestead had served its purpose, he sold it. He then let go his mining shares, regarding the 1920s as a profitable and entertaining decade. He also dumped his Hudson's Bay Company shares, and just in time: the shares paid investors between 19.5% and 40% each year during the 1920s, but dividends dropped to 17.5% in 1930 and there were no profits at all from 1931 to 1937.

Marigold also brought expectations to the marriage. As was the custom of the times, her family provided her with a marriage settlement, or an investment fund, which made her about $1000 per year.[2] She and Patterson also dreamed up another source of income for her: "We took out with us a pair of little dogs, Border Terriers, and I was to remain in the house, wherever it was, and breed Border Terriers." They also bought a bull terrier in Canada and named him Shrovetide—something to do with Rabelais, no doubt, but they always called him Snork. It perhaps made sense in 1919, but reflecting on the scheme in 1999, Marigold shook her head and said, "Thinking back on it, I can't think of a sillier plan."[3]

"Plans, in this imperfect world," wrote Patterson in *The Buffalo Head* twenty-five years later, "have a habit of breaking down."[4] Patterson always wondered what would have happened had he returned to the North after the wedding. As it turned out, Gordon and Mollie Matthews eked out an existence in the frozen wastelands for most of the 1930s. Frequent letters from Wrigley, the next fur trading post north of Fort Simpson, filled "George" in on northern news. "Our old cabin was turned into a 'hunting lodge' last fall for a party of Yanks who were taken into the valley by the Commercial Airways. Mr. Peffer had charge of the grub; procuring guides, etc. Jonas Lafferty & Carl Arhaus being the guides. The 'sportsmen' were taken up our old Baldy & there they were lucky enough to kill eight good Rams, returning to Simpson & the States in due course with the fixed intention of telling their friends all about it. In the newspaper write-up our cabin is described 'as the roomy, comfortable lodge erected for the Commercial Airways.' The pilot of the plane tells me that everything is exactly as we left it. Cache, stove, bunks, tables, etc. etc."[5]

Had everything gone according to plan, these letters would have reached "Patterson the Prospector" as he wandered the Canadian west in the employ of an exploration and mining company. The investments should have continued to grow, exponentially, compounding his wealth and providing a good life in the newlyweds' adopted country. But luck took a little holiday at the end of 1929 and the prospecting job disappeared just as the returns on investments faltered.

Then the stock market crashed and the tough decade of the 1930s began just as the Pattersons invested in a sheep ranch called Buckspring west of Calgary. It overlooked the Bow River and had a panoramic view of the mountains. Although completely unskilled as a sheep rancher, Patterson did his best, took his lumps and boldly pursued the new venture. Unfortunately, the price of sheep plummeted in a downward spiral that eventually took it to 25% of 1929 values. Marigold recalls that in 1931, "The price of wool didn't pay the shearers' wages, by quite a long way."[6] Cochrane sheep rancher Dick Wright suggested "this depression is going to continue," and sold out. Patterson wisely followed suit, but others hung on longer and found buyers for neither the wool nor the animals. Patterson said he "crawled out from under, one of the lucky ones, battered but not crippled, and cured for good and all of any hankering after sheep…. From then on, all I have ever asked of those perverse animals is mutton-on a plate."[7]

The Pattersons sold their first place to R. C. Burns, Q.C. He promptly sold it to Jim and Lillie Scott who operated it as a dairy farm, milking purebred Ayrshires.[8]

Although Raymond and Marigold spent almost four years at Buckspring, few stories from this period appear in his books. A local history recalls that Patterson bought the ranch on the SW 1/4 Sec. 32-25-3-W5 and "rescued it from ruin." He put a new roof on the house, painted the house and barn, planted a row of spruce trees as a windbreak between the house and barn, replaced the fences and stocked the ranch with saddle and pack horses. The terriers, apparently, developed a habit of killing neighbourhood cats, so Patterson attached string harnesses to their shoulders and a tobacco tin in which a few small stones rattled as the dogs walked. In another story, Patterson deterred thieves from breaking into a nearby vacant house by digging holes with a crowbar and freezing stout spikes in place with warm water. When the crooks returned in the dark, Patterson's trap flattened their truck tires and they drove away on the rims, cursing all and sundry.

Despite the hole it was making in their bank account, many good things happened at Buckspring. On May 21, 1930, Marigold presented her husband with the first of three children, Janet Murray, who was born in Calgary. Mail being what it was in the North, Gordon's congratulations did not arrive until February 1931. "We are very glad to hear of the small Janet & I shall be proud to Godfather the young woman." Today, Janet fondly remembers him "as a person of considerable charm." The Matthews also had news of the family sort. Legendary bush pilot Wop May flew Mollie south to Edmonton on March 12, 1931, for the delivery of their firstborn, G. Richard "Robin" Matthews, who arrived safely on

Buckspring sheep ranch near Cochrane, Alberta.

April 20, 1931. In return Patterson was glad to be his godfather. Included with these notes from the North came a marten pelt that Gordon sent to Marigold as a wedding present.[9]

In Alberta Marigold developed the habit of taking a holiday from the cold weather. In the days before natural gas or central heating, the long winters were easier to take when broken up by an annual escape to Vancouver Island.

Perhaps while riding the train through the mountains to Vancouver, Raymond and Marigold caught the vision of a cabin by a river in a mountainous gorge. Or perhaps it was the view west through the gap of the Bow River that prompted them to search for a retreat in the Rockies. However, evidence sug-

Buckspring cook Mrs. Sheppard, Marigold Patterson and daughter Janet in 1932.

gests Patterson bought grazing land on the Ghost River to augment the pasture at Buckspring. The newlyweds purchased riverfront property on this tributary to the Bow River before their first anniversary. "Well, it is a nice spot, isn't it?" recalled Marigold in late 1995, then with classic British understatement added, "One went down a rather precipitous slope to get to it…. We were pretty busy at the time, but my husband loved the feeling of being on a river again. I think that is part of the reason he bought that bit of land."[10] Of that unique property Patterson wrote: "Though that glen of the Ghost was only a bit over two miles from the Calgary-Banff road, yet it was like some little piece of the wild mountains that had wandered out into the foothills and liked it there and stayed."[11]

Photos of a winter scouting trip to the Ghost River property show bare ground and balmy weather. As they stomped about the steep ravines, they sought the perfect location for a cabin. Both above them and below, steep cliffs jutted into the river, affording privacy. One can easily imagine their growing excitement as they paced out the cabin dimensions on the dry grass just above flood level.

Rather than cut trees from their own property, Patterson arranged to buy logs from the Eau Claire Lumber Company. Its spring log drive ran right by the cabin site on the Ghost River, headed downstream to join a massive flotilla of trees that came from various mountain streams into the Bow River and on to its lumber mill on Prince's Island in downtown Calgary. And so in July of 1930, Raymond, Marigold and a hired man named Hamish Begg stood watch on shore as the flooding Ghost River filled with logs. Hamish roped straight logs suitable for cabin walls while Raymond waded into the chilly stream and secured them with a logging chain. He then hooked the chain to the team's double trees and Marigold drove the horses out of the river. After they had peeled the logs and brought windows, roofing paper, shingles and other supplies from the city, Guy Gibson built a square structure, fifteen feet by fifteen feet. Boasting one comfy room, the Pattersons called it the Ghost River Cabin.[12]

Before they could run sheep on the quarter section, they had to fence the property. With downstream neighbour John Gillies, Patterson walked up and down the precipitous slopes, deciding just where the fence should go. In places they attached it to large trees. Elsewhere they moved it from its legal placement to a more logical line where people and animals might find a footing. Even so, driving fence posts into rocky ground was labour that Patterson vividly recalled three decades later: "Guy Gibson & I put up the fence—and every time he hit a fence post with the post maul he

Marigold Patterson at the Ghost River Cabin.

said: 'Son of a bitch!' Every single stroke!" Just as they finished the job, the spring flood began, threatening to wash out much of their hard work.[13]

According to Marigold, they never set up permanent residence at the Ghost River Cabin. It was, though, the perfect place for Raymond to show her the life he had come to love in Canada. By contrast to Buckspring, where there were farms and ranches all around them, the Ghost River Cabin was isolated. Even getting there was an adventure. During winter months they negotiated slippery slopes down from the prairie a few hundred feet above the river. In summer, paddling upriver in the canoe from Ghost Dam was their favourite approach.

Just a few bends below the cabin, the Ghost River runs into the still water of the Ghost Reservoir. On that lake Patterson explored the islands, bays and coves. Other times he ascended the Bow River to the short-lived Hudson's Bay Company 1832 trading post at Bow Fort Creek. There the mountain river forces its way through a dramatic sandstone formation as it rushes out into the plains. Then as now, the Stoney Indian Reservation borders the river; land unfenced and untouched, looking much as it was thousands of years ago. On these waters Patterson recreated for Marigold and others a sense of the mystery of river travel that first consumed him on the South Nahanni. Along these banks he saw bear, deer, elk and even an occasional mountain sheep. Once he flailed away in the dark with his canoe pole, smashing thin ice on the lake under a moonless sky while returning to the cabin from a late-night drinking social at a neighbour's home.

DURING these years the Pattersons began exploring the country on their doorstep. Writing to boyhood friend Edwin Fenwick, Patterson explained how, "We both like the range country of Western Alberta where a man can get out with a horse & travel like a Christian. We took saddle horses & pack horses & a packer & banged the trail out into the Alberta mountains at the head of the Athabasca for a week of the most glorious weather & hill colours. Saw beaver, deer, bear—& came 40 miles the last day & ran into the Bighorn Sheep in a rock & snow pass at about 8000 ft. We counted 88 & were within 50 yards of some—a sight one might never see again. I never expected to see more than the 60 I counted at once on the Nahanni. I had never seen the Bighorn variety & Marigold was lucky to hit them in her second week in Canada. We made our second camp fire that day at dusk on a ledge overlooking the old trail from Alberta into B.C.—the fur trail of eighty years ago."[14]

Family photo albums show snapshots of a visit to Maligne Lake in Jasper National Park in September of 1929. That same year they drove to the southern Alberta foothills. "I took her up the Highwood River to the ranch of an Italian friend of mine, Pocaterra. The Eden Valley—& rightly named—about ten miles from the Prince's place, & things happened rapidly—an unrehearsed wild west show. There were cattlemen & cowboys & old time trappers with their forceful vocabularies & quiet jesting a la Virginian: the first snow caught us in there & we took to sleighs for a while till the chinook came...& lastly we swayed through the mud to High River & the plains in Pocaterra's car—more under the mud than in it, & to the detriment of an inquisitive beef & some roving porkers. What a ride—& she never turned a hair."[15]

It is not apparent when George Pocaterra and Patterson met, but early letters between them suggest close ties before 1930. Pocaterra was too much of a showman to miss a Calgary Stampede, so perhaps someone introduced them at the Greatest Outdoor Show on Earth in the summer of 1926. Two more dissimilar people you could not hope to meet. George Pocaterra—better known as Pokey—was five feet, nine inches tall with dancing hazel eyes and salt and pepper hair. He proudly traced his roots back a century to a prominent northern Italian family. Although a pauper for most of his life, he carried himself like the nobleman his title—Count Georgio—suggested, commanding attention wherever he went.

While the spats between Pocaterra and Patterson make for good reading in *The Buffalo Head* and the third part of *Far Pastures*, the two strong-willed individualists actually greatly admired each other and had much in common. They both loved the creature comforts, entertainment and social stimulation that the metropolis provided. But each also craved the solace, the demands on the body and the renewal of spirit that comes from extended adventures far from the crowds. Writing from Milan in 1937, Pocaterra reflected that, "the best arrangement would be to split one's time between the two; in other words—live a life of contrasts."[16]

In 1930 Patterson and George Pocaterra began exploring the Rocky Mountains together. That summer Patterson joined Pocaterra and his ranch foreman, Adolf Baumgart, on a September trip to Upper Kananaskis Lake. Photos show a similar trip in January of 1931. Later that month Patterson and Pocaterra crossed over the Continental Divide and camped in a tepee on the Fording and Elk rivers. In August, Marigold joined them for a six-day pack train trip to Kananaskis Lakes via Flat Creek, Grass Pass, Packtrail Coulee, the Highwood River and Highwood Pass. On the return

R. M. Patterson and George Pocaterra amusing unknown cowboy and Adolf Baumgart
while preparing for the Kananaskis trip, September 9, 1930.

journey, the Pattersons detoured up Flat Creek and explored the north side
of the mountain that now bears his name. "That afternoon—we were on
Flat Creek (Trap Creek on your map) we took our saddle horses & rode far
into the Highwood Range on an old, old Stony trail. We went up & up till
we came to a little lake in a country that men have forgotten. And the last
larches of timberline & the grey limestone above them shook in the heat—
a very drowsy afternoon—& the horses ate the heads of the wild red top by
the lake, & I fell asleep. I needed it, what with bulls & bears the night before. And, my God, George, it's a sweet feeling to feel yourself free in the
sunshine & the little breezes, but was I scorched about the shoulders? Yes,
sir, I was—but not as badly as on the Slave [River in 1927]."[17]

In September and October, Pocaterra, Patterson and Baumgart made
an epic trip through Elk Pass into southeastern British Columbia. Up Flat
Creek they rode before taking its south fork where they camped in
Pocaterra's trademark tepee. The next day began with the usual ritual
recorded from Patterson's point of view. "Soon the tea water was boiling
and porridge was made. I got out some eggs and then set to work slicing
bacon. Adolf came back and sat by the fire. Between us we upset some
plates or something and Pocaterra's voice came from a humped-up sleeping bag, wanting to know what the devil we thought we were doing,

getting up in the middle of the night like this. But the smell of coffee simmering and the sizzling of a fryingpan fetched him out, still muttering about midnight and so forth, but becoming more human every minute.

"I offered Pocaterra some porridge—just to see what would happen—but, as usual, he pushed it from him, turning away his head with a gesture of disgust. 'No, no, Patterson! You know I loathe the beastly stuff!'

"I knew, perfectly well; he couldn't bear the sight of it. So now, in the darkness, under Mount Head, Adolf and I cleaned up the porridge while Pocaterra fried the bacon and eggs. Then, breakfast over, we packed up camp, saddled and packed the horses in the first feeble light of day and rode on towards the Grass Pass."[18]

At the Highwood they headed northwest through Highwood Pass and down Pocaterra Creek—the south fork of the Kananaskis River. Their plan had been to pass unnoticed into British Columbia via an abandoned Indian trail through Elk Pass known only to Pocaterra because of his association with the old Stoneys.

"All seemed peaceful and serene," wrote Patterson, "until I saw the horseman approaching. Pocaterra had seen him, too, and his very attitude expressed acute annoyance that this man had come blundering into his plans. Now, he was thinking, we should have to ride all the way down to the ranger station on the main trail, and from there double back to the Elk Pass. Catch him showing old Indian trails to any stranger....

"The rider proved to be McKenzie, an Australian, recently appointed forest ranger of the Kananaskis country—and he very decidedly got off on the wrong foot with Pocaterra. Instead of dismounting and passing the time of day in the manner of the hills, he sat on his horse and opened fire far too abruptly. 'Are you the guide of this party?' he asked.

"Pocaterra stared at him with all the anger of an old-timer who is questioned by a newcomer. 'Guide?' he said. 'I don't know about that, but I am George Pocaterra. Those are my coal claims down there—that ridge between the two mountains—and this creek was named after me by the survey. And this is a private party.' And, with that, he took a savage bite out of a ham sandwich, thus rendering himself speechless for a while....

"...McKenzie remarked he would ride with us as far as the ranger station—whereas Pocaterra, in a gust of fury, leapt on his horse and set off at a lope across the open meadows of the pass." Tension hung thickly in the air as the party headed down the trail, the horses crashing through the bush and over avalanche debris, steadily increasing their gait as the trail improved.

At one point Patterson saw "Adolf hurriedly whipping his lines round the saddle horn. I wondered why—when suddenly, he leaned out from his saddle and made a terrific swipe at a spruce branch with a willow switch that he held in his right hand. A puff of feathers flew and a fluttering bird appeared. Adolf swung still further out from his saddle and caught the 'fool hen' with his left hand before it could fall to the ground. In one easy, gliding motion he swung back into the saddle, wrung the bird's neck and stuffed it inside his jacket....

"A few feathers floated on the air. I rode through them and turned in my saddle to see if McKenzie had observed anything—but he was only then coming into sight around the bend. 'Does he always travel at this rate?'" he shouted.

"'Always,' I called back to him—and I fetched the packhorse ahead of me a crack with my lines....

"Mackenzie had had enough by the time we reached the Kananaskis Lakes ranger station. A brief farewell—and then we rode away southwards, across the meadows and into the timber, climbing steadily upwards, headed for the Continental Divide. The pace slackened as Pocaterra's equanimity became restored—though still, from time to time, some blistering comment on greenhorn forest rangers would come floating back to us from the head of the pack train. And then, as the sun touched with its dying fire the wall of the Elk Mountains, we crossed the flat meadows of the Elk Pass and came to the brink of a new valley—almost of a new world, for now the water drained to the Pacific."

Pocaterra showed Patterson and Baumgart all the secret treasures of the high valleys at the head of the Elk River that the natives called Nyahé-ya-'nibi, translated from the Stoney as "Go-up-into-the-mountains-country," or as Pocaterra put it when he revised it for the *Italian Alpine Club Journal*, Il paese nel cour delle montagne, "The country in the heart of the mountains."[19]

One night they arrived at a good campsite just as snow began to fall. To save time, Patterson unloaded the packhorses and draped the tepee canvas over the pile to protect it from the elements.

"Pocaterra came out of the bush with a load of tepee poles, singing. He was so happy at returning to this valley after the lapse of so many years that it did one good to hear him. But this happiness was fleeting: the song broke off short and he said, in a tone of dismay. 'My God, Patterson, you've stacked all the stuff just where we decided to put the tepee.'"

"'I know. But you'll find I've left plenty of room to set the poles up around the outfit.'

"'But all that stuff is right in my way. We'll have to move every bit of it….'

"'I think you'll find it's all right. We can set up the poles and….'

"'But damn it, we can't stand here arguing all night….'

"'You mean you don't want that stuff there? You want it shifted?'

"'That's exactly what I've been trying to tell you for the last five minutes.'

"'Of course you have,' I replied. 'Well, there's nothing easier.'"

And so Patterson threw off the tarp and hurled Pocaterra's gear to the four corners of the compass while Pokey did the same to Patterson's kit. When Baumgart happened onto the scene a few seconds later, he just turned on his heel and headed back into the bush for more firewood.

Patterson immediately regretted the incident. "I was kicking myself. Here was this man, my friend, back after almost thirty years in a valley that his youth had made sacred to him—and what did I have to go and do? Invent a bright new way of making camp and then lose my temper because it was not instantly understood. Fool! Idiot! Probably I had wrecked the trip."

In silence they erected the teepee. Later, around the intimate fire, small talk began, nurtured by Patterson's brandy that made healing coffee royals.

Day after day they hiked and rode through remote valleys, climbed mountains and swam in lakes and, being hunters of the old school, ate what they shot. Unfortunately, Baumgart had taken an old billy goat and so for days "what came out of the stew pot or frying pan was nothing but a bunch of indurate shock absorbers."[20]

They also fished. Horsemen pride themselves in doing almost everything from the saddle, and Pokey proved his worth by catching fish while riding his horse up and down trout streams. Patterson usually did well enough on foot, but when a big trout stole his last spinner, he loaded his Mannlicher and shot at the offending fish with the big game rifle. Pocaterra rode up to investigate.

"'You have wounded something, Patterson,' he shouted above the noise of the torrent.

"'No,' I said, perversely. 'I was just scaring a fish.'

"'Scaring a fish? And with that cannon! I have heard you fire it before—but what a devil of a row it makes shut in under these trees! For heaven's sake, man, muzzle the thing—you are not in the Northwest Territories now.'"[21]

In this manner the Italian and the Englishman deepened their friendship.

Picking their way up Abruzzi Creek in quest of a pass into the White River, they left their mounts behind and struggled up moraines below a small glacier. Gaining the ice, they looked back at the lush valley, but what was that? "To the left, in the middle distance, the outlet stream tumbled away from the lake towards Abruzzi Creek; to the right and beyond the lake rose the peak of The Warship; and behind all this ran the sunlit eastern wall of Nyahé-ya-'nibi. But it was the lake that caught and held the eye. In its sombre setting of the fir trees it glowed like a sheet of burnished gold."

"'Lago de Oro,' I said—but Pocaterra said. 'No. It is we who have found that lake. The surveyors can never have seen it: they must have put it on the map from some Indian report—and then wrongly, as we have seen. Let us call it Lake Marigold, after your wife. Her hair is that same colour of gold, and so it is fitting that we should name it for her....'" Sadly, officials refused to honour Patterson's amazing wife and called it Abruzzi Lake instead.[22]

The trip ended with the coming of winter, but not before Pocaterra and Patterson scrambled up a snowy trail onto a shoulder of Mount Cadorna. Still wearing their chaps and riding boots, they had not expected such a long hike as they followed a very narrow game trail toward the Pass in the Clouds—a possible route into the White River. "Above us the scree stretched up to the rimrock. Below, the eye followed it in one unbroken sweep of 1500 feet or more down into the head of Abruzzi Creek. A pack-horse here would be in the same position as those mountain goats we had seen the day before: the first slip would mean death. A man, too, for

R. M. Patterson and Adolf Baumgart at Lake Marigold, 1931.

there was nothing to hold on to, nothing to stop you until what remained of you fetched up in the stony bed of Abruzzi Creek, so far below."

Bad weather moved in, so they quickly descended snow-slicked rocks in a mad race to reach the horses before the thick fog obscured their mounts. "In the end it was a dead heat for we came to the horses just as the first streamers of frozen mist were swirling around them." They vowed to return another year and complete the crossing.[23]

It was during this trip that "...the possibility of my taking over the Buffalo Head" was first raised. "There was a little meadow of bunch-grass at the lower end of the flats, at the point where the quiet stream became the wild torrent of the spruce forest. It was a veritable suntrap, and there we would boil our teapail and let our horses graze while we discussed the business that lay between us."[24]

In February of 1932, Pocaterra and Patterson took a quick winter camping trip to the Kananaskis and visited Fossil Falls. That same year, on June 24, "...I nearly departed this life. I was on my way home from the Highwood to the Bow with two horses & had camped in a lovely valley of the TL. Seven a.m. next morning as I was leaving camp with intent to sleep that night somewhere along the Elbow, over came my black pony on top of me—clean back over & I got the horn in the chest & the high cantle in the tum. Took me four hours to make it back to the TL Ranch house & I was certainly glad to see a human face—the 70 year old dial of the biggest liar in the country.

"For a week I could hardly move but finally the sun cured me & the adhesions vanished sweetly away. Calgary recorded 400 hours of sunlight in July & I used all I could of it without taking the hide off—it's so powerful here—4000 ft. & no haze."[25]

During long trips with Pocaterra, black gold was another of the business propositions discussed. Coal lay in great abundance in the Front Ranges and Pocaterra wanted Patterson to help him develop a mine. According to Marigold, Pokey "was looking all the time for somebody with money to develop them. He thought we might fill the bill: we didn't."[26] Although Raymond had some cash at his disposal, he also knew that underground workings cost much more than his modest fortune could bankroll. His December, 1930, letter to the Italian proves that he wrote a friendly English investor—Edwin Fenwick—on Pocaterra's behalf. The reply from across the Atlantic included all the usual objections to investing in a speculative venture in a distant country: "Development costs over here wd. be around £2,000,000 to equip a pit for an output of a million tons a year but in your case I haven't any idea what wd. be needed." The investor expressed concerned about winter conditions. "The product seems an O.K. loco[motive] coal…, but I fear the main difficulty will be everything getting frozen up in the winter-machinery, condensers etc. Is there any alternative to steam as a source power?" Patterson probably rolled his eyes when he read this question. To Pocaterra he replied, "I wrote & pointed out in no measured language that this was not the Liard & asked him how the devil he thought the lumber camps worked only in winter, & how the C.P.R. & our cars & a few other trifles like that continue to operate all the year. I can say what I please to him, having known him so long…."

Patterson knew only too well the limited state of Pocaterra's resources. "We shall see—but if we can once convince them then evidently money is no obstacle…. Time will show—but he talks of £2,000,000 & in considering that amount your £16,000-cash looks very small. I only wish you were not tied up in such a manner that everything hinges on an 'if.'" He concluded on a positive note: "I feel from this letter that if you deal finally with my friend's group you will benefit financially in the framing of the proposition as you will not be dealing with men to whom a stock slump means a disaster."[27]

As it turned out, a financial disaster and the Great Depression developed out of the stock slump of 1929 and Pocaterra's coal mine had to wait more than another decade. Besides, Pocaterra would be spending most of the 1930s in Italy, managing the operatic career of a Calgary dentist's daughter. In 1932 Patterson's practised eye began to wander from Buckspring and the sheep ranching venture. In August the Pattersons visited the Buffalo Head again, taking time to dip in the bathing pool in the Highwood River and to visit the Prince of Wales' E.P. Ranch. When they returned in November, the foothills ranch lay glistening under a blanket of snow. The lure of the mountains had caught them in its grasp.

And so Raymond and Marigold began toying with the idea of making a bid to buy the Buffalo Head Ranch from George Pocaterra.

Luckily, Patterson's second attempt to find the perfect place to invest his capital and raise a family was more successful than the first. The new ranch, crouched by a hill, was less than a day's ride from the headwaters of the Highwood River. Patterson claimed that Dr. G. M. Dawson of the Geological Survey of Canada called that stretch of the Highwood the Eden Valley, "…the most beautiful valley he had ever seen."[28]

Probably he also read an earlier account of the area by Captain Blakiston, a member of Captain John Palliser's expedition exploring the Canadian west in the 1850s. In the "Report on the Exploration of the Kootanie and Boundary Passes of the Rocky Mountains in 1858," Blakiston described how, "On the 16th [of August 1858] our hunter was lucky enough to procure us some fresh meat in the shape of wupiti or wa-waskasew (red deer) of the Crees. In order to lighten the burthen of the horses and preserve the meat, the bones were taken out, and it was cut into thin flakes and half dried over the night camp fire.

"The same afternoon, as we arrived at Trap Creek, just above its junction with High Woods River, we found six tents of Thick-wood Stone Indians who were just preparing their encampment. We camped along with them, and as usual, when with or near any Indians, my flag, a St. George's Jack, was hoisted on a pole in front of the tent. I gave them a present of some tobacco and fresh meat. The Stone Indians, with whom are associated also a few Crees, and whose hunting ground is the wooded and semi-wooded country along the base of the mountains at the head waters of the Saskatchewan, are a harmless and well-disposed people towards the whites. Education has, thanks to the former Wesleyan missionary, the Rev. Mr. Rundle, and his successor, the Rev. Thomas Wolsey, made some little progress amongst them; a few being able to read and write the Cree syllabic characters, now in general use among the missions of the north-west.

"During the afternoon I held a talk with these Indians. I told them plainly for what reason we had been sent to the country; that Her Majesty was always glad to hear of their welfare, and that any message which they might have for Her, I would take down in writing.

"'We are glad,' said an old man, 'that the great woman Chief of the Whites takes compassion upon us, we think she is ignorant of the way in which the traders treat us; they give us very little goods and ammunition for our furs and skins, and if this continues our children cannot live. We are poor, but we work well for the whites. The Indians of the plains treat us badly and steal our horses, but we do nothing to them, for the minister tells us so.' In addition to questions from myself, they said that they would wish white people to come and live among them, and teach them to farm, make clothes, &c., so that 'their children might live,' for the animals are getting every year more scarce. I may here state, that I have been fortunate enough this year to fall in with many camps of the different tribes of Indians inhabiting this country, from whom I always obtained as much information as possible on their present state, and their wishes as to the future; and I hope to draw up a report on the same information for Her

The Eden Valley from Knife Edge Ridge.

Majesty's Government; for without a doubt, when deciding on the future of this country, some provision should be made for the poor uncivilised beings to whom by rights the soil belongs."[29]

It is no wonder Patterson fell in love with this historic place that was likened to the Biblical garden. Eden Valley was also called by two other names, more descriptive of the unusual inhabitants of this picturesque part of the foothills: Loony Lane and Mad Valley. And the inmates of the unbarred asylum did—and still do—their best to live up to the nicknames. Many interesting characters have called the valley home, but none was more quixotic than the homesteader who pitched a tent there in January of 1905.

George William Pocaterra entered the world on September 22, 1882, born in a town called Rocchette in the Italian Alps. By the early 1900s he was in Winnipeg, "the Chicago of the Canadian West," with $3.75 in his pocket and looking for work. "I saw the Highwood country first in 1904, when I drove a four horse team to help take down from the upper Ings Creek a saw-mill belonging to Billy Channel." Ranch work in the area convinced him to make the valley his home. "My cousin Arturo Talin and I first camped on B.H.R. in January 1905, when we both took up homesteads there, and bought some railway land. All there was on the place then were several sets of tepee poles, standing up, ready to have the te-

George Pocaterra and Janet Patterson at Buckspring, 1932.

pees rolled around them." The next year they built a 14 by 16-foot cabin on the site and named the unfenced land the Buffalo Head Ranch after the bleached skulls they found on the ground. While cutting trees across the Highwood River, Pocaterra met the Stoneys who readily accepted his gifts of tobacco and friendship.

Pocaterra was not a fan of cattle.‡ Horses were his passion, and throughout the 1920s he firmly believed that the demand for them would return. With a few mares and a good stallion, he set up a breeding program. At one time he had a sign on the gate that read "Beware of the mad stallion." A passerby stopped one day and changed the sign to "Beware of the mad Italian." Decades later, foreman Adolf Baumgart described Pocaterra as a strong-willed and eccentric fellow. "He did not like to depart from his horses— that was his grave mistake and that broke him."[30]

‡ IN ALBERTA (Winter 1919-20) by G. W. Pocaterra

There was a lot of cattle,
Then came a howling storm.
And right then started they,
To lose their sleekest form.

The North sent us another,
A-blowing its dismal horn,
That made the poor old cows
Look yet some more forlorn.

Then there came a bunch of them,
Always more severe,
The Stockmen started then,
To feel increasing fear.

With unremitting labor,
Not counting yet the expense,
They kept the hides of some
From hanging on the fence.

Then came the end of April,
The skies all overcast,
A howling blizzard followed
Upon the first cold blast.

The first week of May
The sun shone bright and hot,
Too much for the poor cows,
Knocked down the whole Damned Lot!

Luckily, in 1924 Allen Seymour of the Canadian Pacific Railway tourism department approached Pocaterra and his neighbour Guy Weadick at the Stampede Ranch and asked them to entertain dudes. Since the earliest days, the CPR had actively pursued ways to create business along its tracks. It built fancy tourist hotels in the mountains, irrigated desert-like land in the prairies to attract homesteaders and built demonstration farms to show farmers how to turn the desert into cropland. Dude ranches were just another way to expand the demand for passenger train travel. By the late 1920s, Europeans were paying $50 per week to stay with the multilingual Pocaterra—he spoke five languages fluently, while Americans stayed upstream with the Weadicks.[31]

Poet and writer P. K. Page remembers the Buffalo Head Ranch as a virtual menagerie of personalities when she visited it as a child and teenager. "It was an absolutely extraordinary ranch, with the most incredible collection of people. Adolf was a Prussian. Pocaterra was a real character." She recalls the summer when Pocaterra and Adolf built a boat on the landlocked ranch and christened it the "Velitta." With horses and a cart they dragged the sailing ship through the bush to a slough. P. K. and one of her friends went along for the ride and to witness the historic launch. All went well, until the boat reached water.

"Pokey put on a bathing suit that was enough to make a girl of sixteen blush. It was an old-fashioned one that came down to about his knees but because the moths had eaten all the crotch out of it, he had to put a sort of a pair of canvas drawers underneath it. I've never seen such a sight in all my life. I was slightly in love with Pokey until that event and that put me off him. He got into the boat and the boat promptly sank. He and Adolf were in it and it promptly sank. They ignominiously came out covered in leeches."[32]

That was the character of the Buffalo Head under Pocaterra's command. According to Baumgart, the banks and other mortgage holders were always on his back. What little money Pocaterra made from selling horses and hosting dudes went to cover ranching expenses and finance his endless attempts to develop coal mining properties in the mountains.

Pocaterra's partner in the sailing fiasco was, by contrast, a tall, quiet man. Born in 1903 close to the Russian border in East Prussia, Adolf Baumgart was much better mannered than the Prussian who had applied the butt of his rifle to Patterson's helmet during the Great War.

He arrived in Alberta in the late 1920s, lured from the great plains of his homeland by stories of mountains. As a farm boy he found work easily and met Pocaterra while looking for ranch work in 1930. Employed as animal foreman and general superintendent of building projects, he counted the seven years on the Buffalo Head working for Pocaterra, then Patterson, as among the best of his life. Sixty-two years later, seated in the home he built in Calgary, his skilled hands still looked strong. Around us, packing boxes were ready for the move to Vancouver Island, a "retirement to the Farmers' Graveyard" he called it.

In his warm, thickly-accented voice he recalled memories from that time. A quiet fellow, always busy working on the endless round of chores on a ranch, he found "tourists" distracting, referring to the dudes. But city people on the weekend were "more of a nuisance…." He remembered no wolves, but a few coyotes "ruined some cattle." Adolf shot quite a few and took them with traps. Although he remembered reaping at most half a dozen coyotes in a winter, one photo shows Adolf with more than eighteen hides.

He also shot game. "I had a deer shot, skinned and I give it to the Indians, to Tom Amos, hoping to get a jacket. People like Pocaterra had a nice jacket, so I thought I'd get one too. So I gave that hide to the Indians—'Oh yes, we will do it.' It took half a year, it took a year, nothing came. 'How come, Thomas, you didn't bring me the tanned hide?' Like they speak

Adolf Baumgart.

[Adolf dropped his voice very low and gravely, mimicking an old Indian], 'I'm sorry Adolf, my wife has no brains, has no brains.' I was speechless. What in the world was that, I thought? I came back and told it to the neighbours. 'Oh, yes, they use the brains to tan the hide.'" Then Adolf laughed long and hard.

Adolf also told stories on himself. Each week, someone from the ranch rode to get the mail at a set of mailboxes just south of Longview at a place called English Corners. Once he arrived and an elderly English woman—probably Miss Shackerly—asked him to fix the tangled rigging on her horse and buggy. This he did. She then asked him where he was from and why he had such a strong accent. He replied that he was from

Germany. Her response was a curt "I'm so sorry I spoke to you." As always, there is more to the story. Another time he arrived for the mail and the same English woman was there, refusing to talk to him. Then along came four young women between fourteen and sixteen years old, all dressed in pants and riding western style, not side-saddle. Incensed, the English woman jumped down from her wagon and chased the modern young women with a stick to show them a thing or two about manners. The fence was just two strands of wire, not the usual four, and the young women easily escaped their pursuer. Undaunted, the English woman followed, quickly entangling her skirts in the barbs.

Just then along came the mailman, Mr. Jones. Adolf was not welcome to help because she was not talking to him and help was not likely to come from the girls either. Reading the situation, Mr. Jones offered to lend a hand. "Don't you dare touch me," she replied, "I don't have any pants on." And so they all left her to her predicament.

At this point I poured Adolf some juice. He stopped me almost as soon as I began to pour. "No more for me," he said. "I do not like sweets, except the two-legged kind."

He then told the story about the priest who had trouble keeping wine in his church. When the caretaker stepped into the confessional he asked, "My son, are you stealing the communion wine?" "I cannot hear your question," came the reply. "Why don't you sit here?" So they traded places and the caretaker asked the father if he was making love to his wife. "I see what you mean," said the priest, "I cannot hear your question either."

At the end of our brief time together, I asked Adolf if he recalled his first impression of Canada. "Give me back when I saw Canada when I came to this country. When hardly anybody was concerned locking their doors—that was Canada, that time. People were so helpful and so friendly in those days."[33]

No doubt the friendliness of the people on the Highwood helped the Pattersons come to a decision. As the "Buffalo Head Ranch Register of Guests" shows, they had visited Pocaterra a great many times. They believed they could make a living at the little horse ranch deep in the foothills, and began serious negotiations in 1932. The bargaining must have been interesting because although Pocaterra and Patterson were good friends, each considered himself the better man. Patterson wrote, "Each one of us was (and possibly still is) utterly unpredictable. We each had enormous patience when it came to some long-enduring physical feat—and yet every shred of that patience could fly to the winds over some absurd trifle."[34] These were traits that affected and afflicted them both for life, returning to test their relationship many times. Still, they somehow patched together a verbal agreement in late 1932.

When the Pattersons returned from a winter visit to England in April 1933, they drove straight out to the Buffalo Head through ranching country that had retained much of its character from the days when buffalo roamed the hills. When the decimation of the massive beasts ended the nomadic way of life for the natives, who were settled on reserves, there was no longer any competition for the land and the government issued large grazing leases. For a few decades the range was open, then surveyors moved in and barbed wire divided the flat land and rolling foothills into artificial mathematical sections.

Fences had already arrived in Eden Valley when three-year-old Janet looked out the car window on the drive to her new home. The road the Pattersons took is now a paved highway from Calgary to Black Diamond. South, however, the route lay through Fireguard Coulee, not along the section lines where Highway 22 now runs. For many years a man had driven a team of horses and a plough up and down the broad valley from Sheep Creek to the Highwood River, cutting a fireguard in a bold but

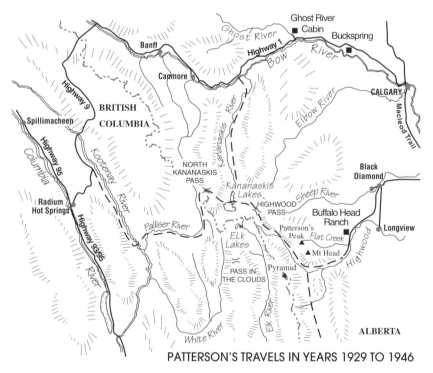

PATTERSON'S TRAVELS IN YEARS 1929 TO 1946

The Buffalo Head ranch house.

probably useless attempt to protect against grass fires. Saddle horses had also used this convenient geographic feature and over time a dirt road had developed that was navigable by cars. For the thirteen years the Pattersons lived at the ranch it was their link to Calgary.

Automobiles finished the horse-powered life George Pocaterra hoped would make a resurgence in the 1920s. Patterson fostered no such illusion. While old-timers held onto their horses, he made plans to transform the Buffalo Head into a cattle ranch. The failed sheep venture taught him to learn something about stock before investing, so his choice of the Eden Valley as a place to live also included a careful scrutiny of its residents. Up the valley from his ranch was Guy Weadick, a great showman, but not a cattleman. Farther upstream lay the buildings of the Eden Valley Ranch. Its owner, Frazier Hunt, knew little about cattle either, coming as he did from New York and being a writer. There was plenty of amusement in these two personalities and their respective wives, Florence Weadick and Emmie Hunt, but little help for a neophyte cattleman.

However, the residents of the Sullivan Creek Ranch alone could have taught Patterson all he needed to know about cattle. Outstanding cattlemen Jim Bews and his son Joe called it their home, and beyond them was Johnny "Rabbits" Brown at the OH Ranch, who earned his Stoney nickname after the rabbits he tried to raise as a sideline escaped.[35] South across the Highwood River from the OH lay the Riverbend, where Bert Sheppard and his father ran another prize-winning Hereford cattle ranch. Elsewhere in the valley were the Hughes, Walter Hanson, Ed Marston, the Riggs,

Tom McMasters and the Runcimans, all of them capable of helping an apprentice rancher. Farther south lay the world-renowned Bar U Ranch just downstream of the Prince of Wales' E. P. Ranch on Pekisko Creek. It seemed the perfect place to cut one's teeth in the business of ranching, even during the 1930s.

The asking price for the Buffalo Head Ranch was not high, and just as well, because Marigold remembers they "had dropped a lot over the sheep." As a result, the early 1933 visit to England was in part related to the new ranching investment. "…He borrowed some money from his Mother, & bought Pocaterra's mortgages, as the latter wanted to return to Italy."

The small amount of deeded land—purchased outright—at the Buffalo Head would not support a cattle operation large enough to feed his family, so Patterson bought an adjacent section of grazing land at 8-18-4 W5 from the Hudson's Bay Company on April 7, 1933. It cost three dollars per acre, with a $960 down payment and a promise to pay the other half in six months. The Bay wisely included a clause "withholding minerals and gypsum" as it did with most of its land sales. This provision allowed it to create a lucrative oil and gas company in later years when geologists and geophysicists found black gold beneath the poverty-stricken province.[36] Six years later, Patterson, together with Bert Sheppard and the Bews, bought the TL Ranch. The grazing leases on Sullivan Creek provided summer pasture for an additional 400 head of cattle.

The October 14, 1933, sales contract in Pocaterra's handwriting included a cash payment of $700 and title to the 170-acre Ghost River property. Patterson also paid off a $500 mortgage to De Palezieux to cover "tourist" goods—dude items such as tents, blankets, saddles, tack and other camping gear. In exchange for these payments, the Pattersons received a few cattle branded XN on the right ribs and twenty horses marked with the Buffalo Head-shaped brand on the right thigh. Pocaterra allowed Patterson to use the brand for eighteen months on the horses, promised to give him the first chance to buy it, but in the end kept the unique brand until his death. The purchase also covered machinery and implements, harness and tack and all other equity in the ranch. Not counting the cost of the Ghost River property, cabin, fencing and other improvements, the Pattersons paid just over $3000 for the Buffalo Head Ranch and the section of grazing land.

Patterson agreed to pasture Pocaterra's twelve personal horses free of charge through 1934. During a transition period, he also agreed to store the Italian's furniture and household items that included "cutlery, silver and plated, all pictures, trophies, Ludieu curios, books, skiis & rugs, stoves, beds etc."[37]

Marigold remembers the condition of the ranch quite well six decades later. The shacks were in poor repair. There were only about seventeen cattle. "There were quite a lot of horses because he [Pocaterra] always kept any horses he had and some were useable but there was a great many that were just pensioners. I'm afraid the bleeding hearts would think it was dreadful, but we sent quite a large number of them down to the fox farms. They were cripples. Most of them would have had a hard time to get through a winter."[38]

Although the cash outlay seems minuscule in retrospect, the investment, mortgages and poor condition of the buildings created a deep hole from which to begin cattle ranching in the early 1930s. Three things helped. First, the grazing land was relatively untouched by Pocaterra's few cattle. The Italian did not believe in exhausting the grass: "...What right has anybody just because he has a man-made deed of property (which he certainly can't take with him on the long, long trail) to utterly spoil land, which future generations will need? After all it's, at best, only a life-long leasehold—the best any of us can have in anything."[39] Next, the low price of beef allowed Patterson to buy calves for next to nothing and gradually build his herd by natural increase. Patterson decided the only way he could turn a profit was

Unknown cowboy, Bert Sheppard, R. M. Patterson, Joe Bews, unknown cowboy and Sam Smith at the Buffalo Head branding, May 1940.

Bert Sheppard of the Riverbend Ranch.

to turn it into a cow-calf operation and with Adolf Baumgart as his foreman, the prospects looked good. "He was excellent," recalled Baumgart of his new boss in 1933, "very straightforward and honest. I don't think there was a better man I ever worked for than Patterson."[40] Finally, Marigold's income from England was a reliable source of cash. In addition to her annual income of about $1000 from her British investments, she contributed additional funds. She used a personal gift of £300—about $1500 at the time—to install a water supply system in 1936.[41] The luck that deserted the family at Buckspring apparently returned when the Pattersons moved to the Buffalo Head.[42]

Branding party with Johnny Brown standing at centre, Joe Bews on horse and Sam Smith at right.

Marigold says her husband greatly admired the Bews as cattlemen. "Joe's comment about his cattle was that he liked to see them looking comfortable. And of course that meant exactly that they were in very good health, with lots of food and water. Joe would say, 'I see them looking comfortable and it makes me comfortable.'"[43] Patterson also valued an educated opinion. His correspondence includes letters with J. C. Hargrave, District Inspector for the Department of Agriculture, Health of Animals Division, Production Service. This Alberta government official offered advice concerning loss of calves and offered suggestions as to possible solutions to their problems.[44] Although Patterson had much to learn about cattle, his keen eye sometimes solved problems for his more experienced neighbours. In Bert Sheppard's book *Just About Nothing* there is a chapter by Patterson describing how he came to the aid of a sick milk cow by using a technique he saw used by a veterinarian at Buckspring.

Unlike some of the larger spreads farther south, the ranchers along the Highwood River ran relatively small operations. Therefore, they often helped each other with seasonal tasks that required extra hands. Photos during this period show Bert Sheppard, Guy Weadick, Joe Bews, Ernest Cox, Cattle Dan, Sam Smith, Johnny Brown and Patterson working together at each other's spring brandings. At the end of the long day—the gathering often started well before dawn—a big meal and lots of beer would greet the hungry men. According to Marigold, Joe Bews did not like his young sons to be around at drinking parties, as the branding parties were for men only and "Some of them got pretty merry."[45]

Some tasks called for experts. Bert Sheppard was an outstanding bronc-buster who had become something of a legend. In the 1920s he had ridden every Sunday to the Bar U from his parents' ranch on the Highwood and collected six wild broncs that he returned, broken, the next weekend. Off and on, he tamed horses for about seventeen years. It came as no surprise, then, when Patterson hired him to break horses for the Buffalo Head.[46]

Bert and Raymond remained lifelong friends and shared many interesting experiences. On one occasion, Patterson, as a member of the Ranchmen's Club, gave Sheppard the recipe for "Tom and Jerry," which included one bottle of rum, two bottles of brandy and three bottles of sherry. To this concoction, Bert added beaten eggs and sugar. The result—sticky and very sweet—pleased Patterson.

Another day the two drinking pals went for the mail. It was late so they decided to visit the Hughes brothers. Patterson was looking to breed his cows and the Hughes' Hereford bulls had a good reputation. Bert recalled the day's events. "Jim Hughes took us down to the corral and said 'There, Mr. Patterson, is a good bull.' Patterson took a long look through his bifocals and said 'I see two bulls.' Jim pointed at another bull standing off by himself and said 'There, Mr. Patterson, is a good range bull which you could probably use for your ranch.' Patterson looked very carefully in the direction Jim was pointing and said 'I see three bulls, which one are you talking about, the bull on the right, the bull on the left or the bull in the middle?' Hughes said 'I think you are in need of a drink, we had better go back to the house.'

"Jim produced a bottle of Scotch and we had a couple before leaving. We manoeuvred back to the English Corner, picked up the west bound mail and headed for Hansons. Just east of the ranch buildings was a pole gate. I opened it and Patterson ran into the gate post, bending the fender down onto the tire. We got a broken fence post and pried the fender off the tire and continued on our way. We staggered into the house with our arms full of letters, papers and parcels, and laid them on the table and in so doing knocked a mixing bowl containing two or three dozen eggs off the table onto the floor. Mrs. Hanson cleaned up the mess and then made us a cup of tea. Having done our duty we went back to the car which I drove to Riverbend. Patterson slept for three hours, woke up right as rain, had a cup of tea and a little food and drove off home."[47]

Home brew was common in the Eden Valley. Fishery warden Sam Smith called Mrs. Marston's home-made wine "bloody awful," but everyone graciously accepted a glass of the potion. She made it with wild fruit, raisins and various other items, including leftover dessert. Bert recalled the ensuing antics. "Everyone that came to the house was given a tumbler full, and that was enough for most people. Patterson of the Buffalo Head always drank his. He said it was rather interesting to find out what effect it was going to have on him this time. No one wanted to offend the good old soul and people had to find ways and means of getting rid of it. I always tried to sit by an open window and when her back was turned would toss it out."[48]

EVERYDAY life at the ranch was complicated. Although Patterson's adventurous wife constantly hid behind her husband's accomplishments and downplayed her role, she admits to being in charge of the household. She planned meals and dealt with the logistics of ordering provisions twice a year from Western Grocers Limited, a Calgary wholesaler. For staples they purchased Highland whole coffee, Sherriff's orange marmalade, Nabob curry powder, Nabob tea, Empire ham, Clover Leaf clams, ginger root, candied peel, onions, Campbell's canned chicken, oxtail, tomato and mulligatawny soups, Five Roses flour, raspberry and strawberry jam, peach jam, Sunny Boy cereal, Eddys Silent matches, Hedlunds pork & beans, Fundy sardines, Bentos corn beef and Sweet Caporals.[49] She tended a large vegetable garden that augmented the semi-annual truckload of groceries and canned massive amounts of fruit and meat, stews and soups, in the process learning to use a pressure cooker to speed up the process. Marigold also did all the washing, except for the sheets that were sent to a laundry. She remembers ironing with a heavy iron heated with gas early in the morning to avoid the heat of the day.

Marigold Patterson.

Over the years she employed a Mrs. Kiddle, an Italian named Roberto, and a "Chinaman" to ring the meal bell. The *Five Roses Cook Book* was the bible of the ranch kitchen, "a true Canadian cook book," according to Marigold. From its pages came the recipe for matrimonial cake, a wonderful dessert confection of a date mixture sandwiched between two layers of oatmeal.[50] The ranch also had chickens and milk cows that Janet carefully avoided learning to milk. Raymond was not fond of the chore either, so milking, for a few years, was left to the hired man Old Bill King. Cattle were butchered on the ranch and what they did not eat fresh Marigold pickled, bottled and put in cold storage in Calgary. Bees provided honey.

Marigold's reserved manner makes it hard to get her to reveal an opinion about herself, but when describing her Aunt Francie she listed qualities that seem like a reflection of her own powerful personality: "My definition of a great lady was somebody extremely intelligent, no fool in any way, very kind and probably organising and running things that had to be organised and run."[51]

Visitors to the ranch today are amazed that the small log building the Pattersons called home was the centre of so much activity. Additions to Pocaterra's original building included a kitchen and porch to the west. A sun porch along the east connected four rooms: a sitting room, two bedrooms and a bathroom. Small cabins nearby housed the nanny, a chore man and other friends as well as guests. The cook had a very small bedroom off the kitchen. Cold running water was the only modern convenience, though hot water was available from a pot on the cookstove or from the reservoir at the back of the stove. Electricity and central heating were luxuries that did not arrive at the ranch until decades later. The telephone hung on the wall in the unheated porch, insuring minimal long-distance charges in the colder months.

The Pattersons wrote many letters on stationery decorated with a Buffalo Head Ranch scene. Plain but tasteful, it included a replica of the XN brand as well as a drawing of an owl—Raymond called the main cabin The Owls' House after a book of the same name by Crosbie Garstin. Pekisko, via High River, Alberta, was the return address. The telephone number was Buffalo Head Ranch at first, then High River 2311. A small drawing of the main gate to the lane completed the package. On this stationery they ordered specialized purchases from England. In 1936, for example, they ordered shoes from Dowie & Marshall, Limited of London. A 1939 order requested a hat, shirts, ties, collars and a sash from Everitt V. Macklin Limited, also of London.[52] Patterson also ordered books from Messrs. Hatchard, Booksellers to their Majesties the King and Queen and Queen Mary. By return post came dozens of volumes including the *Book of Canoeing*, books about British Columbia fish and game as well as maps of England, Asia and India.[53] In 1937, after consulting George Pocaterra, Patterson ordered a Rolleiflex 6 x 6 F3.5 Tessar camera for which he paid £28.16.0 from Wallace Heaton, Limited.[54] The twin lens camera, using 120 size film that produced a 6 by 6 centimetre negative from rolled film, gave Patterson a higher quality image as well as a more compact and manageable photographic system than his heavy English camera.

FROM time to time Raymond and Marigold insisted on getting away, alone and together, into the mountains they had come to love. Shortly after putting out the word they were looking for a nanny, their Calgary physician, Dr. Harry Jennings, arranged for a Miss Cecy Margaret Baldwin to come and take care of their young daughter. Sixty years later, Janet still recalls their first meeting, a day in 1934 when a very young woman came in to get her up after her afternoon nap. They stared solemnly at each other for a very long time. Distrustful, the little girl did not want anyone to look after her except her mother, but they later became fast friends.[55]

A child's perspective on the adult world is always interesting. Janet remembers that when weather and the busy ranch schedule permitted, the family attended St. Aidan's church between the Bar U and E. P. ranches south of the river. Marigold purchased Sunday School lessons for her daughter, but Janet only did them for about a month.[56] She was very much her father's daughter and much preferred setting out a trapline in the garden for which Daddy paid a cash bounty. "I do remember Dick Matthews coming to stay.... My chief memory is that of the mouse trapline which I used to run in the vegetable garden (I received a cent per mouse), and the fact that Dick, tough guy as he pretended to be, could not face taking the dead mice out of the traps, and I could. I was proud of that. Dick also used to sing a song, or a line of a song 'Jeepers Creepers, where'd you get them weepers?' This puzzled me a lot, as I didn't know what weepers were—but I didn't want to ask. I guess Dick never sang the next line of the song."[57]

When a bit older, Janet rode the ten miles to English Corners on Wednesdays to fetch the mail. She loved riding through the Shintz, Runciman and Hanson places along the way, picking up letters to take out. Delivering the mail on the return trip, she carefully timed her stops so as to be invited to stay for lunch at the Hanson's.[58]

Janet's sources of entertainment expanded when brother Alan Noel arrived. Born October 15, 1936, he attracted letters of praise from Matthews in Aklavik and Pocaterra in Italy. The Crown Prince, as Pocaterra immediately named him, started out life in the relative warmth of the Victoria house his mother had rented for the winter. The rest of the family took advantage of the situation and wintered on the coast, not returning to the ranch until the spring of 1937. Patterson tired of indoor life in dreary Victoria and complained to Pocaterra in early 1937 that the weather in Victoria was "nothing very remarkably wonderful." As a result, he often slipped away to the west coast of the island for a visit to the Pacific Ocean.[59] Pocaterra responded that staying away from the ranch at that time of the year was well advised. "Surely you will have more sense than to go back to Alberta before May. I remember always the early spring months as the most disagreeable in the Hills. Warm, almost hot days, and MUD, and MUD, and then again snow, and ice, and hot again, but never anything steady. And I have seen 35 below zero in April more than once."[60]

Once the initial fascination wore off, Janet found her baby brother a bit of a scene stealer. Once, a physician came to the ranch to examine the sick little boy. Doctor O'Callahan pronounced Alan very ill and ordered him to hospital in Calgary. Janet remembers being jealous over this incident. Try as she might, she could not convince the doctor or the other adults that she also warranted special medical attention in Calgary.

But for the most part Janet liked her baby brother. She graciously allowed him to mug for photos in the Chinook Racer, a dashing-looking wagon. She also introduced him to the finer things in life in the "Big City." On one occasion they stayed at the "Paralyser" as many called Calgary's best hotel, the Palliser. Roberto, their old cook, was working there as a waiter, and looked quite dignified. They were pleased to see him again. Their parents, however, were not pleased when they left the children alone in the room. Somehow, Janet and Alan called room service and went wild, ordering adult portions from the main menu. After that, Patterson took the children to a cafe across the street, ostensibly for its prompt service, but also with an eye to the bill.

Alan Patterson.

The family enjoyed many southern Alberta outings. Janet remembers attending the July Dominion Day festivities and races at Millarville in 1934 and picnicking with her parents under the large cottonwood trees. The Calgary Stampede, later in July, always warranted a special trip. Dressed to the nines, the rancher and his family made a day of it in the city, Raymond conducting business in the morning while the family visited friends. Then they reunited for the afternoon events at the Stampede grounds. Alan remembers staying for the grandstand show in the evening and driving home late at night.[61]

At the ranch the family created its own entertainment. They bought a gramophone from the Beaudrys, and with it came a collection of large, one-sided, 78 rpm records, including Fats Waller tunes.[62] When Dick Matthews visited in the late 1930s, he loved playing the windup Victrola.

"I think I drove them nuts," he recalled. The record collection included songs with lyrics such as: "Abdul, Abulbul, Amir" and "Count Ivan Skavinsky Skavar," which Dick played night and day. He also loved "The Lambeth Walk."[63]

Alan also remembers the gramophone. Although his father had sat through the opera in London, he had never developed a love for the art form. One day, when Marigold was listening to an opera recording, Raymond sent Alan in to ask his mother a question. "Who's dying?" asked the little tike who seconds later rejoined Patterson in the yard.

Winter snow allowed the children to learn Nordic sports. Marigold tried teaching Janet to skate on the Highwood River but the ice was often bumpy and, according to Janet, there was usually an open channel somewhere. The children used skis with a spring binding around the heel on the hill behind the house where Raymond cut wide trails to make the skiing easier, but he never had much time to slide down the hills himself. As Janet recalls, "Living in the country is a full time job."[64]

Horses, of course, were one of the reasons the Pattersons bought the foothills ranch. Over time Patterson built up a stable—a horse for most every need. He also was imaginative when it came to naming the creatures. As a result, mounts and packhorses went by such interesting names

Looking up Flat Creek to the Bull Creek Hills and Mount Head.

as Black Jack, Bluebird, Bozo, Brainless, Molly and Rex, Pink Eye, Red, Sailor, Socks, Turk and Mrs. Wood. As soon as the children learned to ride the family took excursions into the mountains west of the ranch: up Flat Creek and into the lush valleys under Mount Head and Holy Cross Mountain that provided summer pasture for cattle and calves. From early June until October Janet helped drive the cattle to and from the summer pasture, making the best of the adventure. "What I used to enjoy, among other things, was when we used to go through a section of Bar U land, we could chase those Bar U cattle as fast as we wanted, but not our own."[65]

Schooling in the Eden Valley posed a special challenge. The Schintz family across the river subscribed to correspondence courses for their sons. To the east, the Bews sent their children to a public school in Longview and later to Catholic boarding schools. The Pattersons tried various solutions. At first, Marigold and Miss Baldwin tutored Janet at the ranch, using correspondence school lessons. Then in the early 1940s Janet was sent to a private girl's boarding school called Strathcona Lodge on the shores of Shawnigan Lake, Vancouver Island. Exquisitely polite, she remembers being "very good" and quite shy. Her habit of always apologizing quickly earned her the nickname "Sorry Patterson." The other girls also made fun of her inability to ride a bicycle, although she could have showed them a thing or two in the saddle. Janet found boarding school a very lonely place, at first, but gradually made friends.

Regular letters from her father helped ease the pain. On October 4, 1943, for example, after returning from a trip to the Palliser River with Rex and Mollie, he wrote: "This with love from your Father who voyaged far beyond the Pillars of Hercules but returned to tell the tale—mainly because the grub was running low & he had to get back anyway." Hearing that his teenager was considering taking up cigarettes, he wrote on November 11, 1945, encouraging her to wait a couple years and then he would buy her some fine tobacco and smoke with her. According to Janet, he had quit smoking about ten years earlier and was considering taking it up again, but never did.[66]

Photos from February, 1941, show young Prince Alan sitting at a desk on the lawn with his mother. Miss Baldwin also taught him lessons, but within a few months he, too, was packed off to boarding school. He arrived at the boys' school at Qualicum Beach in September, 1944, when only seven years old. After two years he moved to Shawnigan Lake School—across the lake from Janet's school—where he remained until he graduated. Both institutions were affiliated with the Anglican Church and

Alan recalls being forced to attend "damned chapel." It is telling that neither Janet nor Alan chose to send their own offspring to similar schools.

Because Janet and Alan were away from the ranch for most of the year, the Pattersons scheduled special summer family holidays. Bow Lake was a favourite spot in the Rockies. Old Jimmy Simpson had lived on the shores of this beautiful lake before the road went through from Lake Louise to Jasper, bringing his guests to Num-Ti-Jah Lodge by saddle horse from the train station at Lake Louise. The packer, guide and outfitter was a decade older than Patterson and in his earlier days had lived the hobo life with

adventurer Jack London. Patterson greatly admired the author of *Call of the Wild* and Simpson probably smoked many pipes of Patterson's tobacco while spinning yarns for his young friend. Marigold recalls getting to know Jimmy, his wife and two daughters quite well on their annual trips in the early 1940s. Janet recalls that he "always looked the part" of the mountain man.

He maintained a superb collection of classic canoes for guests to use on the headwaters of the Bow River. Most days the Pattersons would set off to explore the shore. "…There, in the bays and the shallows toward the outlet of Bow Lake, we would glide…right up to the giant moose as they browsed on the water weed. You moved only

Daughter Mary, Mrs. Simpson and Jimmy Simpson at Num-Ti-Jah Lodge at Bow Lake.

when they were not watching: you made the paddle-stroke when their great heads were under water, and then sat rigid and hardly breathing when they raised them and regarded you—strange, heraldic, almost prehistoric beasts, dripping and festooned with weed…."[67]

On his first drive back to the ranch, past Hector Lake, Patterson's watchful eye caught glimpses of the Bow River. The upper whitewater was too challenging, even for the veteran of the South Nahanni. But at Lake Louise the river looked navigable and farther down by Castle Mountain it looked nearly placid, maps indicating a relatively moderate elevation drop from there to Banff. An idea germinated and grew with each return trip to visit old Jimmy.

Somehow Patterson had to find a boat that would allow him to explore the mountain rivers and lakes. A canoe would have been his first choice, but he could not take it on horseback into the high country. A kayak, especially a collapsible model, was not his ideal either. Indeed, he had often poked good-natured fun at the leaky, metal-tube and canvas contraption that Fenley Hunter had used on the Nahanni in the summer of 1928. Not for him such a fragile craft!

The solution to this problem came in a letter from Pocaterra in Milan, Italy, in February 1937:

> You remember the plans we used to make about a canoe trip through the heart of Europe? Well something like that is being done now often. There are in Germany seven hundred thousand Faltboats, which cruise all over the streams of Central Europe…. These Faltboats are all collapsible, they can be taken apart and put together in a few minutes, and as a boat capable of carrying 700 pounds, and unsinkable, will weigh only about sixty pounds divided in two bags of about thirty lbs. each, you can easily see how handy they can be…. The two-seater, cruising Faltboats are also equipped with a sailing arrangement, with Jib and Mainsail, with rudder and side-boards, like the Dutch sailing boats, to act as keep against side slipping, and in Germany there are many contests for these crafts…. They cost here, that is a cruising boat for two, of the best firms, around $125, with all equipment included, that is sailing arrangement, life-saving cushions, waterproof clothes bags, watertight compartments, and everything else needed. Also a collapsible bicycle wheeled (2) carriage, on which one can take the boat from place to place without having to take it apart when travelling on a cruise. Some of these boats are a bit too narrow for my taste, but others seem alright. In Germany they shoot almost any rapids with them….[68]

Patterson was intrigued and asked Pocaterra to send him a catalogue. By August he was convinced a Faltboat—a folding kayak—was just the thing for Elk Lakes. "My idea for an alpine holiday would be to take a Faltboat & by means of it to relay the outfit up the lake & up Nivelle Creek—sending the horses back with a horse wrangler to the Lower Lake meadows. Could a Faltboat do this? & would the 30 lb. packs that you mention make, say, side packs for a pack horse if well protected?"[69]

In late 1937 or early 1938, Patterson bought a Swedish-made, 16-foot Falcon Faltboat and two double-bladed paddles from Sören Berner of Montreal. As Alan and Janet remember the craft, it was blue, the same shade as Bow Lake, and had an insignia with three crowns on it.[70] "We…discovered that a very quiet pack-horse would pack the broken-down faltboat into the mountains for us; and we took it with us on several month-long trips into the Rockies, assembling it on the shores of lonely lakes, close under the glaciers of the Great Divide—lakes that rarely saw a human being and which had never seen a canoe of any kind."[71]

As it turned out, it wasn't until the first day of October, 1944, that the idea germinated on trips to Num-Ti-Jah Lodge came to fruition. That evening Patterson and Miss Baldwin boarded the CPR passenger train in Calgary and were nearly expelled for taking the Faltboat into the sleeping compartment as hand baggage. Lake Louise was their destination and there the train's conductor gladly deposited them in the wee hours of the next day. The lateness of the season added to the adventure as the craft sped over the skimpy coating of water on rocks,

Marigold Patterson paddling the Faltboat on Lower Elk Lake, 1938.

but they made Banff without accident. Not without incident, however, the story of this remarkable odyssey becoming the second instalment in Patterson's stories about paddling in the dark. After successfully navigating minor rapids by starlight and dodging bugling bull elk as they "slid past within a few feet of them," they carefully beached the kayak on what they assumed to be a friend's garden in Banff. But, when they returned the next morning, they found it sitting in the garden of a Mr. Wresterby, who disliked Patterson intensely. Apparently, Wresterby had once gone to a "tremendous lot of work and trouble to put a boat on a certain mountain lake. The day after he got it there I turned up on the opposite side of the lake with a string of packhorses.... About half an hour later, and much to Wresterby's disgust, the canoe shot out of the bay where we were camped and on to the sacred waters of his lake. A pure coincidence, but I heard afterwards that he was convinced that I had done it on purpose, just to wipe his eye. Said there ought to be a law against me and another one against faltboats."[72]

Meanwhile, Patterson continued to explore the mountains with a vigour that was nothing short of amazing. Though he resided in the area for only thirteen years, he ventured into many unknown valleys, climbed some of the mountains and gave evocative names to features that are in formal or local use to this day.

In 1931, Pocaterra had pointed out a pass to the southeast of Pyramid—today's Mount McPhail—that had been named Weary Creek Gap by the British Columbia-Alberta Boundary Survey after the tributary that ran down the west side of the divide to the Elk River. The Indians had told him a story about it, how in the distant past the elk had held a council out in the plains and decided to leave Alberta because there was too much hunting. So they had travelled up the Highwood and then up a creek and over a pass to the west. Pocaterra thought the mysterious Elk Trail would make an excellent shortcut into British Columbia, a "wonderful private hunting trail. Right close to home, too. But the Indians tell me there's some rock ledge or something that would need blasting out—some step that a horse can't make. I've never been there to see...."[73]

Pocaterra never did get the chance to scout out the trail and it was left to Patterson to take up the search. In October, 1934, while returning from Highwood Pass, Raymond and Marigold detoured up Bunk Creek—now called McPhail Creek—along the logging road to the old lumber camp. "We forded the stream and climbed up onto the open bench that followed

The Elk Trail headwall and Pyramid from The Hill of the Flowers, 1935.

the valley towards the mountains. An Indian trail can be counted on to follow, wherever possible, the point of a bench, thereby avoiding the timber and gaining a good view of the valley. And there we found it—a well-used game trail that seemed also to have been used long ago by men. There seemed little doubt that it was an old Indian trail to Elk River that had been in use probably for centuries, ever since men first came into these hills, and then abandoned when the horse reached the Indians of the plains."[74]

Patterson and Baumgart returned in November and from a base camp in Bunk Creek the rancher looked for a route up the headwall to the pass. He scrambled up a spur on the side of Pyramid and looked down on the gap, but still could not find the trail. Then he spied six mountain sheep, moving toward the bottom of the wall. Could they show him the way? "Sure enough they dipped down towards the foot of the wall. Then they began to climb at an angle on a wide ledge; and then they disappeared from view behind small, dwarfed trees, vanishing into some gallery of the rock. They reappeared higher up, going in the opposite direction, and then they came to a very steep place up which they bounded one by one. And so they went, zigzgging up the face of the wall, now in view, now hidden, keeping always to the right of the waterfall, until one saw them for the last time as they walked sedately over the crest of that barren rampart and vanished into the darkness of the firs."[75]

Writing that fall to Edwin, Patterson painted the venture with a broad stroke in order to entice his friend to come for a visit.

I took Adolf & four fresh horses & beat it for the mountains—upper Highwood this time—for a week, where a good pagan can worship nature in peace in a sunny bunch grass meadow surrounded by the tall spruce. And a long way from all this tohu bohu & whizzing machinery. I took out a bear license & never met a bear, but went exploring & found a wonderful country instead—& a trail, the most perfect I have ever seen— I must tell you about it. I think it must be an old Kootenay raiding trail into the Blackfoot country. It goes up by a waterfall & through a gap in the wall of the divide into the Elk valley in B.C.—a wild country on both sides. The waterfall was flanked with rows of columns of ice like the pipes of many organs. From various signs I had known this gap existed but I never knew of the trail—& now my old I am going back next year & if you want to travel the perfect poachers trail over the top & shoot the 'Kootenay Ram' you had better come too.

I climbed up in at least three feet of snow—I left Adolf camped eight miles away happily riding his war horse after mountain sheep on the dry slopes of the Highwood Range, & took my eiderdown & some grub & mucked about for three nights & two days in the high country on my own. A bull elk showed fight at me & I had to fire over his head to drive him away from my camp. Adolf stampedes a bunch of seven elk out of the willows & later shoots a yearling elk in mistake for a full grown deer. Most delicious. Elk protected south of the Athabasca in Alberta (& rapidly increasing) but we got the meat home allright. And had lunch with the Forest Ranger on the way who had in the meantime shot a grizzly within a hundred yards of the ranger station. I demanded my five dollars back but in vain!

Thank you—I take a less gloomy view of life now when I remember that old, old trail through the magnificent trees & think of next July.[76]

Patterson returned in 1935 to improve the trail in his own unique fashion. "From the meadow back towards the Highwood I cleared out the trail in such a way that no very obvious sign of my work remained for anyone to see. The lower end, towards the river, I left blind: that is to say that no cutting was done at all; I merely made a winding round through the jackpine by dragging out of the way the major obstacles. Nothing was left in plain view that one year's growth of grass and fireweed would not obliterate."[77]

With the trail to his liking, he hiked up a nearby hill. Where the June sun had melted away the deep snow cover there was evidence of many alpine flowers, some already in bloom. A few weeks later Patterson returned with Marigold and climbed the hill again. "...Everywhere, in the open and beneath the thin, green canopies of the larches, there grew, massed as a flower should be for effect, the golden snow lily. Except for the anemones by the snowdrifts there seemed to be no other flower; this most beautiful of all alpines had this slope of the larches to itself and it covered the ground with its golden acres of nodding bloom.... As the

Marigold Patterson on The Hill of the Flowers, 1935.

summit of the hill opened up, we saw that it was one living, shimmering carpet of many colours: here, by God's truth, were flowers beyond all imagining—flowers such as we had never seen. It was the kingdom of the flowers, the garden of the gods." So moved was Patterson by the beauty of the hill he decided to give it a name. He chose to ignore the naming tradition of the peaks along the divide, that "enthroned in stone, a collaborator, a traitor to his country, sundry generals of dubious merit, and a demagogue who, for his own ends, wrecked a way of life which had taken centuries to perfect—to cite only a few of these ill-named mountains." Instead, he imagined the name the old fur traders would have attached to such a special place. "They would have called it, quite plainly and simply, La Butte des Fleurs—The Hill of the Flowers."[78]

In October Patterson returned to The Hill of the Flowers with Baumgart on a hunting trip. From this viewpoint they looked in vain for game. Suddenly Baumgart's eye caught something, and he asked for the monocular. "Surely there is a lake in that coulee to the right of the Pyramid. I can see the sun sparkling on the water...." The next morning Patterson scrambled up the headwall to the little lake and found fossils shaped like a horns scattered along its shores. Consequently he named it the Lake of the Horns.[79]

* * *

IN EARLY 1936 the Pattersons printed up brochures advertising the ranch as a vacation destination. Dude ranches were not a new venture in the Eden Valley. Guy Weadick and George Pocaterra had first entertained greenhorns on their spreads in 1924. When dude-agent Richard de Zeng Pierce first approached the Pattersons, they passed the business on to the Weadicks because it seemed like too much work, and the prospect of cluttering up the meadows with sleeping and eating barracks was disagreeable.[80] But by the middle of the Depression the Buffalo Head needed a cash infusion, so after long deliberations Raymond and Marigold took the plunge and opened their doors to the world. That first summer of 1936 dudes paid only $5 per week, compared to the $50 per week Pocaterra took in during the 1920s. Nevertheless, the speculative venture turned into "a small private gold mine."[81]

As with any mining venture, there was work to do and capital to invest before the profits poured in. In a flurry of activity the staff tore the roofs off the old cabins and stripped the walls down to bare logs. Frank Horrell then fixed up the interiors and artist Roland Gissing from Cochrane helped refurbish the cabins and build a new one.[82] In July they purchased a Bungalow Tent 9' x 12' with side wings for $52.50 from Western Tent and Awning Company, Manufacturers and Jobbers of Tents, Awnings, Blankets, Camp Beds and Camp Supplies in Calgary.[83] Into this temporary shelter Patterson kept his promise of an unlimited water supply by piping in water from a spring. Warm water for showers came from a metal drum that soaked up the heat of the sun just outside the tent. A stove provided hotter water.

As a result of the increased activity, the Pattersons had a large number of people on the payroll: a cook, a foreman, a chore man, a nanny and an engineer. Perhaps the most interesting was The Major, Corny or Major Cornelius Foreman—he went by all three names—who had been on the Mackenzie and Liard rivers with Patterson in 1927. This mechanical genius operated the small blacksmith shop and fixed just about anything around the ranch, including the plumbing. Not all his mechanical devices were a complete success, recalls Alan. "He had that dreadful old car, an old Model A or Model T, that he fixed up and painted, and it burst into flames at one stage." The Major merely rebuilt the damaged vehicle, adding a nice red wooden box.[84] He also arranged for winter wood. An engine from an old Model T Ford powered a vicious-looking circular saw that cut firewood to various stove-sized lengths. At an abandoned mine up Flat Creek Corny retrieved coal both for the forge and to keep fires going throughout the long winter nights. In the days before rural electrification it was his job to see to the oil lamps that supplied light. In his spare time he made his own wine and beer, painted water colours and played the piano well, even though his hands had been badly damaged years before by rope burns. According to Janet, the Major had once been in the choir at Salisbury Cathedral. He lived in a small cabin on the property, took meals in the main house and was considered part of the family.

When Albertans ousted the United Farmers of Alberta political party in 1935, Janet recalls Corny arguing about the virtues and faults of the new Social Credit government and its policies. In the depths of the Depression, employment was a major concern, but the emphasis on creating work made no sense to Janet. "I can recollect sitting at the dining room table and listening to the adults arguing about it [Social Credit] and listening to Major Foreman talking about everybody needing jobs. I wondered why, because to me jobs meant that you had to clean your teeth and pick up your pyjamas and things like that. Who would want those tasks?" The radical policies of the new government probably did not sit well with Patterson, a lifelong Conservative, so the discussion was probably quite entertaining.[85]

In June of 1936, Patterson had a lucky escape on a mountain above the lake at the head of Flat Creek. Years later he pointed out the peak to friend Mary Pope while changing a flat tire at the top of Sullivan Hill on the way to the ranch. "That peak's nameless on the map.... It's an orphan mountain and I just adopted it," he said, and went on to explain why the locals called it Patterson's Peak.

Seeking a few hours of escape from all the work going on at the ranch, he had ridden up the Flat early one morning and lunched at the lake. Suddenly he decided to climb the peak and kicked steps up a steepening snowslope. About 800 feet up from the lake he got stuck. "The snow came to an end and the rock above was overhanging." By this time the sun had melted his steps and without an ice axe or pole he felt unsure how to descend. "I had a bright idea. The rock that I was hanging on to was loose and slabby. I thought that, if I could dislodge a large chunk of this without pulling anything down on myself, I could slide down, face to the snow and using the rock as a brake.... It took me ages, but in the end I eased out a slab three feet long and up to five inches thick—a heavy brute and I couldn't manage to turn it over to see what the underside was like."

Janet and Marigold Patterson near the lake at the head of Flat Creek, July 1943.
In the background rises the north slopes of Patterson's Peak.

The rock, however, did not slow down his descent. "The rock travelled even faster than I did and it took charge right away. There were some fierce acrobatics that I don't really remember—you see, I was absolutely terrified—while the rock by-passed me. But I had a death-grip on the thing and I hung on—and there we were, plummeting down that snow-slope, the rock in the lead and me hurtling after it, too frightened to let go. Thank God I lost my grip in time and the rock went hurtling on ahead.... I just slid gently into the rocks at the bottom, soaked—and then I was sick. Not without reason....

"I got back to the ranch in the evening to find people obviously wondering where I'd been all day. I didn't enlighten them; my wife was safely out of the way—in London, celebrating King George's Jubilee. Just as well, probably: no awkward questions, no reprimands for behaving like an idiot. All in all it was a memorable day, and I still feel I have a sort of squatter's right to that mountain."[86]‡

---

‡ After decades of lobbying by Gillean Daffern and Dave Birrell, the Alberta government officially assigned his name to the mountain on March 1, 2000.

Unaware of what happened that day, Marigold was in London for the King's Jubilee. She liked to keep connected with England, its traditions and current events. She watched the procession from Picadilly Square and recalls "the whole Empire was represented" and that it was "really marvellous." Returning to the ranch with pictures of the grand event, she talked about it but found that, "my goodness, nobody gave a damn...I could have killed the lot of them. And it was then I realised I lived in two different worlds: I was English and would always be and they, curse them, didn't give a damn. It was a real shock, it really was." To be fair, Patterson and the construction crew were busy rebuilding the kitchen, remodelling some of the cabins, building others from the ground up and erecting a shower house. It was her worst recollection from life at the Buffalo Head and one that reflected a part of her husband's personality she did not like. "I could have wrung his neck, and stamped on it."[87]

Later that summer, unsuspecting dudes—mostly from the United King-dom—arrived in Calgary expecting cozy cabins, an unlimited supply of hot running water, showers, sumptuous meals and adventures on horse-back in the mountains with a man some called "Rocky Mountain Patterson." Up the Highwood Valley along the river they came, stopping to open and close more than a dozen gates, each one separating them farther from their urban lives. Once at the ranch they approached The Owls' House along the tree-lined drive called The Lane that featured a quaint bridge spanning a creek. After introductions, Patterson escorted guests to private accommodations, small but well-appointed cabins on their own expanse of grass, or tucked into the trees with a special view. Usually, dudes arrived in the summer and stayed well into October or even November, the fall often being the most pleasant season in the foothills.

Dudes that first summer were in for more excitement than they could have imagined. To Patterson, canoeing the canyons of the Highwood along his ranch boundary seemed an eminently reasonable adventure. If he could just find the right craft and an unsuspecting dude to go along for the ride, there might be a story in it. Correspondence between Patterson, who loved Chestnut canoes, and H. S. Chestnut himself in early 1936 discussed the best craft for the Highwood. Amazingly, the canoe maker had examined the river at the town of High River and speculated that it might be even faster water at Patterson's ranch. Sure enough. He suggested the Ogilvy Special canoe instead of the Prospector. The rancher took his advice and bought the green Chestnut and put it through its paces in the early summer of 1936.[88]

The canoe trip was a drenching success. Paddlers and onlookers revelled in the action as the canoe slipped down the canyon, tipping the occupants a few times. Patterson had suckered a dude into paddling in the bow, an adventurous dame named Lois with hair, "the semblance of an osprey's nest—a first attempt, I mean: one that has been built by a learner." On they paddled to Sullivan Ford, where they cached the canoe above high water and walked home "under the burning sun." News of the escapade quickly raced through Loony Lane. "Been drowning any more dudes George?" became the standard question asked of the Buffalo Head owner by his Eden Valley friends.

BY THE mid-1930s, drought had made the entire country a fire hazard. Finally, the inevitable happened. In August, 1936, a fire that began in the Elk Valley blazed up the western slopes of the Continental Divide and crossed into Alberta. People at the Buffalo Head prepared by cutting the grass very short around the house and arranging a water supply to fight the fire. Patterson faced a quandary: should he entertain the guests at the ranch or spirit them away out of harm's reach? Some questioned his judgement, but in the end he took the dudes to Mount Assiniboine. As far as he was concerned, there was nothing more he could do to help fight the fire, "Having left everything as complete as possible, & with Sam's & Adolf's assurances in my ears, I was most relieved to get six dudes off to Mt. Assiniboine with George Harrison—we had a peach of a trip & I returned to a slightly breathless but rain washed & fast greening valley."[89] Fortunately for the ranchers, after incinerating much of the headwaters of the Highwood, the fire had been slowed in its progress by heavy rains.

Somehow, visitors and hosts survived the first season and the Pattersons were in the dude business.

In the fall, Patterson returned to his beloved Elk Trail, but with a heavy heart. Because he could neither ride a horse through the charred and toppled forest nor find feed along the way, he travelled on foot with a light pack to survey the damage. To get a better view he climbed almost to the summit of Pyramid where dive-bombing eagles forced him to defend himself with his knife and a map. From there he could see that a large part of the country to the west was charred, but that Elk Lakes had somehow escaped the inferno.[90]

The sight made him mad. In a letter to Pocaterra he condemned the Alberta Forestry Department that "wished to create the impression that they got a ready-made fire on such proportions on their hands that no man could do more than check it and guide it." He thought them "a poor, cheap, shoddy lot to be in charge of a beautiful country & of magnificent forests of first growth such as you & I have seen in those hills." As far as he was concerned, politicians on both sides of the border were to blame by refusing to fight the fire because it threatened no communities. "Between the two, in the interests of economy, they have burnt off the watershed of a continent—however, the money will be available for paying the weed inspector, or straightening out the corners on the Cochrane Hill. We must look on the

Fire wreckage at the summit of Elk Trail Pass after the 1936 fire.

bright side of things."[91] Patterson was still writing to his friend about the incident twenty years later. "By the way, I got the B.C. Forestry Dept's final estimate for the loss in the 'Philips Fire' as they call the 1936 burn—900 million board feet—i.e. enough to floor 32 square miles 1' thick—as near as dammit that was 33% of the total B.C. cut for 1936! This, of course, takes no account of the Alberta loss."[92]

In 1937 he wrote Diamond Jenness in Ottawa, encouraging him to establish a national park around the Elk Lakes. Jenness was Chief of the Division of Anthropology at the National Museum of Canada in Ottawa and had written *The Indians of Canada*, a standard text continuously in print since its first release in 1932. Although Patterson's letter met a sympathetic eye, the reply did not hold out much hope. Jenness wrote: "…there was not the slightest chance of interesting the present government in the Elk River country, because it [the federal government] was already operating large national parks in all the western provinces, but none at all in the east…." Instead, he suggested Patterson contact F. C. Green and see if the Surveyor General of British Columbia in Victoria might be interested in the idea. Perhaps he was, because today Elk Lakes Provincial Park protects that special part of the mountains.[93]

* * *

Marigold Patterson near the head of the Palliser River.

IN EARLY June of 1937, the residents built a new bunkhouse and bath-house to upgrade the previous year's temporary facilities. Patterson turned down income by postponing visits by dudes until August. The fire of 1936 had shocked him into the re-alization that the wonderful country in his backyard was not necessarily safe from devastation. As a result, he left the ranch in Adolf's capable hands, and headed for the hills with Elmer Jamieson and Marigold. "It was the only way to go, & the result at that lovely season of the year was such a success that I hope to do it again & again. We made the first tracks everywhere, got the first grass & saw more game than I have ever seen before. We went to the Elk Lakes, Upper Kananaskis, Three Isle Lake, Palliser, Spray & Palliser Pass & ex-plored the side valley & byways with some care. I also spent some time in hunting up hidden meadows & camps & ways into them for future refer-ence, away from the trails—& it was in this pursuit that I came, late one evening on foot, to the main head of Pocaterra Creek, about a couple of miles off the trail & right under the wall of the Elk Mountains, & there, in the highest meadow, found five of the finest bull elk grazing & lying down together. I came close unobserved—it was a beautiful sight, the great red animals in the green, flower starred meadow under the larches."[94]

While Patterson was exploring, Marigold was left to her own devices. One hot day she climbed up from their camp by the Palliser River to Tip-perary Lake. "The lake looked most inviting and it was not long before she was swimming in it. Almost immediately a family of black bears arrived on the shore and took charge of her clothes for her. This might have been rather awkward if these had not been remarkably well-mannered bears. The swimmer emerged lower down the shore and says that she looked at the bears appealingly. They, realizing that they were not wanted, ambled shyly off into the bush—which, I think, was very decent of them, even if they did, occasionally, look back over their shoulders."[95] Patterson, from his perch a thousand feet above, had not noticed his wife's adventure.

Back at the Buffalo Head, the Pattersons settled in to entertaining their guests. Indoors, the dudes amused themselves with only the finest diversions. For example, Patterson ordered a dozen darts at a cost of £2.7 from E. J. Riley Limited, Willow Mills, Accrington, England.[96]

But, of course, almost every visitor expected time in the saddle. Because many were accomplished riders, the Buffalo Head Ranch provided English as well as Western saddles.[97] A popular outing involved a ride up Flat Creek, then its south fork to a meadow near the headwaters of the creek now called Wileman. There, "Coulees ran back into the heart of the mountains, deep-shadowed even at noonday; one by one we explored them as the years went by, finding always something new in those green depths—old, bearded forest, mountain sheep, ice caves, the fairest of alpine rock-gardens, mountain goat in their incredible white breeches, bears; it was truly amazing how much of beauty this little mountain world could hold and hide."[98]

Leaving their mounts to graze, Patterson and the dudes would hike up a small valley to the headwaters of the creek that drained Mount Head Coulee. A narrow band of trees between two cliff faces led them "Upwards again to the green plateau where the marmots and the rock-rabbits live and conduct their methodical and orderly haying operations—and from there up a spur of the main ridge, with the valley of

Nancy Bennett on the ridge between Holy Cross Mountain, in left background, and Mount Head.

the South Fork 3000 feet below and the Bull Creek Pass sinking lower and lower till it became nothing but a hollow in the rounded, stony Bull Creek Hills. Climbing in the deep shadow of the ridge where the Chinook thrummed through the crannies and the crevices, until the last set of legs had safely kicked and struggled itself over the crest and into the sun and the crest and into the sun and the bellowing wind...."[99] From the ridge between Holy Cross Mountain and Mount Head the view to the west was all mountains, the backbone of the continent separating Alberta from British Columbia, with the lofty Mount Assiniboine far away to the northwest.

The exhilarated group would then pick its way back down to Marmot Plateau where Patterson would boil up a pot of water in a little rocky firepit. Hot, sweet tea went down well with the sandwiches they devoured before descending to their mounts for the long ride home. What a day!

Patterson probably made the first ascent of Mount Head. "We—one or two of us from the Buffalo Head—probably climbed Mt. Head first about 1934, & there were no signs of a cairn or anything. In the forties a party from High River climbed the mountain & left a stencilled tin plate saying, rather mistakenly, 'First Ascent.' Somebody pitched it overboard." He climbed it many more times, alone and with Baumgart, Miss Baldwin and Nancy Bennett, the daughter of Jim Bennett. "We used to scramble up Mt. Head often after packing salt up to the cattle in summertime and relocating them, so that the sun wd. be in the S.W. & straight into our eyes."[100] On another ascent in July, 1937, "Adolf & I took a Sunday to ourselves three weeks ago & climbed Mt. Head. We dealt with it thoroughly, chased a billy goat over the head & then followed the main ridge to the highest peak of the mountain."[101]

He climbed Holy Cross Mountain in August of 1937. "Last Monday Miss Baldwin & I rose at 2:30 a.m. & got our own breakfast, riding away with the first light to the valley of the South Fork. By nine a.m. we were finished with the cattle &, making tea & a second breakfast, we rode up to the timber line & tied the horses. We followed an alpine valley into the heart of the Mt. Head massif, marvelling at the show of pentstemons & yellow & blue columbines, clawed our way up by a waterfall nearly treading on a sleeping deer, & then dealt thoroughly with the Holy Cross Mountain, lunching on top, 9000'. I climbed down to a snow drift & we melted snow in tin cups in the hot sun for drinking water. Thunder clouds gathered on a level with us but moved off north along the range. Sitting in the shade of a great slab with my feet dangling into space I watched, through your glass, a few of the cattle moving slowly, seeking deeper shade, nearly 4000' below. The whole foothill country was in a haze of heat & I became drowsy & nodded into a dream, waking suddenly with a snatch of terror. Damn nearly I had nodded into the abyss.

"We made the curious discovery that if on a mountain peak, you stand on all fours & look backwards between your legs—upside down, you understand—things become insanely reversed. You are, as it were, in the

Miss Baldwin on the summit of Holy Cross Mountain, August 1937.

centre of a vast bowl of country & in grave danger of giddiness & of taking to yourself wings—fleeing from your gyrating perch into the blue safety of the bowl."[102]

MANY city friends also visited the ranch. P. K. Page, a regular visitor in Pocaterra's time, remembers pitching her tent by the river. Her father was Colonel Lionel Page whose command of the Strathcona Light Horse ingratiated him to all military types and people of British origin. Old remittance men regularly visited the Colonel and his wife Rose in their Calgary home. Patterson, too, quickly added their home to his visiting list in Calgary.

P. K. thought Raymond a most unusual man. He charmed her and always "looked so professorial and spoke so quietly." But he also "had an astonishing sort of wild streak in him." For example, after a night out on the town, he boasted to Rose Page, "I danced like a stag, I danced like a stag!" On occasion, Raymond and Rose went to fortune-tellers together, but they never revealed their findings to young P. K. Marigold, by contrast, had no time for soothsayers.

Marigold remembers the day the Buffalo Head served a particularly good quality roast to the Page family. After finishing his portion, young son Michael blurted out, "That's the best bit of bear I've ever eaten!" The boy, who was only seven or eight at the time, had watched it being cooked and was very pleased with the result. Marigold recalls, "Mrs. Page was shattered, for the time being, but had to admit it was very good eating."[103]

When P. K. spent a year in England in the early 1930s, Raymond and Marigold entertained the wide-eyed teenager in London. From a flat in Queen's Gate they showed her a once-in-a-lifetime night on the town. "They were very dressed up," she recalls. "It was astonishing to see them in their London guise.... Raymond took me to dinner at Scotts, a great and very famous seafood place in London. Then to a famous restaurant after the show. I was pretty dazzled, I can tell you, by it all.... Marigold was always so cool, such a good sport.... She used to look absolutely impeccable."[104]

Closer to home, Patterson enjoyed his creature comforts at Calgary's exclusive Ranchmen's Club. Founded in 1891, fourteen years before Alberta became a province, it began as a place for ranchers to stay while in the city on business. Over the years it grew into the city's most august social club, where the oldest money met and socialized. Usually a sombre place, it could kick up its heels when the occasion warranted. For example, when Edward, Prince of Wales, visited Canada in the summer of 1919, there was a party in his honour at the Ranchmen's on September 12. On this occasion the Alberta government relaxed strict liquor laws in deference to the Prince, and everyone reacted in proper spirit, a provincial judge leading the crowd in a song with the chorus "another little drink won't do us any harm."

Alan and Janet recall Patterson's sciatica improved in warm places, so he liked to stay at the Ranchmen's and read books. He visited the club often enough to hear stories and experience events that became part of the mythology of the place. For example: "Old Dudley"—The Rt. Hon. William Dudley Ward, P.C.—once concocted a most unusual recipe on a hot plate in his room, "a privilege

Marigold and R. M. Patterson dressed for going to Calgary.

that was unique and not likely to be accorded to anyone ever again." The Affair of the Boar's Head involved simmering the skull of a pig in a small quantity of water for an extended period. "Time went by, the water vanished in steam and things began to happen to that boar's head, spitting and writhing in its almost incandescent pot. By slow degrees the hellish fumes spread and penetrated first the doors, then the dreams, and finally the nightmares of the sleeping Ranchmen. It began to dawn on them, one by one, that all was far from well in the old shanty. Doors were opened and anxious men peered out into the reeking corridor. Some genius, inspired, cried out, 'By God, it's coming from Dudley's room!' and a rescue squad charged along into the north-west angle.

"They flung the door open and groped their way, coughing and choking, into a blinding reek of oily smoke and burning flesh. They felt round for Dudley's charred body, thinking to drag it out into the corridor; and they were guided into their search by a sound that came from the corpse itself—an unexpected sound—a long, contented, bubbling snore!"

Ten days after the event Patterson checked into room No. 23, oblivious to its charred history. Sleep came quickly to the tired rancher, but it was sleep tainted with a certain odour. "A faint but still frightful smell greeted me on the third floor of the Club, and in the morning I asked one of the servants what on earth had happened. 'Just one of Mr Ward's little experiments, sir. We're living it down gradually. This is nothing to what it has been....'" This story and others of Patterson's adventures in the city on the banks of the Bow River would later appear in an article titled "The Foothill City" in the November, 1960, edition of *Blackwood's Magazine*. It still remains a wonderfully amusing window on Calgary during its early boom years. "And now Calgary, raised on beef and grain and, in recent years, swollen with oil, has burst its small-clothes; the stockaded fort the Mounted Police built beside the two clear rivers has sired a sprawling city of over a quarter of a million people.... Where is it going? Where will the Foothill City end? No one can tell. But Kipling, no mean prophet, numbered Calgary among the fortunate Towns, and—it is on its way."

Patterson's connection to the Ranchmen's lives on today in a piece of art hanging on its walls entitled Nahanni Rams. In early 1943, Patterson asked his friend, outstanding wildlife painter Carl Rungius, to paint a scene of his adventure on the South Nahanni when he shot the Dall ram. Although Rungius often painted commissioned works, Patterson's request came as an unusual challenge to the man who painted about a dozen canvases a year. The artist prided himself in firsthand research of the topic, usually sketching the scene himself or working from photos he had captured in the field. But for this commission Rungius agreed to use the rancher's photos of the canyon and the head of the ram, relying totally on Patterson's recollections of shading and colour.

They corresponded in late 1943, Rungius offering to paint "a 30"x40" for $800.00, 28"x36" for 700.00, a 25"x30" or 24"x32" for 600.00 and a 16"x20" for 300.00. "The prices quoted are 1/3 below regular price. I would paint the picture next summer in Banff." By January of the next year they had agreed on a size and price. "It will be a pleasure to paint that Ovis Dalli picture for you and I will try to work something out on the land of your photos or from what you told me about the country. In any case I shall send you a rough sketch before I start." A July letter stated, "The rocks seem to be rather rich in color, small spruce and shrubs, roses etc. growing up the canyon walls, and are the sheep white in summer or somewhat stained in spots? I commenced the painting and think I have a good start." In the fall came news of the completed work. "Your painting is boxed and will go down to Calgary tomorrow. As I stated before, the price is $600.00, the cost of the frame was too small to mention, but I think it will be satisfactory for the time being. Please send cheque to Wilfred V. Goddard, Imperial Bank of Commerce, Banff, at your convenience. I had a good trip, shot a Grizzly and a very fine buck."[105]

The Rungius painting was loaned to the Ranchmen's Club through the late 1940s and early 1950s. Finally, in 1954 club members pooled their money and purchased the unique piece of art for $1,400. The honorary secretary treasurer of the club thanked Patterson for the gracious loan of the painting for so many years and concluded: "I must say on behalf of all members of the Club, how much we appreciate your consideration in making the picture available, as we understand your personal associations with 'Rungius' and the fact that you shot the ram which was used as a model."[106]

IN 1939, just prior to the outbreak of World War II, the Pattersons voyaged to England on one of their regular winter visits paid for by Mother. The family album shows photographs of Janet at Gaddens, Cowdray Park, Pevensey and at Bochym in Cornwall. But the visit was tinged with sadness, as Mother had suffered a stroke. With sad hearts they boarded the ship back to Canada on April 20, 1939, never to see the wonderful old lady again. She died less than a month later, in May.

The threat of war was the first major intrusion affecting the idyllic life-style of the residents of the Highwood Valley. Ranch foreman Adolf Baumgart chose this inopportune time to visit his family and friends in East Prussia. The Pattersons were sad to see him go, but sent him off with instructions to have a good time and with a wager that the Pocaterras would meet his ship when it docked in Genoa. "Yes, Mr. Patterson," he wrote on February 26, 1938, from his home, "you won the bet." For their part, the Pocaterras were thrilled to see Adolf. George had doubtless told Norma many stories of his hired man, raising expectations for the day they met him off the ship. "He looked exactly the same as when I last saw him in 1935, only better groomed…. We took him to see some of the most famous places in the city. Most important the Camp Santo, the wonderful city of the dead, celebrated in the whole world as the most magnificent for natural position, high up amongst the hills, and for the thousands upon thousands of the most gorgeously artistic monuments imaginable. Miles upon miles of statues and large groups of statues, interspersed with semi-tropical gardens, and rows of cypresses and other trees. We took him there in an open carriage, horse-drawn, as something different and more attractive than the usual taxi."

Adolf's eye was open to the opportunities in the Pocaterra household in Milan. "We have a very attractive-looking maid, a typical Italian beauty, large dark eyes, with long lashes, lots of wavy brown hair, and poor Adolf could not keep his eyes away from her. It was funny to hear them trying to make conversation together…. It was rather sweet. Of course Ena has a fiancé, and it was all so guileless."[107]

Baumgart then set off for his home, encouraged to see firsthand that all the stories he had read and been told about Italy were nothing more than lies. Passing through Munich, he drank a beer for himself and another for Patterson before boarding a train for Berlin. He found Germany much changed, and in spite of 500,000 unemployed men in the streets looking for work, he was impressed with the improvements Hitler had made to the country. "The people so far as I can see are satisfied and happier. Hitler I believe is more for the poorer Klasse, for the mass. It is strict all right but is order. It is more work, more business. Many have their own cars, Autobusses going to beat hell. But for myself it is hard to get a start here…. I am only here for a short time and can not tell you for sure what I am going to do. But it is more likely that I will come back once more to you, only if you want me and does not interfere with your new man. Then life is not quite so easy for anybody in Canada."

On a lighter note, Adolf wrote four months later: "I found that beer tasted far, far better when good looking girls are serving." Accustomed to the saddle, he had picked up the knack of chauffeuring an automobile. "I have learned to drive a car and find pleasure in it, not getting seasick." Always the gentleman, he inquired after Sam Smith, Janet, Alan, Miss Baldwin and Mrs. Patterson and sent them all his greetings.[108]

Into his hometown of Aulowönen he slid easily into a routine, too easily perhaps, because he found himself trapped far from freedom when war erupted. Nine years it took him to wriggle out from behind the evil grip that held Europe in its grasp. Sixty years later, the man who played such an important role in the Buffalo Head remained cautious and quiet about his time back home, suspicious lest anyone misinterpret his actions during those lost years. But Patterson always believed in the man, and later wrote that, "after a period of energetic and successful poaching on an estate in Holstein, Adolf returned to Canada older by nine eventful years."[109] Although Patterson, Smith, Weadick and others wrote letters of reference to Canadian officials in support of Adolf's application to return to Canada, Baumgart still had to write a letter in October, 1946, to convince the Custodian of Property of Occupied Countries in Ottawa that his seized bank account should be released.[110]

Long before Adolf's successful repatriation to Canada could take place, many of the other characters in this story lived through some very trying times. The always emotion-filled relationship between Patterson and Pocaterra took on added intensity in the late 1930s, even though civility largely prevailed in their correspondence. For his part, Patterson described himself in January, 1937, as a "confirmed European" and as a result of his Great War experience, not one to take the current problem lightly. In a letter to Pocaterra, he recounted the discussion of the "European problem" at a recent party, and his proposed solution: "So I suggested—& made a strong case for it—that Canada should be presented to Hitler, Mussolini or anybody else with a territorial grievance. My reasons, elaborated, were that it was a thinly (not necessarily under) populated country & that consequently only a few wd. be affected by the transfer—that its present inmates had made a frightful mess of it and, by their inability to elect one honest government of ten, had proved themselves unfit to run it, & finally that any connection between it & my own country was, as far as I could see, only a source of expense & weakness to the latter, of or from which I should be glad to see England disembarrassed.... What I was driving at was that a country should either do something for the organisation to which it belongs or get out. Not try to keep one foot in the trough for purposes of trade benefits alone, & the other three firmly outside—& then try to dictate the policy of the whole."[111]

In April of 1937, Pocaterra responded, "I have been able to check many of the deliberate lies in no uncertain manner myself, and have come to the conclusion that if one sees something in the Press, it is a wise policy to wonder at once how far from the truth any statement actually is. Seeing it in print puts at once a profound doubt in my mind about its authenticity."[112]

Patterson replied confidently in early 1938, assuring his Italian friend that a solution was at hand. "But at last, as far as Italy and Britain are concerned, they seem to have arrived at an understanding.... If, as everyone hopes, France follows suit, Europe will be guaranteed a long spell of peace which was absolutely impossible of achievement as long as the monstrosities of Versailles were allowed to stand. This IS the general belief in Central Europe and I believe now in England."[113]

By 1939 the situation was looking quite desperate, but Patterson still trusted Pocaterra's people. "I quite believe all you say about Italy being normal & quiet. Nobody here, that I have met, believes anything to the contrary—in fact the fact is never even discussed. There are many good friends of Italy in this country." He too thought the only way to solve the problem with Germany was to muzzle the press. "My only suggestion for peace perfect peace in Western Europe would be to muzzle absolutely all the press & radio for six months, & then have the coming conference calm & secretly & present the various nations with a fait accompli. There will, of course, be no war—nothing wd. be left this time but the ruins—but the incessant nagging of these damned newspapers should be made to cease. The Canadian ones are, as they have always been, sensational & absurd."[114]

Once the war began, Patterson and Pocaterra engaged in a battle of wits, words and interpretations of reality. In response to Pocaterra's lecture to him about European history, Patterson wrote, "For my sins I had to make a specialised study of European history for five years of my life—& furthermore, 1917 is not yet forgotten." He also warned Pocaterra, who took out Canadian citizenship in 1909, to be very careful when he returned to the Eden Valley. It would be best to keep all conversations clear of politics, he warned the Italian, as there is "a growing hostility towards Italians which has recently found open expression in this Highwood country & from people who used to be among your best friends. I won't go into details except to say that, in this instance, naturalisation papers made not an atom of difference."[115]

Some of the letters between the men are missing for this period, but there is no doubt that World War II caused a terrible strain in their relationship. Reacting to Patterson's letters, Pocaterra wrote that his old friend's letters were "showing me, who know you so well in most of your changeful moods, that you are far from being a happy man." Offering a branch of peace, he added that "pleasant memories rush to my mind, when I knew you as a very different man, gloriously happy in a very simple way during our mountain trips and our first times together."[116]

During this time Pocaterra had much more to worry about than his relationship with Patterson. His very life and that of his opera diva Norma were in jeopardy. Penniless, they abandoned their home and possessions and boarded a ship bound for America, two of 1300 passengers on a ship designed for 700. In a summer 1940 letter to Patterson he reviewed the details: "When the whirlwind struck Europe last September, I was faced with a terrible problem. My wife had many offers of operatic engagements, with very good returns, but to stay on might have meant at any time being interned. Try to put yourself in my place. I decided to get back if we could possibly get passages, and for two weeks I lived in hell. Finally, at tremendous expense, I managed to get a small petty officer's cabin, and we got back to this city [Montreal] in October.

"For the last ten months it has been so unsettled, and at times so hectic, that the old Highwood and the mountains beyond seemed like a haven of rest. But apparently even there one cannot escape altogether the effects of the madness that is blotting out old Europe."

Already, the old friends were working out their differences by mail. "But I do want to say that I sincerely appreciate your letter and the way you have written it. It seemed to have brought back the old days when I first knew you, when our friendship ripened into something that I have not known before or since."[117]

After trying unsuccessfully to introduce Norma into the opera world in New York, Pocaterra and his wife travelled to Montreal on July 31, 1940, and returned to Alberta at the end of August. They moved back into Eden Valley, "right across the river from the old Buffalo Head Ranch. Mr. Harper Sibley, whom you must remember, gave us the much appreciated privilege of living here until we could get our own place properly fixed up." His goal was still "the success of the lyric career of my wife, a success already achieved in Europe before we left, and which gave promise of even greater achievements in her chosen line of endeavour." In the meantime, they intended to lick their wounds and dream of the new home they wanted to build on the old Patterson property on the Ghost River. To that end, they spent a lovely month in the spring of 1941 in the little cabin. "Quite sufficient for our present needs," was Pocaterra's description, "as this place is only about 45 minutes from Calgary."[118]

The old friends renewed their acquaintance on Monday, January 27, 1941, at 8:00 p.m. Patterson was delayed by a visit from Bert Sheppard, and as a result, Pocaterra and Patterson talked late into the night about their favourite topic "The Mountains." Pocaterra complained of a headache the next day and blamed it on the chinook.[119]

On February 1, Pocaterra made his first inspection of the Buffalo Head since selling it in 1933. At exactly 7:45 p.m., according to his carefully dated letter, he inserted two pieces of paper with carbon paper between them into his typewriter and pecked out the following inspection report to Norma: "This morning after the usual things that have to be done, I caught Darkie again, and went over to Patterson arriving a little after 11 a.m. Patterson being the cook, pro tem, Janet and I went and made a round of all the new and old cabins. P. did make quite a few improvements, some of them I like, others not quite so much, but taken all in all he has done well by the place. Everything is kept up, outside of the kitchen linoleum, which is holy (not sacred!) in several places. The best thing he has done, is the arrangement of the water supply. They also have a practical shower-bath cabin, by itself, where also the hot and tired men, in the summer, can cool themselves off with a fresh shower. After a pleasant lunch, P. J. and I, we went for a ride all over the place. There are also some improvements, but not so many as I half expected. All though, are good ones. One can see that P. really loves country; as such, and hates to do anything which might spoil it. We finally rode part way up Bellavista and down Vallombrosa. There is now a much plainer trail down it, than when I left, and it looks lovely. One of the things I did not care for, was the living room, which has had all the walls and everything possible, stained dark, sort of dark oak stain, and it makes the room, which was once too bright and cheerful, rather gloomy. It is positively extraordinary, how English people always go for dark coloring, and love their places of abode sad and gloomy. It's the same in their country, overseas."[120]

The Pocaterras moved to the Ghost River cabin later that year, built a larger log cabin and named it Valnorma—after Norma, calling it home until they bought a house in Calgary in 1955.

Baumgart and Pocaterra were not the only ones whose lives were affected by "Hitler's War." Demand for petroleum prompted the government of Canada to produce oil out of the Turner Valley oilfield at unprecedented levels, for a time making it the most productive field in the British Commonwealth. In a way, that dirty group of shacks eventually landed Patterson some work in the war effort when all other avenues he pursued came up empty.

When war broke out, the great wanderer rubbed his hands with glee. Here was a custom-designed opportunity to see the world as part of an expeditionary force that he expected would travel the globe. Gordon Matthews, a year his senior, got a commission at the outbreak of hostilities. With Marigold's blessing, Patterson not only enlisted the day England declared war, but began pulling strings to make sure he got a post as soon as possible. And then he waited. And waited. And waited. Finally a letter dated April 30, 1940, arrived from The War Office in London, informing him that he was registered in connection with the Royal Artillery in the case his services should be needed. In other words, he was too old.[121]

Patterson did not give up easily. He next called upon his mentor from the Bank of England, Sir Edward Peacock. In August, 1941, came the reply: "I have just received your letter of August 3rd. I understand your anxiety to get into the war somewhere and I shall do my best to find an

"The Duchess" Rafaelle Kennedy in 1941.

opening for you, but I have my doubts. I think the authorities here would be inclined to say that your natural entry would be through the Canadian Army, and I fancy you feel that this channel would not give you an opening for your particular training." Peacock added a note on the same page, dating it August 25, 1941. "I am now in receipt of an official reply from the War Office, of which I send you a copy herewith. I am sorry not to have been more successful."

The attached note from The War Office bore the date 22nd August, 1941, and was unsigned by the Director of Recruiting and Mobilisation. "Mr. Patterson was originally classified for the Royal Artillery but since that category is now overfull, he has been placed in the General List and there appears to be very little prospect under existing conditions of his being called upon to take up an appointment."[122]

Patterson temporarily suspended his quest in the middle of 1941 when Rafaelle Kennedy decided to visit her old boyfriend on his ranch in the Alberta foothills. She had returned from England after war broke out in 1939 as the Duchess of Leinster. She still quite liked The Urchin—her nickname for Raymond—and with two failed marriages behind her, she needed a break from her tumultuous life. With her maid Maureen, she spent four August days and nights crossing the continent on the train. Her sour mood brightened gradually and she delighted in watching prairie dogs. "Never had I seen anything like them, nor will I ever forget their moment of happiness. Hundreds and hundreds of them lived in holes in the ground. One would come up and sit on its hind legs on top of his burrow and look and look and look, then he would raise his small face and let out a long, shrill, piping sound meaning 'all clear.' Thousands of others would rush up from their tunnels and join in with the whistle. I couldn't get over this haunting, stolen moment of sheer happiness. There they were piping to their hearts' delight to the evening star. Fancy settling for that as their golden moment of life."

Patterson met them in Calgary and escorted them to the Buffalo Head where they moved into small dude cabins, or "crude huts" as Rafaelle called them. The two city women were terrified by the sounds of the night: coyote howls, the quiet rustle of quills as a porcupine waddled past, the sniffing of a bear and the patter of little squirrel feet on the roof. Such was their fear that Miss Baldwin slept outside their cabin in a tent for protection! Come daylight, Rafaelle rode the packhorse Mollie, while Patterson led the way on Rex up Flat Creek, where they explored the canyons and creeks and made tea in a billy. Storms frightened her, particularly lightning that sent her scrambling under the bed for cover. For his part, Patterson took close-up photographs of the stunning beauty against the mountain backdrop. And then she was gone, back to a life in New York and London until her passing on December 28, 1993.[123]

DURING the war years expeditions based at the Buffalo Head were all that Patterson's lifestyle allowed. Photographs show a camp at Highwood Pass and the Faltboat in Three Isle Lake and Elk Lakes. Another image records an unusual event in Canadian mountaineering, something

Patterson called "The canoe horse" with the folded kayak aboard. September, 1939, photos show the family once again camped up Mount Head Coulee. On June 27, 1940, Patterson and Miss Baldwin climbed Holy Cross Mountain for the second time and took pictures of each other from all points of the compass. That November Patterson took snapshots of Steamboat Mountain and the Columbia River marshes and bulrushes at Spillimacheen in British Columbia, evidence that his wandering eye was already scouting land farther west.

In July, 1942, Patterson captured on film the fascinating image of a gnarled tree on Fir Creek Point—a favourite family destination located on a ridge near Grass Pass. The ridge, which boasted good springs and "all that cattle could need in the way of grass," formed the southern limit of the Buffalo Head grazing lease, its steep sides serving as a natural fence. "Away out on this point stood a very old limber pine. It grew, like all limber pines, almost completely in the rock, and beneath it, in July, the barren-looking gravel was alive with flowers. The old pine had been blasted by lightning; now, on its massive trunk, instead of a full crown it carried only a quarter of the greenery that once was there; and out of one

The canoe horse Peanuts and ranchhand Jay Wickle.

side there reached to skinny, skimpy branches that somehow gave the impression of a witch's arms and claws. It was the Boundary Pine."[124]

In September, 1943, Patterson returned with his two favourite horses, Rex and Mollie, to Nyahé-ya-'nibi, intent on attaining the Pass in the Clouds that had eluded him in 1931. It was a long trip to the west side of the pass, over 200 miles. Up the Highwood he rode and down to the Kananaskis ranger station where he deposited his rifle for safe-keeping owing to a hunting ban. Then they climbed over North Kananaskis Pass, followed the Palliser River downstream and started up a tributary, Joffre Creek. Travel proved so diffi-

The Boundary Pine at Fir Creek Point.

cult he established a base camp above the canyon and continued on foot to Sylvan Pass. To Edwin he later wrote: "I got there & I saw the White River valley at last & it was worth it, and what a devil of a country to come at! There is gypsum & weird salts in those mountains & there are circular springs in the forest that look like pots of boiling gruel, &, to these, deep old game trails lead from all points & tracks of goats, deer & elk are legion. In fact you'd think the ground had been churned up by a herd of cattle. It's devilish hard, at time, to sort out the old Indian trail from the game trails (our own Indians from here hunt there no longer & the old trails are disused & the timber falling in & blocking them) & as for old blazes, yellowed over with gum, you can see a hundred would-be blazes shining in the dark woods owing to the damned elk rubbing the velvet off their antlers against the trees."[125]

From a perch above the pass he spied out the new country. To the east stood a wall of rock: mountains called Joffre, Nivelle, Cadorna, Abruzzi, Lancaster, Marconi and Minton. As he ran his monocular over the rock, his heart stopped. "That wall on the east was not unbroken. Five or six miles south there was a gap in it—hard to see in this afternoon glare but definitely a gap. It had to be the gap that led to the Pass in the Clouds, there was no

Rex and Mollie at Lawson Lake on the trail to North Kananaskis Pass, 1943.

other break in the wall. I studied it for some time: it had all the lure of distance, it was difficult to get at and it led to something I had never seen...."[126]

Back to camp he dropped and made preparations. He barricaded the horses into the little valley so they would not wander off, stashed most of his gear up a tree, then set off with three days' food over Sylvan Pass into the White River. It was a long day and that night he camped at "Wilcox' alpine lake," 1500 feet above the main valley. His report to Edwin continued: "However, Bronzo navigated with accuracy & saw great marvels of forest, game & beauty. Some notable climbing & hoofing was done (not for nothing did old Frenchmen call these Montagnes Rocheuses) & my favourite pair of mountain boots (by Dowie & Marshalls of Garrick St.) look as if they had tackled Kangchenjunga. Something will have to be done about that...."[127]

An early start the next day put him on the pass at 8500 feet. "Then came the dip over into Nyahé-ya-'nibi and the valley of Abruzzi Creek—after all these years! "Anxiously I looked down. Below me, in the head of Abruzzi Creek, was green forest. And the summit of The Warship was green forest.... Everywhere else rose the grey skeletons of the burnt forest. I had never been able to get a sight of this valley in the intervening years since the fire—but somehow I had always thought of it as a green valley, protected. It was a place where, like Pocaterra, I had been happy when I was young, and now my vision of it had been destroyed. And when that happens you lose something of yourself. 'Never again,' you say, 'will I give my heart to a valley in the mountains. Never again will I be that young.'"[128]

Crossing steep scree slopes, Patterson went on down the trail into the sad valley until he could get a glimpse of the tarn that should have been called Lake Marigold. And then he turned his back on Nyahé-ya-'nibi and climbed out over the Pass in the Clouds and returned to his horses. He varied the trip home from Kananaskis ranger station, returning by way of Elbow Pass, Sheep Creek and the high pass into Misty Basin where he hunted sheep for a couple of days. Leaving "virgin bunch-grass and coming in one day's ride to the overgrazed range land of the upper Highwood...spoilt the pleasure of my return,"[129] and he did not even stop to visit when he saw tepees along the trail near home.

"There's newt to beat it," he reported to Edwin, "—the telephone never rings & the mail never comes in. There are no men, no blatting radio. You have no house, no cattle, no family—no use thinking about them because if they were all wiped out you wouldn't be a penny the wiser. The safety of your outfit & yourself depends on you—you have only yourself to blame (and don't try any of your wild, fancy swiping with an axe, for instance! Keep that for near home). Every night you eat a good supper & fall asleep under the stars, & every morning up comes the sun (it did on this trip, anyway) & another golden day is yours. The trip was about 240 miles & I saw two men in Alberta & none in B.C."[130]

A few weeks later Patterson found Stony friend Paul Amos in his kitchen. Why, he wanted to know, had Patterson ridden right past their camp at Cat Creek a few weeks before? And so Patterson told him the story of his adventures in places known to only a few natives and fewer whites.

"'You go that country all alone?' he asked."

"'Yes, Paul.'"

"He began to laugh. 'I think never stay one place too long,' he said. 'All the time travel—just like old bull moose, alone in mountains!' And a gust of laughter shook him as he sat there by the sunny window. Quite certainly he understood."[131]

* * *

MEANWHILE, Patterson had once again applied himself to the task of finding a posting in a war machine that considered him "over the hill." He even went so far as to make an unsuccessful application to join the French Foreign Legion. It was at this point that the oil industry came to his aid. After Pearl Harbour all eyes in western North America scanned the horizon for the feared Japanese invasion. A land and air route to Alaska had become a wartime necessity and it was Patterson's skills as a northern traveller that landed him a post of sorts in 1943. "Men decided to build a road through that vast hunting park—through to Fairbanks in Alaska. They started—and a ponderous screen of secrecy descended upon the project. A child could have penetrated it, I found later, and no doubt the Japanese High Command was fully informed; but in Canada most people couldn't have cared less where that road went, and the few, like myself, who knew a bit about the country and were interested, were too busy to take the time to find out."[132] Then an oil company called the ranch and the next thing he knew, Patterson was headed north to supply his expertise to the job of installing gasoline storage tanks along the Alaska Highway. While thin-blooded Americans froze in unheated trucks along the route, Patterson and his buddies stayed warm. Not for them the counterproductive strategy of huddling by the fire; they walked from one camp to the next, letting their internal furnaces provide a more lasting warmth than any red-hot oil burning heater could provide.

Running off to serve the war effort was fine in the depths of winter, but come summer there was a shortage of labour on the ranch. As a result, every adult helped put up the hay; Miss Baldwin drove the stacker and Marigold drove the rake. From across the river came Dutch artist Ted Schintz who lived with his wife Janet and three sons in a house with a stunning view of the mountains. Every day the painter went to a small studio, with only east and north-facing windows, and put paint to canvas while carefully avoiding the distracting scenery to the west.

Life by the Highwood River made for strange initiation rites. Eldest son Mike Schintz remembers his father tieing his boys one by one to a long pole and dunking them repeatedly in a hole in the river until they learned to swim. He also recalls the day Father Bowlen of High River tried to pay a clerical visit. After parking his car across the river from their home, he began wading. Ted Schintz suggested he step only on small rocks. Believing in divine guidance, the Father slipped and fell. Scrambling to his feet, he heard Ted yell, "See, I told you not to step on those big flat stones. If you'd listened to me instead of the Lord you would have got over here safe."[133]

By late 1943 another complication presented itself when it became apparent a new Patterson was due about the same time as the spring calves. Marigold moved to a house that William Dudley Ward lent them in Calgary and on May 15, 1944, young Robert George—always called Robin—entered the world. The youngest Patterson child, unfortunately, experienced little of life on the ranch because in 1945 the family decided to sell the Buffalo Head.

Patterson's restlessness had been increasing for some time. Each time he recounted stories from the Nahanni, the Liard or the Mackenzie, his heart was pulled to new adventure. An exploratory trip to the head of the Livingstone River in September, 1945, provided a chance to see new country, but often weeks and months passed between escapes into the mountains. Luckily, the Bull Creek Hills were close to home. Located between the ranch and the Mount Head massif, they were for this restless soul "the true untouched wilderness of the wild hills. That, in times of stress, was what held me there on the Buffalo Head. That was what made a settled life possible for one whose conception of the perfect home was a camp."[134]

Patterson's wanderlust also expressed itself in other ways. Given his preference, Patterson would have driven a Daimler or a Bentley all his life. Indeed, while in England for a visit in 1939 he splurged and rented a Daimler, later writing it was "a joy after driving a Chev—& one needs a powerful car on these twisting Cornish hills."[135] But living on a Chevrolet budget while aspiring to a Daimler lifestyle did not prevent him from making automobile ownership into another form of adventure. Every few years he sold off his current model and boarded a train for Detroit. Picking up a new car at the factory saved shipping charges and gave him an excuse to drive back through the United States, not necessarily by the most direct route. Janet recalls his fascination with the Taos and Santa Fe region of New Mexico and that he had lots of old Santa Fe Trail books. He was also fas-

Robin and R. M. Patterson.

cinated by the American mountain men. The family photo album shows images of the Grand Coulee Dam in February, 1946, though Patterson wrote no stories of this trip.

No doubt the changes that had been creeping up the Highwood Valley also contributed to the decision to sell. During the 1940s, the Pattersons felt increasingly squeezed by the people they sought to avoid. Landowners seldom held title to mineral rights, so their interests often came into conflict with those of the oil companies. Although some ranchers worked the rigs or benefited when an oil company drilled a successful well on their land, most had little use for the oily bunch. Marigold called them "a pest." No exploration occurred on the Buffalo Head while she lived there. "It wouldn't have been at all welcome. Those people seemed unable to close gates and they disturbed the animals tremendously and they were just not welcome."

The influx of city folk was becoming another problem and like other ranchers, the Pattersons often found themselves helping pull cars out of the ditch or a snowbank. "Once in a while, not very often, whoever was being pulled out would offer to pay a little something towards it, but not too often. They thought it was the farmer's pleasure to come pull them out," recalls Marigold. Just to balance the equation, there was also the case of the farmer who regularly watered the mud hole in the road and assisted people for a fee.

Because people were camping indiscriminately on Buffalo Head property, Patterson fenced in a piece of land for campers where Flat Creek entered the Highwood River downstream of the old bridge. Still, he had to patrol the campground like a park warden, encouraging people to control their fires and keep the place safe and clean. Marigold recalls one solution: "Once my husband found a really super mess, and a car there, and he picked it all up and stuffed it under the car's hood. Well, something has to be done." Another time hunters shot the family pet. They claimed innocence, saying they thought it was a coyote, but Patterson prosecuted and the hunters were fined for their careless mistake.

Then came the day when the children's pet dog Kerry went missing. Fearing the worst, the adults mourned the lost animal. Luckily this story had a happy ending. A few days later, while Marigold and Alan were walking through the barn, they passed a feed bin. Alan piped up, "Kerry's in there," and sure enough, older sister Janet had hidden the pet in the feed box. "There were feathers in the bin," she recalled decades later, "and I thought it looked cosy. Later, I forgot. I got into a lot of trouble…."

Later, Patterson summed it all up in a letter to Pocaterra: "Comparing these present conditions with those obtaining in, say, 1929 on the Highwood, I'm glad I moved on, from the point of view of sporting & residential amenities, though I don't ever expect to see any place that I shall like so much again.

"…You go to a place because you like the people, the wild country at your back, the way of life—and in fifteen years it is all gone. Roads, oil wells, logging camps, coal mines, deaths, the break-up of ranches, forest fires, your friends moved away, lease regulations changed from security to imperma- nence, government officials nosing around taxing your springs—(beat that one: I was on the top of a haystack when he turned up &, secure in the knowledge that I was selling, dealt myself the luxury of telling him what I thought of him & his miserable outfit. One is not always so fortunately placed.)—time to pull up stakes & move on while the memories are still good. Never will any place or countryside be home to me as that was. Never before, in all my life, have I lived so long in one place."[136] With his wander- lust pulling him away to greener pastures, Patterson was, perhaps, using the excuse of an itchy foot as justification for leaving the Buffalo Head.

Marigold and the children were also part of the decision to move west. With Alan still at boarding school on Shawnigan Lake, a new home at Shoal Harbour would allow closer contact. Vancouver Island schools would also ease worries as Robin approached school age.[137]

Patterson did well on the sale of the Buffalo Head, receiving $55,000 for 1182 acres of deeded land and 5200 acres of lease. Forest reserve per- mits allowed sixty-five head grazing rights on Flat Creek for 5.5 months each summer and an additional seventy-six head the chance to feed for six months of the year at the headwaters of Sullivan Creek. The offer of sale mentioned 1944 taxes totalled $374, including forest reserve and lease payments.

In addition to ranch buildings, the sale included ninety-five breeding cows, seventy-five yearlings, three bulls, forty-four two year-olds and three dry cows for a total of 220 cattle, not including eighty-three calves. Three teams of workhorses, six saddle horses and two yearling fillies also came with the ranch. Tack included three half sets of harness, seventeen collars, five pads, seven nose nets, twelve halters, six old halters, two saddles, a pack saddle and two bridles. Machinery was all horse-pow- ered, including two No. 4 John Deere enclosed gear 5' mowers (1940 and 1941), two John Deere 10' rakes (1941), two stackers, a pushpole, a sweep, a bullrake, three wagons (one low, steel wheeled), three sets sleighs (one bought November 1943), two wagon boxes, two hayracks, a democrat, a slip, a walking plough, an International 8' disc., one set tooth harrows and a No. 2. McCormick Deering cream separator.

All ranch tools went with the sale, "excepting Hudson's Bay type saddle axes of 3 lb. and under, and one breakdown Swede-saw and one fixed grip one man crosscut (these forming part of pack outfit)." The ranch included seventeen stoves and the kitchen range, Quebec heaters and a jacket water heater for the bathhouse.

"Reserved from sale all personal property, furniture, kitchen and household equipment, bedding, personal saddlery, camp, dude and packhorse outfit, excepting bunkhouse furniture and mattresses, and certain cook's room and cabin furniture and mattresses (less bedding) and all kitchen and pantry tables."[138]

George Pocaterra expressed remorse at the sale of the old place in a letter to Harper Sibley in early 1946. "Patterson sold the Buffalo Head Ranch to P. Burns and Co. I heard for $60,000.‡ Patterson has bought a place on Vancouver Island. Burns now controls almost all the valley from the O.H. Ranch (Ing's) to Marstons. The Lucks also sold to Burns, and now there remains only old Guy Weadick of the settlers we knew. 'Oh, jerum, jerum, jerum, of! quae mutatio rerum!'"[139]

---

‡ The Buffalo Head Ranch, still a working cattle ranch, reverted to Italian hands when Louis DePaoli's father bought it for him and his new wife Betty in 1949. Burns and Company parted with it for $35,000, not including stock. Ranchers still run cattle up Flat and Sullivan creeks, though the lease only allows them to graze for three months each year. The DePaoli's land holdings are about the same size as when Patterson owned the Buffalo Head. Most of the things mentioned in Patterson's bill of sale to Burns became DePaoli property when they bought the ranch in 1949. The slip is still there for moving dirt. Says Louis, "You get a team of horses in front of it, and it has two handles on it. A good way to break your neck." They used the Patterson walking plough to break up the garden. They still use the disc in the riding arena.

Life was primitive at the Buffalo Head when she and Louis arrived in January, 1950. Somehow they survived the chivaree the locals and friends threw for them and, once the house was warmed, the ranch never looked back. In some ways, little has changed since 1949. Most of the cabins and outbuildings remain and the cabins in the woods remind the visitor of the time when dudes visited each summer.

From the day the DePaolis bought the ranch, they wanted the classic Buffalo Head brand. George Pocaterra retained it his whole life and Norma held onto it after he died in 1972. So one day Louis and Betty paid Pocaterra's widow a visit in Calgary. The opera singer served them coffee so strong you could almost eat it with a spoon. When time came for negotiations, Louis was willing to go as high as $1000 for the brand, but all Norma asked was $100. "I sure gave her the hundred dollars in a hurry," said Louis when telling the story years later.[140]

Life on the DePaoli Buffalo Head Ranch has had its own unique flavour, one that Betty has typed into a diary since 1950. There are many more fascinating stories to tell, enough, perhaps, for a book called Another Buffalo Head.

Others wondered what would become of Patterson—if he would ever be content to settle down on only one piece of land. Pocaterra wrote Cochrane friend Dick Wright in May, 1946, putting his opinion on the record. "Since my last [letter] to you Patterson has left my old Buffalo head Ranch for his new place on the coast of Vancouver Island. I wonder how his restless nature will stand that most conformist and traditionalist atmosphere, and restricted environment? Last time I saw him, late in the fall, he showed me several snaps he had taken of two different places in the Columbia valley, above Golden, which he wanted to buy, but could not make up his mind which one he wanted most. P. is great at having more than one place at a time.... I somehow can't see him contented and settled down on a small site on Vancouver Island...."[141] That fall, Patterson—who had a continuing desire for a place beside the wilderness—bought a small ranch at Spillimacheen.

Though the Pattersons had officially vacated the Buffalo Head in early 1946, they left behind five horses. In October of that year Raymond and Marigold left the boys with Miss Baldwin in Victoria—Janet was on a horseback adventure of her own to Telegraph Creek in northern British Columbia—and returned to Alberta fourteen months after selling the ranch. Their plan was to leave it as they had first experienced it—on horseback.

Patterson saddled up his horses on the Buffalo Head for the last time on October 8, 1946, for the ride to the new Patterson ranch on the Columbia River. Snow covered the ground much of the way, nearly trapping them in the passes. In a letter to Dick Wright, Pocaterra pronounced his judgement on the late fall adventure. "They took their horses over the mountains from the Highwood to the Columbia in October, and they just, just made it, and with some difficulty. All I can say is that P. took an awful chance to go that way with his wife. However, all's well that ends well."[142] The Patterson's ride west was more than a crazy stunt; it was consistent with their quest for a life of great adventure in the midst of busy family routines.

They covered the first few miles in deep silence, Patterson wondering more and more why "he had been mad enough to exchange these friendly hills and meadows for a few acres of mountainside in the East Kootenay and an orchard by the sea." On the second day, deepening snow on Highwood Pass "rather shook our gay confidence.... 'If it's like this here,' we said, 'what's it going to be like on the larch plateau and the North Kananaskis Pass? Quite a bit higher, too, and in a deeper snow country. And then the Palliser—d'you think we're absolutely crazy?' A unanimous 'Yes' was the answer to that question."

"Waka Nambé and the mountains of the Divide were hidden by a swirl-ing smother of snow and cloud" as they descended to Kananaskis Lakes on the fourth morning. They decided to camp and see whether the storm cleared. Then Patterson surprised Marigold by ferreting out the key to the Kananaskis Lakes ranger station and hosting her in cozy comfort for the night. "Very soon the horses were grazing in a swampy meadow and the two humans were sitting down to afternoon tea at a real table com-plete with chairs. Outside a fine snow whirled and eddied on a roaring wind. Inside all was warm and snug."[143]

Luckily, the next day was clear as they followed the trail alongside the Kananaskis River to the forks and up the avalanche slopes. The ascent to North Kananaskis Pass was going well until Bozo, a dedicated routefinder even when not in the lead, wandered off the trail and in an attempt to rejoin the party, fell on a steep slope. Down he rolled to the edge of a cliff where "one small clump of alpine firs" arrested his fall. Patterson went to investigate and found the horse unharmed though upside down on the packs. Unpacking him, getting him back on the trail and repacking the load all took precious time.

They had hoped to reach the Palliser River that night, but just short of the pass they had to admit defeat and make the best of a bad situation. "We flung the tent down on the wind-packed snow and spread our eider-downs on top of it. I unlimbered the Swede saw and got to work on some

Marigold Patterson holding the horses on North Kananaskis Pass, October 1946.

dead larches. I built a winter fire of eight-foot logs; soon the flames were leaping high, writhing in the wind like crimson snakes. We cooked our supper on a few coals raked out from the blaze; then we sat there on the eiderdowns, warm and comfortable, idly talking, watching the shining mountains under the pale light of the moon….

"We slept—and a beastly dream held me in its grip. There was a low growling noise and I knew that a great grey bear was in camp, sniffing at this and that, coming closer and closer and I couldn't move…. I woke with a frightful start and looked around. There was no bear to be seen but the growling noise was real enough. It was coming…from the humped-up eiderdown and a pile of saddle blankets on my left. Then I knew that at least one member of the party was sleeping serenely, unperturbed by thoughts of yesterday or of the day that lay ahead."[144]

Drifts barred the route the next day and they had to rest the horses every two to three hundred yards, but with perseverance they struggled up to the pass. A fine, cold snow was falling as they floundered into British Columbia through waist-deep snow "lucky that no horse had lost his footing and gone down." After a thousand feet they ran out of snow, only to encounter an obstacle of another sort: a grizzly, that reared up on his hind legs to check them out. "The welcoming committee, do you suppose?" asked Marigold.

That was just the first of several encounters with the curiously edgy denizens of the Palliser River valley. "A madness seemed to have got into them; as the afternoon wore on the elk struck up their bugling, screaming noise…. The moose were worse. They would run past us close to the opposite bank and then, in turn, would stick their great Roman-nosed heads and massive, palmated horns through some screen of willow or small spruce, and stare—just stare silently with a thick-skulled, imbecile curiosity. Or was it menace?" Patterson ended the nonsense by shooting an elk and all the animals disappeared.[145]

Whatever it was that was bothering the wild animals seemed contagious. Patterson's horses flinched at every sound, shied from every movement and Marigold was not much better. When Patterson returned to camp that evening after harvesting the meat from the elk, he had a near-mutiny on his hands. "'Take me out of this place,' she said. 'Now. At once.'"

Try as he might, Patterson could not comfort her. He assured her that she was never in any danger and that he had been within sight of her the whole time. "'You were not. You rode straight into the sun and disappeared into the shadow of that mountain. I couldn't see a sign of you

The Royal Group from the Palliser River valley, October 1946.

against that dazzle, not even if I shaded my eyes. And all those insane things probably still watching us—and that mad horse. Get me out of here....'" A candlelit supper in a tent warmed by the little stove provided a place of solace. Still, Patterson approached the tent carefully after doing the last chores of the night.

"'Aren't you in bed yet?'"

"'Yes, I am now—all tucked up, warm and snug. Come back in.'"[146]

At the mouth of the Palliser they crossed the Kootenay, turned upstream and travelled on without incident to Spillimacheen. At Radium Hot Springs, while Patterson held the horses and looked into Sinclair Canyon, Marigold phoned interested friends in Calgary to assure them everything had ended well.

"...Ahead of us the warm glow of the sunset streamed into the western gateway of this arching canyon. In the shadow of the rocks we rode on towards it, leaving behind the Buffalo Head and the mountains that had been home to us—wondering if it had been wise to leave Alberta for this strange new province where they met you on the frontier with a grizzly and a bunch of moose and elk that ran around like mad things and stared insanely at you from the cover of the trees."[147]

Gone West: A Writing Life
1947 to 1973

RANCHING had sustained the family quite nicely through the Depression and the move west promised the chance of another ranching adventure. The Spillimacheen property was more than just a place to park the horses; it would provide an opportunity to get away from the new home on Vancouver Island at regular intervals. Not for Patterson a life tied to a house in a suburb. The place on the Columbia River promised to become a good ranch if only he could find the right man to run it. Patterson and Pocaterra had successfully repatriated Adolf Baumgart back to Canada and the new British Columbia resident had plans for the talented cowboy. "Tell Adolf for God's sake to get married and then he will be mobile. I always considered that marriage immobilised a man but then I'm looking at it from a different angle." Indeed, Patterson's letter to Pokey proved the years at the Buffalo Head had not cured his wanderlust.

It was more than itchy feet that catapulted the ex-rancher out of his chair in the pleasant house in Shoal Harbour. Edwin's suggestion of a writing career held real attraction, and good historical writing required research: an intimate knowledge of geography, a fine ear for stories and most of all, an unquenchable thirst for adventure. Many of his articles and books would rely on research collected over many years, sometimes decades. Summers, therefore, usually included not only a family holiday but also an annual foray into the wilderness and speculative jaunts throughout western Canada for fun or research.

That first summer out west, Raymond, Marigold and nine-year-old Alan left the Shoal Harbour house to the workmen and set out to explore the west coast of Vancouver Island. Up island they drove and across to Port Alberni where they encountered strange animals wandering the streets: elephants, llamas, dromedaries and other curious beasts. A circus was in town. There the Pattersons boarded the coastal ferry, the *Maquinna*, bound for Ucluelet, and the next day drove down the winding road toward Tofino—one moment surrounded by thick bush, the next coming into view of surf crashing onto a beach. "Many know of these beaches &, as usual, few ever go to see...," wrote Patterson to Pocaterra. For five days they camped on the beach in perfect weather. Patterson, of course, fell in love with the place and vowed to buy property there soon. "It was the relaxed, happy feel of that western sea that got one, I think." Driving back from Port Alberni, Patterson spied Mount Arrowsmith and returned a few days later with Miss Baldwin to climb the peak. The family then moved into the newly renovated house at Shoal Harbour as workmen finished up the last details on the house that would be the Patterson home for the next fourteen years.[1]

The Shoal Harbour house on Vancouver Island.

What with his investments, the sale of the Buffalo Head, perhaps a bit of income from the new ranch on the Columbia and even some income from fruit and vegetables from the Shoal Harbour acreage, the Pattersons hoped to retire early and in comfort. The nine acres of hay meadow and apple and prune plum orchard produced an incredible bounty. In a June, 1946, letter to Pocaterra, Patterson bragged, "Green peas, big head lettuce & new potatoes out of the garden here & I hooked & caught a 19.5 lb. Salmon." But tellingly he went on to say, "but I prefer the mountains to the roses & strawberries."

Family members also entertained themselves on the property in the Columbia River valley, where the horses grazed in another Eden called

Marigold Patterson working in her garden at Shoal Harbour, October 1949.

Spillimacheen. Plans for a ranch never took hold, so it was used as a centre for hunting and riding trips. Patterson bought a 14-foot Chestnut canoe and used it to hunt ducks on the upper Columbia.

Toward the end of the 1940s, the exchange on the Patterson's English investments suffered owing to the devaluation of the pound sterling and exchange controls, and their income dropped by 50%. As a result, they sold the Spillimacheen property and consolidated their real estate holdings at the single Vancouver Island property. Patterson also went to work as a seasonal surveyor for a couple of years.[2]

Robin and Alan Patterson messing about with the rowboat, Shoal Harbour, 1952.

Patterson would later write of Samuel Black's personality profile in the infamous H.B.C. Character Book: "Desperate ventures are best placed in the charge of desperate men.... Those who fit neatly into the routine of an old-established trading post, who are content with a humdrum business life or who venerate the jargon and the ponderous processes of the law, are best left at home."[3] The adventures that filled the next three decades of Patterson's life called for just such an obstinate personality. Luckily for him, television and the theatre had not yet eclipsed a good adventure story. Hundreds of thousands of readers would wait with bated breath as his pencil scratched its way across paper.

Patterson's third career began in earnest when *The Beaver* brought out his first article "River of Deadmen's Valley" in its June, 1947, issue. Written from memories nearly twenty years old, and spiced with quotes from the diaries and illustrated with his own photos and specially drafted maps, the South Nahanni piece was a precursor to the book *The Dangerous River*. Columbia University's history professor Dr. J. B. Brebner, a Rhodes scholar and friend from Oxford days, had introduced Patterson to *Beaver* editor Clifford P. Wilson, and Patterson's prose did the rest. And so began the writing career of a gentleman with many lifetimes of stories to tell.

Immediately after the article appeared, Fenley Hunter wrote Patterson, upbraiding him for not mentioning he had been on the South Nahanni in the summer of 1927. Until 1947, Hunter had been under the impression his trip to The Falls of the Nahanni in 1928 was a first for a white man, and that his photos of the cascade were the first ever taken. The 1927 photos of The Gate, the incredible canyons and the Falls themselves must have shocked and dismayed the self-possessed explorer.[4]

Public reaction to the piece overwhelmed Wilson and in September he wrote, "I think an article on your trip between Ft. St. John and the Sikanni Chief sounds like a good idea. If you could have heard the comments I heard on your Nahanni article, I am sure you would sit right down at your typewriter and pound it out."[5]

Patterson, of the old school, never pounded anything out on a typewriter. In fact, he never learned to type. Instead, in beautiful, carefully stylized printing, he wrote out his manuscripts by hand. The left-hand page of each spread in a notebook he kept blank for notes and corrections. Granddaughter Julia, Janet's only child, recalls that Patterson's work habits were regular and "he was usually in his study or busy at something when I visited there."[6] In this manner he began a series of articles for *The Beaver* that included a review of a return trip to the Nahanni, retracing explorer Butler's steps on the Omineca River and accounts of trips on the Liard and Peace rivers. Payment of between $200 and $250 followed the publication of each article. The last *Beaver* article appeared in the Summer issue of 1961.[7]

British readers were the next ones blessed with stories from Patterson's pencil. *Country Life*, a "Journal for all interested in country life and country pursuits," printed "Trails of the Canadian West" in its June 25, 1948, issue. "The green years have gone by, and there are so many pictures to choose from...," began Patterson's review of hidden spots. "Poplar seed and butterflies flickered between the shadow and the sun, a moose stood in the shallows, a man drew his canoe on to a sand bar and lit his evening fire." For three pages he wrote about ranching, exploring rivers, packing into forgotten valleys and through unknown passes, always searching for new places to explore. Five photos illustrated the text, all vintage Patterson: the Boundary Pine, The Gate, Upper Kananaskis River, Horses at a Lake, Matthews dogsledding on the South Nahanni.

Twenty-five months later, the July 28, 1950, edition featured a story titled "A Thousand Miles by Canoe." The four page article, illustrated with seven photos and a map, told of a journey in 1949 from the headwaters of the Parsnip River north of Prince George down the Peace River to the town of the same name in Alberta. This extended trip also scouted out the Finlay River, the Peace's other major tributary, necessary field research that enabled Patterson to write various pieces including the introduction to Samuel Black's 1824 Journal and his 1968 book, *Finlay's River*.

Mentor at the Bank of England and warm friend Sir Edward Peacock wrote in August, "I have just read your article in Country Life of July 28th with the greatest pleasure. I congratulate you on a first class story, told in just the right way. It is direct, moves swiftly on, avoiding side issues—it is told simply but vividly. The best piece of yours that I have seen—more power to your words.... I hope you & Marigold are enjoying life. My love to her and my best to you."[8]

Letters from Peacock always included solid advice on whatever topic Patterson sought counsel. For example, when Raymond considered sending Alan to England in the late 1940s, the Canadian blood in Peacock rankled at the suggestion. "You speak of Alan's schooling and the question whether he should come to England or not. I have no hesitation whatever in saying that he should not come to an English school. After the life that he has led, it would be in any event dull and uninteresting to him; under existing conditions in England it would be worse than that. Everybody suffers from inhibitions on every subject, and a boy who has led as free a life in as free a country as Alan I think would find it almost unendurable."[9]

Peacock's affection for the younger man reflected the fact he had almost become Patterson's stepfather. According to Janet, the man later knighted by the Queen courted Raymond's mother for a time, but eventually married her cousin, Katherine Coates, instead. Born in Ontario in 1871, he attended university where he excelled at philosophy and political economy. After quitting teaching school in 1902, he joined Dominion Securities in Toronto who transferred him to London in 1907. There he rose in financial circles and in 1921 became the first Canadian appointed to the Bank of England. He also held positions on the board of the Canadian Pacific Railway and the Hudson's Bay Company. Unable to have children, the Peacocks adopted two daughters formally and treated Raymond as a son. Sir Edward died in 1962, but not before encouraging Patterson's writing career in many ways.

Another influence from England was those monthly *Blackwood's Magazines*. Year after year they came as a gift from Jim Bennett. "Blackwood's Magazine—A Scottish literary magazine founded in 1817, was strongly Tory in its political sympathies and violently opposed in its literary outlook to the so-called Cockney School of poets. John Gibson Lockhart and James Hogg were well-known and influential members of Blackwood's staff."[10]

Although Patterson was busy with many canoe trips in the late 1940s, he found time to write an article called "Back Door to the Mackenzie." G. D. Blackwood himself was so kind as to write the rejection letter personally on March 7, 1950. The article was too long, exceeding their maximum of 6000 words, but his comments were encouraging. Two years later Blackwood accepted the revised manuscript, retitled "Interlude on the Sikanni Chief," for publication. It ran as the lead article in the July, 1952, edition and at a rate of £2.2.0 per magazine page, netted Patterson about £30.[11]

Peacock's letter in April, 1954, complimented his friend on his next *Blackwood's Magazine* article, titled "Fort Simpson, McKenzie's River." For the March, 1955, edition, Patterson described the fur trade post as he found it after struggling in from the winter cabin on the South Nahanni. Antics of life came alive in this partial retelling of the story that would become *The Dangerous River*. The article ended with Patterson climbing on board the Fokker Super-Universal and leaving the North in 1929 to wed Marigold in London. "You know, Gordon, there's a sort of miserable fascination about this northern country." His trapping partner replied, "There is, old man." Patterson looked him straight in the eye and said, "One will probably be back." "One probably will," said the man Patterson did not see again until 1938. Ranching and tight money prevented the friends from meeting again in the North until the early 1950s.

Five more articles by Patterson appeared in *Blackwood's*, the last in 1960. "The Beaches of Lukannon" in 1957 brought to life the discovery of the Pribylov Islands in the Bering Sea in 1741, and the sealing trade that developed in the area as a result. "Springtime in the Rockies" in 1958, described life at the Buffalo Head and "The Calgary Road," "The Foothill City" and "The Bow River," all in 1960, expanded upon the fascinating world the Pattersons experienced in southern Alberta. Many of these articles appeared later in his book *Far Pastures.*

Appearing in 1951 as a privately printed edition of only seventy-five copies was a seventy-eight page booklet bearing the title *Dear Mother: A Collection of Letters Written from Rossall Between May 1911 and March 1917 by R. M. Patterson.* Dedicated to his Housemaster of Maltese Cross House, A. B. Kingsford, Esq., it states at the bottom of the title page, "'Let us now praise famous men'—Men of little showing." The edited collection of letters home constitutes a fascinating perspective of life at a British public school just before the Great War and served as much of the research for Chapter 1 in this book. Patterson's 1951 commentary reflects on his personality while at school and explains the nature of his friendship with his beloved Mother. The letters arrived at Vancouver Island "in the drawer of a little escritoire that once stood in a corner of the drawing room of my Mother's flat in Prince's Gate." He wrote the introduction on June 6, 1951, from a ranch near Fort Macleod, Alberta.

Always on the lookout for a way to get back into the potentially profitable ranching business, Patterson joined his cousin Robert Coates and major investor E. M. Wilkinson of Calgary in the purchase of Big Coulee Ranch in early 1951. The place came well equipped with horses and 740 head of Hereford cattle for a total price of over $275,000. To Patterson fell the task of arranging financing for 20%. "There will be a lot of work to start with," he wrote in a letter to Curtis Smith, "routine calving of 300 cows and heifers and the branding in early June. Rebuilding of corrals, re-organisation of the whole place, dehorning of 160 yearlings that should have been dehorned a year ago—a literally bloody job—and a hundred other things."

Cattle prices were strong enough to support wages for Patterson as part-time general manager, his cousin Robert Coates as manager of day to day operations and Adolf Baumgart as foreman.

All went well for a time. Later that summer Patterson guided Smith to the Falls of the Nahanni, then returned to the ranch for the remainder of the year. Slowly the ranch began turning into a farm and the rancher gradually worked himself out of a job. In 1953 Patterson sold out to Coates and returned to Vancouver Island. As luck would have it, foot and mouth disease broke out, cattle prices dropped, and all concerned—the Bank of Montreal included—suffered financially.

Not all was doom and gloom during this period. Summer trips on northern British Columbia rivers in 1948 (the Stikine, Dease and Liard) and 1949 (the Parsnip, Peace and Finlay), prompted Patterson to send written accounts of these expeditions to friends, including Peacock. As a member of the executive committee of the Hudson's Bay Records Publication Board, Patterson's mentor knew of its plans to publish an edited version of Samuel Black's journal of exploration on the Finlay River in 1824. Who better to write the introduction to that volume than a man with all the kinks of the river fresh in his mind? So Peacock forwarded Patterson's letter recounting his Finlay River trip to the honorary secretary of the society, R. A. Reynolds, and encouraged his friend to take on the task. General editor E. E. Rich of St. Catharine's College, Cambridge, most pleased with Peacock's recommendation, responded, "it is clear that Patterson could fill in the topographical commentary with a real personal interest." He also asked Peacock to formally request Patterson's participation in the project.[12]

As with all demanding research projects, the writer must complete months or years of exhaustive investigation before setting pencil to paper. But, finally, in 1955, The Hudson's Bay Records Society published *A Journal of a Voyage From Rocky Mountain Portage in Peace River To the Sources of Finlay's Branch And North West Ward In Summer 1824* by Samuel Black, edited by Rich and assisted by Hudson's Bay Company archivist A. M. Johnson. The title page acknowledged a ninety-eight page introduction by R. M. Patterson. In the preface Rich wrote, "Mr. Patterson, bringing to his task the enthusiasm and the knowledge of one who had himself travelled the same route, has without any doubt put the Journal, the journey, and Samuel Black into their correct relations." Because libraries and academics were the main recipients of the subscription-only volumes, less than a thousand copies of Patterson's first seriously researched publication reached the library shelf. Dr. Douglas Leechman read the volume with great interest. As president of the Glenbow Foundation, he wrote Patterson immediately to commend him on the project. Patterson wrote Pocaterra, "I'm glad he was pleased-writing that d___ introduction took me, on & off, four years of work & correspondence & was worse than writing 2½ ordinary books."[13]

Publication in 1954 of Patterson's most famous book, *The Dangerous River*, predated the release of Black's journal, but Patterson's work on his blockbuster apparently began during or after he had completed the introduction to the fur trader's diary. He loved its success, but its popularity puzzled him. In fact, he had tossed off the manuscript between other assignments to fulfil a demand by various friends, acquaintances and several complete strangers. Its conception came in the dark at the old Alberta ranch. Almost thirty years later, when friend and publisher Gray Campbell sent over a flagon of Chivas for Patterson's 80th birthday, the author responded with a complete account of that whiskey's affect on his life, "it was really the Father of The Dangerous River. On summer evenings, around eleven p.m. when the zoo had all gone to bed, [regular ranch visitor and friend] Jim Bennett & I used to foregather by a certain window in the Buffalo Head livingroom well equipped with a bottle of Chivas, glasses, soda water, & ice—a block from the ice-house neatly split, out on the lawn, by me with a sharp axe.

"Thus equipped we would go at it—& it wd. not be long before J.B. had me telling stories of the Nahanni country & all that went with that. He loved them. They opened up a new world for him.

"Then he began badgering me. 'You must write these things down!' he wd. say. 'Write one for my favourite magazine, anyway: Blackwood's Magazine.'

"'Oh, I might, someday. But I doubt if I could.'

"Bennett would go on urging. Then he put me on the Blackwood's mailing list, he had enjoyed his times on the Buffalo Head so much. And he never came without several bottles of Chivas, a bonanza in a wartime, rationed world.

"Finally I yielded. I had to wait for hours between the boat from Victoria & the departure of the bus from Seattle one mid-winter's night [probably in early 1951 while travelling to the Fort Macleod ranch in southern Alberta from Victoria]. Forewarned of this, I took an old notebook along to while away the time. And there, in the Seattle Bus Depot I sat, lost to the awfulness around me, & writing a story about the Sikanni Chief River in northern British Columbia....

"But now you have it all, set down in a fair hand—pretty fair, anyway—just how telling stories in the old B.H. living room, inspired by Jim Bennett's liberal doses of that great whiskey, somehow dragged out The D.R. By means of whiskey & sheer bullying.

"P.S. In 1954, when The D.R. was published & I sent him a copy, Jim Bennett said he had had to work harder to get that book out than for almost anything in his business career. He claimed unofficial proprietary rights in it, & wrote rude things about 'getting blood out of a stone,' & 'I told you so.'"[14]

To read the octogenarian's words, one would think he just dashed off the classic, sent it to the publisher, and watched royalty cheques flow into the bank. But even this most charmed of projects involved considerable research. Sir Peacock received regular letters from Patterson and often encouraged him to write more. "Your letters have always been quite exceptionally interesting and good, and your life of course is quite out of the ordinary and of interest to almost anyone who lives in a more humdrum part of the world. I think you ought seriously to consider the question of writing an account of your part of the country, the life there, and particularly your own experiences, not with an eye on the publisher but just with the kind of zest which prompts these admirable and lively descriptions in your letters to your friends. Think it over and try a note every now and then, keeping them together until you get a collection, and then see how they look—& let us see also!"[15]

In 1951 Patterson landed a job guiding Curtis Smith of St. Albans, Vermont, to The Falls of the Nahanni, a return engagement that would enable him to do further research for the book. Fenley Hunter apparently knew Smith and had recommended the author as a suitable guide. "My old friend, Raymond Patterson, is a wonderful man and a wonder with fast water, even with a leaky, rigid canoe which I think he bailed with a frying pan."[16] Hunter's character reference for Smith was guarded. "Fine personality and most enthusiastic about the Nahanni, decisive, but after all it's your decision. Rex Beach once wrote me 'You never know a man until you eat a sack of flour with him' and there is a lot of truth in that."[17]

With financial problems nagging at the family bank account, Patterson hesitated when Smith first approached him about the venture. "As to my coming along (if 52 years has not put that out of court) I want to thank you very much for the offer." Patterson helped Smith with the logistics, arranged food and even secured the services of a local to transport the men and canoes to the Falls by motorized scow. "I cannot tell you how much I appreciate your offer. I will do all I can to help you organise, and if I can I would like to come...."[18] Once committed to the venture, he even sacrificed his stomach to the cause. "I found some canned 'pemmican' in Seattle & brought a small tin back—Emergency K V it called itself. Yesterday, in the interests of science & the Nahanni-farers, I ate it warmed up with a little butter. No meat in it—rather like a Christmas pudding with split peanuts through it—but dynamite is an understatement. I feel confident of recovery—& one K V will last me a lifetime." By this time, hunting was prohibited in the South Nahanni (it was part of the Mackenzie Mountains Game Reserve), so they had to pack every ounce of nutrition into the food they took.[19] Patterson's recipe for bannock became standard fare on this return trip to the South Nahanni.‡

Smith's plans for the trip changed with time. He originally intended a party of five with Patterson as the guide. In the end, his sons and others dropped out, leaving only himself and a recently resigned F.B.I. agent, Frank C. Woods from Burlington, Vermont. For scientific reasons, Smith brought along a Geiger counter that weighed ten pounds, and to record the highlights, a Bell & Howell 16-mm movie camera. Patterson met them on Friday, July 13, at Fort Nelson airport, near the Hudson's Bay Company Landing where canoes awaited them, one 16 feet long and the other an 18 or 20 foot freighter. In weather that reminded Patterson of the glorious summer of 1927, they sped north down Fort Nelson River,[20] then east down the Liard to Nahanni Butte where they arrived on Thursday, July 19. There, "Curtis made a deal with Fred Sibbeston & his helper David McPherson to take us & the outfit to the Falls & back to the Flat." Sibbeston told Patterson that muskrats had become a nuisance to river boats on the Mackenzie. Under the cover of darkness they often pulled the caulking out of scows, sinking them by morning.

Smith and Woods did not always get along with their guide, but for the most part the trip was a success. After visiting the falls, they returned to the Flat River. On Tuesday, August 7, Patterson renewed his

---

‡ PATTERSON'S BANNOCK RECIPE

2 cups flour
1 big tablespoon lard
1 big tablespoon sugar
1 1/2 teaspoon salt
3 teaspoons baking powder
almost 1 cup water
have frying pan buttered & bake slowly

friendship with the old Minnesota trapper at Irvine Creek. "In all that lonely country there was, as usual, only one man in that summer of 1951—my old friend, Albert Faille, the man who had taught me the ways of a canoe. And equally as usual, nobody knew where he was, and no man, white or Indian, had set eyes on him for a year. Situation absolutely normal."[21] Inadvertently, Faille had been in the wolf business that summer. Seven had tried to get him; all became carcasses. Some were quite large, "brutes the size of Shetland ponies" was how Patterson described them.[22]

The next day the men caught huge fish for breakfast. "Dollies caught in this pool with up to six mice, one fish & one salamander in them."

Sometimes, Smith and Woods took side trips, a pleasant change for Patterson. On August 28 he wrote in his diary, "Up at six & it straightaway began to rain. Rained on & off with cold wind. Good breakfast—porridge, bacon, trout, bannock, hot cakes. Baked bannock." He then wrote a quirky little story, perhaps suitable bedtime reading for some brave child.‡

September 13 found Patterson and his clients back on the Liard River, headed for Fort Nelson. Ed Cooper ran them upstream from Nahanni Butte on his 44-foot boat powered by a 93 h.p. Chrysler Marine pushing a 47-foot scow. En route they stopped in at Netla River trading post where

---

‡ "The Princess was very sleepy.

"As so was the Lady Daffodillia.

"'And in the cave lived six little dwarfs' she was saying, '& they all had funny red hats & ugly damned great noses & then all had everything alike—six porridge bowls & six wash basins.'

"'What were the washbowls for?' said the Princess sleepily. She had been bathed in her lovely bath of mother of pearl, & had had the outer coat of grime, at least, successfully removed with the royal scrubbing brush. And now she was listening, with one eye open & one eye shut, to her bedtime story.

"'—six washbowls &—er towels...' went on the Lady Daffodillia, nodding, & bashing her nose on the cot rail in consequence.

"'I said, WHAT were the washbowls FOR?' the Princess broke in peevishly.

"'For washing in, of course, dear,' said the Lady Daffodillia.

"'Then why in hell couldn't you say so the first time?' said the Princess, & inadvertently closed both eyes.

"'I think you're getting sleepy, darling,' said the Lady Daffodillia. She tucked the Princess carefully in & tiptoed gently out of the royal nursery, slamming the door behind her with a crash that fetched down two expensive Corots & several yards of plaster in the upper gallery, & sent the King's state crown tumbling off the hat rack in the hall below.

"'Pesky little b-h!' muttered the Lady Daffodillia, smiling tenderly—an untimely reverie, since, at that very moment, she tripped over a fallen Corot & holed out in one, landing with a torn skirt and a rip snorting, grenadier's oath on the hall floor right at the feet of the Lord High Chancellor...."

they were greeted with open arms by trader Dick Turner "a very pleasant fellow." It was the beginning of a long friendship.

"Late in the evening, after coming up the Flint Rapids, & by the light of an almost full moon & an average aurora, I made my bed up by the bollards, coiled rope & cases of lubricant on the forward deck of the scow that Cooper's boat is pushing. A magnificent bed platform—I lay there & watched the Mackenzie Mountains march by to the rhythm of the swinging stars. Soon the swish of the water sent me off to sleep."

Monday, September 17 was their last day together. Patterson wrote, "Perfect morning. Negotiated the bar & proceeded, with further bars & riffles, towards Nelson. Packed gear, & had late lunch—finally arrived at H.B. Co. landing below airport, at about 3.0 p.m.

"Photos taken:—156 colour stills, 132 black & whites."[23]

Smith, disappointed at not finding Strontium 90, the reason for the Geiger counter, was to return four years later to continue the search.

Back home, Patterson quickly condensed the thirty-five pages of trip notes and stories into an eight-page article with ten photos that appeared in the June, 1952, edition of *The Beaver* as "Nahanni Revisited." On that trip he saw The Falls of the Nahanni in sun for the first time, a rainbow arched in front of them. The old cabin he had shared with Matthews was gone, washed away by a change in the channel they called Wheatsheaf Creek. Fresh fire scars annoyed him, as did the garbage they encountered everywhere. "Homo sapiens, it seemed, had been trying to ascend the Nahanni that very summer, and his traces greeted us when we landed to make camp at Twisted Mountain. Before this was possible Frank and I had to burn or heave into the river a collection of cartons, newspapers and tin cans that would have done credit to any National Park campground in tourist season. Civilisation was evidently coming closer...."

Blackwood's Magazine published his "Interlude on the Sikanni Chief" in the July, 1952, issue. The reaction to the two articles was enough to send any author into seclusion in glee. On June 26, 1952, the director of George Allen & Unwin Ltd., Publishers & Exporter of London, wrote Patterson c/o Blackwood & Sons. "Your article in Blackwood's 'Interlude on the Sikanni Chief' makes us wonder whether you have not sufficient material of this sort for a complete book? ...If you are thinking of writing at greater length we should very much like to see the typescript and it would be much in our line." Before the month of publication was over, Patterson had replied with a package of photographs and a suggestion that the book should cover his northern explorations and life on the ranch southwest of Calgary. The publisher wrote back on July 18, "At first glance, we agree with you that most of the book would consist of the account of your 'Dead Men's Valley' and 'Buffalo Head Ranch' periods. However, we shall write to you again as soon as we have had the opportunity of thinking the thing out more carefully." A July 25 letter asked for a couple of chapters upon which to form an opinion and wondered if he had thought of a title.[24]

This was heady stuff for a man whose ranching business was a bit down in the dumps and whose other investments were withering. But there was more. Helen King, associate editor for William Morrow & Company, Inc., Publishers of New York, was a bit slower off the mark, not writing until October. She more than made up for her slow start with compliments on Patterson's work, sight unseen. "J. B. Brebner has spoken to me in the most glowing terms about your work, and I am writing to inquire if you have a book in mind, and if so may we see it when it is completed.... I confess that my request springs from blind faith in Brebner's words, for I have not had the pleasure of seeing your published articles. I believe you are being published by Black [sic] in London, and if you do not have an agent then I should like to write to them expressing my interest. Will you let me know?"[25]

With so much mail coming from publishers for forwarding to Patterson, G. D. Blackwood was kicking himself. "I most certainly remember 'Interlude on the Sikanni Chief' and the only regret I now have is that my firm did not make the same suggestion to you as Allen & Unwin. I should have been quicker off the mark!"[26]

In the months that followed letters flew back and forth between London and New York and Shoal Harbour. The British publisher warned Patterson to stay clear of his American counterpart, while Peacock steered him away from the London company. Sensing a competition in the making, Patterson took money from both. The resulting batch of letters makes an interesting peek into the intrigues of the publishing world. In a letter dated May, 1953, the British publisher tried to force Patterson to change the name of the book to "The Silence and the Sun," "because it reads so well." It offered as a subtitle: "Adventure on and Around the River of the People who Speak like Ducks." They also suggested including maps on the end sheets.[27]

Meanwhile, Patterson wrote madly. The little South Nahanni diaries came in handy, as did the collection of letters he wrote Mother and Edwin that were later returned. Taking stolen moments, he wrote

Matthews, Pocaterra and others with detailed questions. Gordon, who was most helpful, answering everything thoughtfully, then extended an invitation, "Why not come over & we can jam in the peace & quietness together, whole bloody tribe away. Dick home late to sleep, Michael same. Eat cheese, beer, kitchen table, no fuss, few dishes, no manners, wot you say eh?" In spite of such distractions, Patterson completed the book in the fall of 1953, and dedicated it to Gordon.[28] As was his wont, he wrote the foreword last on October 6, and sent the typescript off to two distant addresses.

The London and New York publishers both released *The Dangerous River* in 1954. The London edition demanded subsequent printings in each of the next three years, the 1957 product being the first paperback. The New York publisher followed up its inaugural volume with another for the Outdoor Life Book Club in 1955. A Dutch translation titled *Dodemansvallei* came out from Prisma-Boeken about the same time and Editorial Hispano-Europea of Barcelona released *Rio Peligroso* in Spanish in 1955. Fellow Vancouver Islander and publisher Gray Campbell released the first Canadian edition in 1966 with reprints in 1969, 1972 and 1980. Since then, numerous editions and reprints of the book have come off the press. It has never been out of print.

Response to the book was immediate, positive and widespread. Dozens of clippings fill the Patterson files in the British Columbia Archives in Victoria. From England came glowing reviews published in *The Times*, *East Anglian Daily Times* of Ipswich, *Times Literary Supplement* and *Yachting Monthly*, to name a few. *The New Yorker*, the *New York Times* and the *Carmel Pine Cone-Cymbal* of Carmel, California, gave it similar praise in the United States. In Canada it was recommended by the *Winnipeg Free Press*, and closest to home, by the *Victoria Daily Times*, which reviewed the book on Thursday, October 21, 1954, in an article written by Pierre Berton titled "Headless Valley Mysteries Pooh-Pooh-ed by Rancher Guide." Tony Dickason wrote, "'Who,' said R. M. Patterson, who has a book coming out on the entire area October 27, 'ever heard of a valley without a head?'"

To review the book for its summer issue *The Beaver* chose none other than P. G. Downes, a Harvard-educated school teacher whose solo canoe trip through northern Manitoba and the eastern Northwest Territories in 1939 was captured in his 1941 classic, *Sleeping Island*. So when he wrote, "With honesty and admirable frankness, Mr. Patterson reveals himself as an able and remarkably fortunate wilderness traveller," the reader had good reason to believe the volume was worth a read. "The physical battle itself [against the Dangerous River] is told with such detail that this reader for one breathed a sigh of relief that Mr. Patterson ever got out alive." Downes concluded, "This is an exciting, virile, technically absorbing account of a skilful and courageous feat of northern travel.... As a final triumph, how many readers can put this down without wishing Mr. Patterson would poke into the same region again."

The spiritual father of the project sent his praise, though, ever the gentleman, Jim Bennett never mentioned his role in the affair. "I was talking the other day to General Sir Neil Ritchie about Blackwood's and he mentioned your article on the seals [The Beaches of Lukanon]. I asked him if he had seen your book 'Dangerous River' he replied 'Indeed I have, once I started reading it I couldn't put it down.' This is in line with what other friends have said about your book. It should have a large circulation. I hope it has."[29]

The other legitimate influence on the bestseller was Sir Edward Peacock. "I have now read 'The Dangerous River' and can say to you without any qualification that it is a splendid book. I found it absorbingly interesting from start to finish and thought it all exceedingly well done. I do hope it will have a success. It certainly ought to. What an adventurous life you have been able to crowd into the intervals between more prosaic things! Don't press it too far."[30]

Then came the personal notes from friends and acquaintances. Pocaterra wrote from his second home in Calgary, thanking his friend for the complimentary volume, "I pick up 'Dangerous River' every now and then, in times of leisure, and I find it like a dip into the Past. I was reading over some paragraphs a short hour ago, and I felt a sudden and almost overwhelming sensation, what the German call 'Sehnen,' a much stronger and deeper-down and more lasting kind of longing for that kind of life I have known for some thirty years of my life, that feeling of being on one's own entirely, under primeval conditions, unaffected by the turmoil of human passions, of greed, self-seeking, akin to the first nomads, making their first way into totally new lands. You certainly have captured that feeling, and I have never enjoyed reading a book of the kind as much as yours, the descriptive style is simply wonderful. One lives with you through your experiences...."[31]

In a return letter to Pokey, Patterson mentioned he had received a letter from Spike Hunt, "welcoming me into the ranks of the 'finest & most unprofitable profession in the world—the writers of non-fiction.' He seemed to be happy.... He was all for something on the Highwood-Eden Valley—he says 'the material would be inexhaustible.'"[32]

Another valued reaction came from farther north. Vera Turner wrote from their new trading post at the mouth of the South Nahanni on January 4, 1955, "Dick is reading at it now and we hear laughs and comments coming from him. He's getting a great 'kick' out of it." Six days later Dick added: "As you probably know from my ornery nature, I am very critical of everything I read, but I have no averse criticism at all to offer of Dangerous River."[33]

Curtis Smith wrote, "The news of your book is stupendous. You know I shall always claim a certain responsibility.... I can recall, in my innocence I once sent you a book on how to write, as if one could grasp the art like downing a cocktail."[34]

But the reaction he valued the most came from his old friend Faille. Well into his seventh decade, Faille wrote using his own unique dictionary:

Dear Patterson.

I was plest to rosevd the Book yu sound mie thanks lot for the book i rid the book ridewaysur an mad me yong agen brod like all manners long ago wn wie bot was yung on tof on frst time on the Daengrus river.

I shul rite runer bot you now hou i am en riteng do dam god i resived letter from Curtis an wont mi and Yus Kraus to go an luk in to a prospect i found gers ago so i am going op nex sumer i am teaking aerop And place for the winter hilbec en Vancouver boy now an stping at Angelus Hotel winter her es coll bot no snow to speicof i weant op river to geth wood Moris almost raicp the camp nok the run over step en the frieng pan ocn eth the salt.

I am fileng fine hope yu an yur Famelle is the saem.

Yours truley,

Albert Faille[35]

From Ottawa came a letter on the official-looking letterhead of The Association of Canadian Clubs, dated October 11, 1956. Its national director, Eric Morse, is well known to all historians as well as to paddlers of Canadian waters for his seminal work *Fur Trade Canoe Routes of Canada—Then and Now*. First published in 1969, it lists some of Patterson's writings in a section titled "Suggested Voyageur Reading." Born in 1904, Morse was Patterson's contemporary and well placed to comment on *The Dangerous River*.

Dear Mr. Patterson,

I have just finished reading your book 'Dangerous River' and, though I do not recall ever having done this before, I feel I must write the author to say how very much I enjoyed it. It is the best tale I have read for many a month. I went straight out and bought a copy.

I am one of a party of six who spend our summer holidays retracing the old explorers' routes by canoe across Canada.

Cameron Ware, who I believe is a mutual friend, tells me you are in Sydney. It is likely that I shall be in Victoria again during the course of the next year, and if so I should like very much to meet you if it could be conveniently arranged. I will be sure to let you know when I know my travelling plans.

Congratulations once more on the book.

Yours sincerely

Eric W. Morse[36]

Although Patterson would make many new friends through his books, one famous Canadian would never become his close acquaintance. Liberal Prime Minister Pierre Elliot Trudeau flew to The Falls of the Nahanni in the summer of 1970, and though an avid paddler with a birchbark canoe in his private collection, motor-boated out to Nahanni Butte at the mouth of the river. Later that year he wrote Mrs. G. C. F. Dalziel of Watson Lake.

Dear Mrs. Dalziel:

It was thoughtful of you to remember that I did not have time to explore the Nahanni River in great depth last August.

I am looking forward to reading Mr. Patterson's book, The Dangerous River, which, I am sure, will provide me with a wealth of information. I would be grateful to you if you would kindly convey my grateful thanks to your friend, Mr. Patterson, who has kindly inscribed his book to me.

Will you please accept my warm thanks and best regards.

Sincerely,

P. E. Trudeau"[37]

When contacted in 1996 for an impression of the area, the late former prime minister recalled, "I had done some reading about the Nahanni in the years before I visited the river, and I came to it with high expectations,—which were to be amply fulfilled....

"As to your question about the creation of the Park, I remember that my enthusiasm for the idea developed when I came off the river at Nahanni Butte, and heard that prospecting for oil had already begun in the area."[38]

As a dyed-in-the-wool Conservative, Patterson never marked an "X" anywhere near this prime minister's name on the voting ballot, but when it came to preserving this wonderful wilderness river, Patterson and Trudeau were of one mind. Both were instrumental in helping create the South Nahanni National Park Reserve in 1971.

Patterson did not rely on accolades to feed his spirit. He already had an interesting six week trip planned for the late summer of 1954. He ordered a 20-foot Ogilvy Special Canoe from the Chestnut Canoe Company, complete with square stern and keel at a total cost of $208.00, and had it transported to Dawson Creek, B.C., where British Yukon Navigation loaded it on a truck bound for Fort Nelson.[39] There, he set off for the Nahanni again, this time accompanied by twenty-seven year-old cousin Christopher Paterson who was related by marriage through the Coates side of the family. Down the Fort Nelson River they motored to the Liard where they turned upstream and motored through Hell's Gate to the mouth of the Beaver—Patterson's objective. They explored the narrower valley by tracking, then it was back down the Liard to the South Nahanni where they hiked to the top of Nahanni Butte for an impressive view of the Splits. Christopher, an active fisherman and outdoorsman, remembers working hard to keep up with fifty-six year-old Patterson. After visiting with the Turners on the Netla, they hitched a ride on Dick's river boat to Fort Simpson where they connected with Albert Faille, a man Christopher later described as an "understated guy."

On the long trip back to Fort Nelson the weather turned cold with snow flurries. In a letter dated the next January, Dick Turner wrote, "We were glad to hear from you and that Raymond and Christopher got to Nelson without too much trouble. I had no idea that you spent the night not far from the mouth here. We heard the kicker that evening and the next day but thought it was someone going up from Simpson. Did we hear a few words of comment on the motor drifting to us on the evening breeze? I understand that dogs and kickers are conducive to such things."[40]

Back at Shoal Harbour, Patterson received a stream of emotional letters from the Italian on the Ghost River. Pocaterra was back into the coal mining business in the Kananaskis. For the time being, dudes would have to wait while he sought the shiny black gold. Norma's operatic career was making a comeback of sorts, as a voice teacher in Calgary. And Pokey had got run off the road by a gasoline truck, of all things, his Jeep rolling a few times in the ditch. Gentleman that he was, the truck driver had helped retrieve the vehicle. But mostly, Pocaterra was showing Norma the life he had come to love in the Canadian west. Longing to be there in 1937, he had written Patterson, "Oh, I am longing for some of my old camping places, and to show Norma that kind of a life too. Curious isn't it, that I, an Italian born, should be wanting to show Norma, a Canadian, a feature of purely Canadian life!"[41]

During this period Pokey got wind of Patterson's visit to the South Nahanni and encouraged his old friend to allow others in on the riches promised by a flashy mineral on the Nahanni—copper. Ever since the late 1920s, Patterson had been vague about his success as a prospector and many suspected he was just waiting for the right time to cash in on his discoveries. When Pocaterra mentioned the project to friends, they asked, "'...would your friend agree to give us as close a description of the location as he could, make an agreement with us for an interest if we succeed, and let us have a try at it?' So here it is for you to decide. These people ARE competent, and I have found them reliable and go-getters."[42] Patterson replied the next month. "Regarding the Caribou Hole, my hands are not entirely free. I can explain better when I see you which, I hope, will be sometime in the coming year...."[43] We may never know the reason for the secrecy, or whose commitments had Patterson's hands so tightly tied.

In May, 1955, promoter Curtis Smith was writing Patterson every few days, trying to convince him to return to the Nahanni and show the American and his geologists some of the choicer mineral finds at Prairie Creek and up the Flat River and at Irvine Creek. "On advice of counsel I am forming a Quebec company of 50,000 shares to be known as the Nahanni Mining Company to take the business out of my personal hands.... My associates and I, including Kraus, Faille, you and Gordon and all my family will have 50% interest. Having spent much of my own money and considerable time and effort, I am taking the lion's share. I hope you don't mind. If the thing is good at all, you will have enough for free so you will need worry no longer.

"'Bornite,' my friend, is an extremely rich copper ore, better than 50%. There may very well be Bornite there, but the sample you gave me, says Mr. Ledoux, is naught but lowly zinc of a high quality. But even lowly zinc is very desirable."[44]

Smith continued the coaxing throughout June. "I also sense that you and Gordon don't want to disclose any of the possible 'finds' which you made during your trip together. With this I can sympathise, but in spite of the size of the area, I feel you are wrong in your supposition that no one will find them. To-day I received a letter that Kennecott and Shell Oil both have gasoline caches at Skin Boat Lake and two helicopters with every kind of instrument to comb that country this summer. If the anomaly is of any size, some one is sure to find it in time.

"The whole country this summer will be something like Fifth Avenue and Forty-Second Street. Awful—but inevitable and if there is anything there, I am going to get a share for us."[45]

And so, a bit unsure of what he was doing getting involved with Smith again, Patterson returned to the Nahanni in the summer of 1955. He left Vancouver on Tuesday, July 12, at 8 a.m. and flew via Fort Nelson and Watson Lake to the Nahanni. Try as they might, he and Beaver pilot Vic Maguire could not spot Smith and his river boatman, Gus Kraus. So they landed at the hot springs and found the mosquitoes "frightful." Mrs. Kraus knew nothing of her husband's whereabouts either, but offered them supper and a place to stay. The search the next day was similarly unsuccessful, so the pilot deposited Patterson at Faille's Island on Landing Lake beside the Flat River where the crew of N.W. Explorations welcomed the author into their camp.

On Thursday, July 14, he wrote part of the text for his next book before lunch. Then his hosts put him to work loading and unloading freight. On Sunday, July 17, helicopter pilot Al Smiley took him for "a flip over the Flat River in the chopper," an experience he described as "a wonderful method of travel." On Tuesday, July 19, Patterson "Waited for plane all day & wrote away at the Buffalo Head." The next day Patterson went up in the Beaver. When they landed at Prairie Creek delta, the swift current required the pilot to keep the engine turning at 1000 rpm to keep the plane parallel to bank. Out stepped Patterson onto the float and in the process of getting the plane tied to shore, nearly went into the history books as the famous writer who lost his capacity to reason in a most spectacular fashion in Headless Valley.

Meanwhile, Curtis Smith, his geologist and crew were stuck in an eddy in Lower Canyon, warding off the debris-laden floodwaters that threatened to demolish their rig. Invisible against the canyon wall, they could only watch helplessly as the Beaver flew overhead.

On Thursday, July 21, Patterson gave up on Curtis Smith and after writing the prospector a letter explaining his decision, flew out to Watson Lake. Engine trouble delayed the airplane at Fort Nelson but eventually he flew on to Fort St. John and then to Vancouver, arriving in the dark at 3 a.m. "Futile trip but interesting in spots." But even a wasted trip had enough material in it to become the chapter he called "A Cook's Tour" in his 1963 book *Far Pastures*.[46] And he had been rewarded by some wonderful new stories told by his hosts at N.W. Explorations. "One of the prospectors told me he'd seen it—the mating of grizzly bears. I said 'What did you do?' He said, 'Do? I didn't do anything,' he said, 'I climbed the nearest cliff.'"[47] In another story a trapper habitually banged his head on a knot as he went through the cabin door. "On leaving for the last time he shouldered his pack, picked up the axe & rifle & took one last look around. Then he banged his head according to custom. Removing his pack and the cover to the axe, he cut off the knot. 'You G.D. bastard, that's fixed you. I've been meaning to cut you off these last 18 years!'" Cook Oscar Schmidt also related to Patterson the hilarious tale of Big Paul and the bear who loved canoeing, which was eventually fashioned into a story called "The Bear Voyageur" in *Far Pastures*.

Fall found Patterson on an expedition of his own into the headwaters of a tributary of the Peace River. From September 6 to October 4 he explored the Pack and the Parsnip rivers, collecting research that eventually helped form the 1968 book, *Finlay's River*. The text for his current manuscript also went along on this trip. On Saturday, September 17, he took a camp day while waiting for the weather to clear and " wrote about 1500 words of the Buffalo Head & walked around intermittently to loosen up the sciatic nerve."[48]

The immediate success of *The Dangerous River* prompted Patterson's furious writing of *The Buffalo Head*. It appears he completed a rough draft in 1956. Early that year he wrote Pocaterra with a special request: "If this damn thing at which I work ever becomes a book, would you allow me to dedicate it to you? Seeing that it was you who made clear for me the intricacies of the diamond hitch & so opened the mountain trails for me? One thing I do know, & that is that it will be better written than 'The D.R.' One learns...."[49]

That same letter apologized for the tardiness of his correspondence. "I am sorry not to have written before but I have been very busy & hindered in my work by straining a hip muscle &, when that was on the mend, by getting flu. Thank God they did not both come together as, had I sneezed, coughed or otherwise jerked myself with that hip as painful as it was, I think I should have been looking around for a loaded gun." Loaded guns were not much in his hands by this time, however. "I am more interested in travel & a camera these days & I can take care of myself anyway & take my own risks." Not all his friends agreed with him, but he continued travelling alone anyway.

Pocaterra's letter by return mail provided permission for the author to dedicate *The Buffalo Head* in his honour. "As I do share everything with Norma, I asked her if she objected to you dedicating your new book to me, and she, woman-like (I have a sneaking notion that women are a bit more vain, than their lords...and masters??????) seemed actually pleased with the thought. So fire away, if you feel so inclined."[50]

It seemed that Calgary Power had recently besmirched Pocaterra's reputation as a lover of wilderness, without obtaining the permission that his friend Patterson had requested, by naming the massive hydroelectric dam on the Kananaskis River after the Italian. "I knew nothing about all this, until I read my name in large letters in the Herald, on the front page. Many of my friends thought that I must have made a pot of money. Nary a cent, as a cowboy would say." Both Pokey and Patterson expressed outrage at the eyesore caused by the project. Even though they believed in progress, their letters revealed a different opinion as to the appropriate scale of development projects. Were they to visit the Kananaskis Valley today, complete with golf courses and campgrounds that boast electricity, running water, sewer hook-ups and even American satellite television, they might shake their heads in wonder, or disgust.[51]

Although it had got off to a quick start, delays postponed *The Buffalo Head* book project. Between writing shorter pieces for *The Beaver* and *Blackwood's Magazine*, Patterson laboured away at rewrites and revisions. Marigold's cousin, Andrew Forbes, recalls Patterson finishing off the text for one of these versions at the Forbes home in England in the late 1950s. And still the publishers rejected the manuscript. Perhaps stories from a struggling cattle ranch in southern Alberta lacked the siren song of the North. Even the hilarious tales of the dudes, the bears, snits with Pocaterra, the devastating fire of 1936 and the romantic ride west in 1946 failed to move the editors. In early 1960, Helen King of William Sloane Associates, New York, wrote to explain her company's delay. She apparently suggested Patterson add an autobiographical sketch to the book to be titled Part One "Destination Unknown."

In his foreword Patterson credits genetic wanderlust inherited from his father with partial responsibility for his restlessness. For the most part, however, he points the finger at environment, or the nurture side of the nature/nurture equation. The German prisoner-of-war camp followed by detention in the Bank of England fostered a claustrophobia that catapulted him from the centre of the Empire to the far reaches of one of the colonies. Thus, he explained his motivation for ranching in the Canadian West. The American publisher waffled. Trying to figure out how to market it, King wrote, "The trouble is that we like the book.... And please forgive our slow-wittedness." Negotiations continued into the summer, with Patterson deleting about 30,000 words to reduce it to publishable size.[52]

Finally, *The Buffalo Head* hit the bookstores in 1961. In a letter replying to a review written by his friend Gray Campbell, Patterson related details of his research for the book. "Before writing any of The B.H. (& long before I met you) the first thing I did was to buy and read your 'We Found Peace.' I saw the reviews & I thought—now here's some fellow gone & written a book about the Foothills. Let's just make sure we're not going to overlap. And, from memory, I don't think we did."

As thrilling as it was to hold the first copy of *The Dangerous River*, Patterson was even more impressed when he held the first copy of *The Buffalo Head* in his hands. "Both Macmillans and a friend in Victoria sent me copies of your review of The B.H. Well—I know it was The B.H. allright because you quote from it—but I felt like the young North Sea Fisher boy in George Graves' picture in Punch in the last war: German plane plunging into the sea, shipmates cheering, boy still hanging on to gun triggers with amazed look on his face. Caption: "Did I do that?!" I hope you meant some of it?"

Upon reading the text, however, he was dismayed by the publisher's sloppy production values. "Too bad it got loose with all those printers errors." Patterson was on his way to Europe when the proofs came off the press and the galleys never caught up with him in Tenerife. As a result the book was rushed into production and the lack of promised proof-reading showed in the final text. "Some seventy errors, & many of them changing the sense. Spoilt it for me, & for a time I wondered why I had even bothered to write the thing. I have slightly recovered now & hope that enough may sell to justify a second printing. Sloane should by now have an amended copy with my compliments."[53]

Reactions once again came in fast and furious. Pocaterra wrote from Calgary, "I have had little time to read, but did browse enough to be quite taken by the very interesting style of your writing, and I wish to really compliment you about it. It is a most attractive, flowing style, easy to read, and to visualise in different experiences."[54] On the Liard, Dick and Vera Turner thought it "very well written but not quite so interesting to us as Dangerous River. By God, I just about died laughing at Pocaterra, Adolf and you—putting up the tent [teepee]. Every time I think of Adolf's face, seeing you two fools pitching things madly into the bush, I just go into spasms. Two normally sane men gone mad he must have thought. (I had to stop for a minute & wipe tears from my eyes.)"[55]

Newspapers spoke highly of the book, *The New Yorker* review stating, "Mr. Patterson continues the story of his joyous flight from the twentieth

Robin and Alan Patterson with their father at Shoal Harbour in 1957.

century—a flight that took him from Oxford and a comfortable post in the Bank of England to the widest, loneliest, most inaccessible spaces of the Canadian Rockies."[56] The author would respond to that comment in the final pages of his next book, *Far Pastures*. "But if the old times and the old ways are not worth keeping, they still may be worth recording for the benefit of a mechanised, enlightened posterity to whom a horse will have become a snob 'status-symbol,' a plaything in a show—or have we reached that point already?—and a canoe nothing but an unsafe craft that Indians use in races, on days of festival, for the entertainment of the alien race that has taken away their lands, their fish and game, and their way of life."[57]

For a few years a book about Albert Faille's life had been simmering at the back of Patterson's mind. Back in May, 1955, Dick Turner had written with a suggestion: "I have been thinking of a title for your book about Albert. And was wondering if the words Courageous Man could be incorporated in the title. It does not seem perfect however. The words seem better in the mind than they do written down. Out of a lot of suggestions you might make something."[58]

In July of 1958 the old trapper nearly died in the bush, the incident resurrecting the idea of publishing something about Faille, this time to help him replace a bankroll that disappeared into muddy South Nahanni waters. Loaded with a year's worth of supplies, Faille's 26-foot scow had capsized in Lower Canyon. He escaped with three matches and starting hiking out in the rain. The local RCMP were too busy to aid in the search, so Dick convinced E. J. Tassoniyi, a geologist working for J. C. Sproule, to loan him a chopper on lease from Vancouver Island Helicopters. Dick supplied the gasoline from his cache at Nahanni Butte. For two hours on August 8 they searched the Splits and the Lower Canyon without success. The geologist allowed them another flight the next day, with instructions to return by 10 a.m. Dick recalled, "The next morning when we took off to have another look it was with the strongest feelings of urgency, hopelessness, anxiety and a wonderful feeling of friendliness for this fine lad [pilot] Bob Taylor. Right above that high gravel bank on the left bank near the trail to Jackfish Creek, Bob shouted 'There he is!' And there he certainly was—trudging along the beach with a stick in his hand. We landed close and I rushed to him. 'When did you eat last Albert?' 'Eight days now,' he said except for berries and mushrooms.' His hands were cold as ice.... Anyway we were home in 20 minutes. Vera cried when she saw him and so did Albert. He is in Fort Simpson now and back to normal."[59]

Not one to believe in banks, Faille had more than $500 with him in cash before the accident. Dick wondered if he or Patterson could parlay this saga into a popular story and use the proceeds to replace Faille's lost nest egg. As a result, in April of 1959 Patterson thanked Cam Sproule in a letter for his company's assistance in the rescue and informed him that Turner possessed a tape-recorded interview with Faille about the incident. He asked the geologist if his company could make use of the tape and story as publicity and provide payment so Faille could head south "to get his teeth fixed." Both Turner and Patterson wanted compensation from such a venture to go directly to Faille as they knew he would not accept charity. "This publicity business is a sealed book to me—but I do thank you for your peoples' assistance to my old friend—a man to whose teaching of the ways of a river I owe a great deal. If his experience can be turned into cash in any way I know the old-timer will be delighted and will proceed once more to tackle what he calls 'his river.'"[60] Sproule replied that his company would assist Patterson with information if he chose to write the story, but that he could not see using the story himself.[61]

No book was ever written about Faille. But luckily his American World War I pension and income from fur sales kept him financially solvent. The

Faille story, however, took some unusual turns and reappeared in another format. According to Dick Turner, the old prospector spent the better part of two months in the summer of 1961 on the Nahanni under the watchful eye of cameraman Don Wilder. Working for the National Film Board of Canada, Wilder shot 20,000 feet of film—about four hours—of which twenty minutes made the final cut. Albert found filming hard work: crucial scenes of slogging up rapids were sometimes reshot as many as ten times. At one point Faille's outfit wallowed and filled with whitewater in George's Riffle at the top end of Lower Canyon. Downstream it floated, submerged, until the other two boats caught the sunken scow and towed it to shore more than a mile downstream. The result was a short film titled "Nahanni," produced by Nicholas Balla and released in 1962.[62]

Faille survived into his 92nd year. Raised near Duluth, Minnesota, this outstanding river man died on the frozen shores of the Mackenzie River at Fort Simpson on January 1, 1974. In 1959 Patterson predicted, "He will probably end by dying up in those mountains in some way or other—but that is what he would wish, for to put him in an old man's home would be like putting a battered old eagle in a cage."[63] Faille's actual demise was slightly less glamorous, but still on his own terms. Living in Fort Simpson for the winter, he accepted a daily hot meal from Anna Lindberg. When she knocked at his cabin that New Year's Day, no hunched bachelor opened the door. Instead, she found Faille a few steps to the west, dead in his privy.

Today, Faille's cabin overlooking the mighty Mackenzie stands as a tiny museum. Retired school teacher Stephen Rowan—"I was born in England and have never recovered from that"—guides interested visitors around the community that dates to the early 1800s. Drinking tea in a coffee shop while a violent thunderstorm rattled the windows, he introduced the author to Edward "Fly" Villeneuve. Fly had helped Faille move the kitchen wing of the Indian agent's house to lot 61 that he purchased from the Catholic church on March 4, 1957. Dating from about 1920, this small structure had become Faille's home when he was not on the Nahanni. Recent repairs to the footings had disclosed an envelope found tucked behind a cupboard. In it was $1000 in twenty dollar bills and a single American dollar. Faille's other bank was an account with the Hudson's Bay Company, where he left the balance to his good friend Dick Turner.

* * *

SIDE by side with trips taken for research were adventurous family holidays that continued through the 1950s. After the family sold the Spillimacheen place in the late 1940s, they frequently camped at Shuswap Lake midway between Calgary and Vancouver. Although Janet recalls her father never really liked water enough to enjoy swimming, he often waded into the lake to cool off on hot summer days.

Patterson continued his habit of solo expeditions with a canoe trip on Shuswap Lake between October 1-15 in 1956. From Vancouver he rode the bus to Kamloops where the big canoe awaited him at the Canadian National Railways freight office. From there he motored up the South Thompson River to Shuswap Lake, explored Anstey Arm at the east end of the lake to the mouth of that river, then canoed up Seymour Arm to the family's camping spot where he looked in vain for the remains of the H.B.C. Shuswap Post. On the return trip disaster nearly claimed his camp when a tent peg let go and the stove, candle and hot supper almost made a torchy mess of his temporary abode in a windstorm.[64]

In July, 1959, outdoor writer Roderick Haig-Brown contacted the Shoal Harbour resident to discuss publishing ideas. He was heading off on a trip with his son to the North Saskatchewan, to the Fond du lac River, Reindeer and Woolanton area. He wished Patterson and his family success on their trip to Athabasca Pass. "Hope you find the Committee's Punchbowl all it should be and perhaps manage a word or two with the shadows of David Thompson and George Simpson."[65] By all accounts, the Patterson trip went well. Raymond, Marigold, Robin and a few friends ascended with packhorses from Athabasca Falls to Athabasca Pass. After sending the horses back, they camped for three nights, and when the food ran out they walked out, wading the Whirlpool River many times.[66]

On October 15 of that year, D. A. Russell, Dean of St. John's College, Oxford, wrote with commendations. "I have pleasure in informing you that the Degree of M.A. was conferred on you in absence today." The same file in the archives in Victoria states Patterson had in advance paid Annual Dues in the Oxford Union Society for the rest of his life.[67]

The degree came at a good time, just as Patterson decided to sell the Canadian property and move back to Britain. According to Marigold, they had always intended on retiring back to the old country and the early 1960s offered them a chance to move on a temporary basis. Janet was married, with a daughter, and living in North Vancouver. Robin would be going with them and Alan was already in the U.K., attending university in London. The move would also allow Raymond and Marigold a base from which to tour Europe. Patterson's plans for the next few years involved researching a book about Napoleon's horsemen.

Patterson's American editor wrote the next month. "So you're really pulling out. Will it be Scotland for good? Or a place on the Liard? Is Kirkendbright near Edinburgh? If so, you must look up two of my favorite people—Mary Stewart, who writes fiction, and her husband, who is Regius Professor of Geology at the University."[68]

But first, Patterson took advantage of Dick Turner's longstanding invitation to visit in the winter. Departing Vancouver on March 4, 1960, he flew to Fort Nelson where Turner picked him up in his Piper Super Cub and spirited him off to his new trading post at Nahanni Butte. Along the way they checked Dick's traplines. "Once out of the plane, one donned snowshoes immediately. In fact, nothing had changed on the trapline— lynx & marten in a pack are no lighter than they ever were, a fire in deep snow still goes best on a base of green poles & tea made from snow & flavoured with spruce needles tastes as good as ever." He took photos, watched the temperature fluctuate between 37° below and 56° Fahrenheit above and, best of all, spent twenty-four hours with old friend Faille at Fort Simpson. The trip got his wilderness blood moving again and he began dreaming of another season or two on the trapline.[69]

The sale of the Shoal Harbour property was eventful. According to Alan, his father constantly had offers for the place. In the end a Mr. Ross purchased the land in a private deal and a realtor sued for loss of the commission in the Supreme Court of British Columbia. Patterson lost the first round—"Dad always said it was that damned Irish judge..."— but won on appeal.[70]

Shortly before leaving Canada, Patterson wrote his daughter on May 23, 1960, asking her to join him for a week-long canoe trip on Shuswap Lake. It was a hard time in Janet's life: she was working as a secretary to support daughter Julia and husband David who was wheelchair-bound through illness. Her boss at Lafarge Canada was understanding and sent her on her way with his blessing. Janet and her father had many adventures in the big freighter canoe, poking about the more deserted reaches of the lakes, camping on isolated beaches and cooking up wonderful meals. On September 5, 1960, he wrote again, thanking her for joining him on his last canoe adventure before leaving the country. "That was a nice trip & I shall always remember it with pleasure—you make a most nice travelling companion."

The Pattersons eventually took up residence in England. Alan still remembers meeting his parents at the train and marvelling at their most unusual "Canadian" accents.[71] Robin attended grammar school and joined his parents for holidays.

For the better part of two years the Pattersons toured Europe in their little Ford Zephyr, researching the lives of Napoleon's couriers. Writing Gray Campbell, he commiserated with Gray's wife, "I can well understand Eleanor's viewpoint on museums, complete with ancient bedrooms fitted with candlesticks & genuine authentic chamberpots. Marigold is the same, & for her there comes a limit...but in Europe I can go through country houses in any western country, especially France, Spain & Austria, world without end, marvelling at the beautiful things, and absolutely drunk with the architecture & the setting. Marigold weakens: 'Not another schloss/château/baroque library or whatever it may be. I'll get my book & read in the gardens.'"[72] While Patterson tracked down every possible lead of a neglected part of the Napoleonic story, Marigold went along for the ride.

And what a ride it was. On January 16, 1961, they sailed from London to Tenerife in the Canary Islands, where they stayed until March 6. Then they crossed to the continent, finding useful information in France, Austria, Switzerland and northern Italy, finally returning to England on October 5. In a letter to Pocaterra, Patterson wrote, "I don't know how many times we have been just into Italy because we set out to cross every high Alpine Pass we could—& there are 27 notches on the steering wheel...& twice over 9000'." There are sly hints in the letter that Patterson refused to spend any time in Italy.

In early 1962 the Pattersons returned to France and Spain, then boarded a ship that docked in Montreal on May 2. Arriving back in Victoria, they bought a home within walking distance of the university for Robin.

Sir Edward Peacock, writing from the Royal London Homeopathic Hospital in June, 1962, thanked Patterson for his detailed accounts of the extended research trips: "What a lot you have managed to get out of it, and all done so comfortably and effectively. I give you top marks as devisor of pleasant journeying! And you have picked up a good deal that will be useful background to you if you decide to write about Napoleon, as your New York publishers have suggested."[73] Patterson's old friend and mentor died later that year on November 16.

Patterson's next book, however, grew out of a friendship with British Columbia's first book publisher. Fourteen years younger than the well-known writer, the late Gray Campbell remembered Patterson "took a fatherly interest in what I did." In the foreword to four Patterson reprints, Campbell recalled the gentleman's writing system. "He honed his writing style, patiently and laboriously, it seems, in this impatient age of computers and electronics. Writing in school copy-books with pencil, there were many words scratched out. He was fussy about finding the right term, strove to be literate but lucid, striking out a long word when a short one would do. He had tremendous admiration for the English author, Norman Douglas (1868-1952), and admired his style."

While Patterson was in Europe, letters had kept their friendship alive. Writing from Spain, the writer had suggested a collection of edited articles culled from his *Blackwood's* and *Beaver* submissions. Canadian in content, the project seemed tailored for the west coast publisher. Once approved, Campbell sent a request for approximately 60,000 words and made suggestions for titles: "Vintage Patterson," "Range With Patterson from...to...," "Pull up a Chair to Adventure." "Eleanor says the right one is bound to come up."[74]

Some of the material was new, but for previously released articles Patterson sought permission from Blackwood and Malvina Bolus, editors of the respective magazines. The copyrights all belonged to the author, replied Blackwood, also sending along his best wishes on the project.[75] *The Beaver* reply was similarly helpful: "It is satisfying to have the articles gathered up in more permanent form. By all means use 'Nahanni Revisited' from the June 1952 'Beaver.' An acknowledgement will be appreciated. This copyright business is very odd—I have been going into it lately. We are the 'proprietors' of the copyright of articles published in 'The Beaver' but, while we could re-run them in the magazine, we could not publish them in any other form without the author's consent: but neither may the author republish them without our consent. So it is a matter of agreement and usually that is not difficult, except that some authors vanish—or even die—and then it is hard to obtain their approval."[76]

"You & I had fun with that book," wrote Patterson to his new publisher many years later. "Remember my being stuck with a strained ankle, & up at Shuswap Lake, & writing to you, saying 'Time we sawed it off, Gray: it's getting too long.' And you replying 'No-no! This is great stuff. Write some more.'"[77] But the project was not without at least one tense moment, caused in part by the fact Campbell had to mortgage both his house and car to pay the printer's bill for the book they finally called *Far Pastures*. "It was to be our first book in hard cover and he did not learn that as an unknown I had to sign a demand note for the printer which could have lost us our home.

But with R.M.'s fame and skill the risk was not really there though you could smell the fear and uncertainty. We remained friends in spite of my mistakes. He sniffed at the contract we presented because in no way was it like the contracts with his London and New York publishers. I very foolishly, but ignorantly, registered the copyright in my name, but perhaps that had something to do with the demand note. The author let it go."[78] According to Campbell, Patterson just wiggled his nose from side to side for a moment.

Patterson completed the project on August 26, 1963, and dedicated it to Sir Edward Peacock. The public liked the book and in 1978 the Alberta government included it as part of its Alberta Heritage Series commemorating Alberta's 75th Anniversary. Gordon Matthews liked *Far Pastures* the best of all Patterson's books, as did many other retirees. "Well, the old-timers loved Far Pastures when we finally did saw it off & you [Campbell] & John [the printer] got it out. That was the book that rang the bell with them: 'Made me feel young again—ready for a basket social, a good couple of fiddlers & the Red River jig.' I got some wonderful letters—and, as for my wild ride with Johnny Arnold for the rum, that story apparently made people laugh from P.E.I. to Whitehorse, not excluding members of Victoria society, old enough & respectable enough to have known better."[79]

Patterson included a review of the stories with a complimentary copy he sent to Pocaterra. "Did you, for instance, know that I once lay face down for an appreciable length of time face-downwards on an enormous ant-hill, on top of what, only a few seconds before, had been a dozen fresh eggs? If I could bring a libel action against myself I surely would bring one for that! I must have a light heart—or mind?—because it is always the absurd that attracts my attention."[80] Always honest with his emotions in letters to Pokey, he blasted the entire spectrum running in that year's federal election. "I shall not vote in this election: I will never forget that Diefenbaker united with Nehru & N'Krumah (of all people!) to help S. Africa out of the Commonwealth. Pearson wd. promise anybody anything just to get his party in—the very worst type of politician. Soc. Credit, with Quebec making use of it, is a mess. And I don't trust the N.D.P. I shall just take some sandwiches & walk up Mt. Newton or Mt. Finlayson, & to the crocodiles with their damned election. I have spoken."[81]

He did not reject everything associated with government and in 1963 followed Faille's lead and became a television star. Norman Caton of the Canadian Broadcasting Corporation called and asked if he would agree to being filmed paddling on an Alberta river. With typical movie-industry timing the request came in mid-winter, so Patterson had to convince them to shoot on Vancouver Island instead. He called February 18 "a most interesting day...fooling around in a light canoe below the outlet from Lake Cowichan." Two riverboats held nine crewmembers complete with cameras and recording equipment. A cable under the canoe ran up through his clothing to a microphone hidden in his sweater. While Len Macdonald filmed the event, the director interviewed Patterson as he negotiated the current. "Just how the hell any man could be expected to give a sane answer to an impromptu question under those circumstances I do not know." All pronounced the day an amazing success. Ten days later the film crew was dead, smashed against the Front Range of the Rocky Mountains while filming from a small plane.[82]

Meanwhile, the Pattersons continued their western Canadian explorations. They visited Alberta for much of August, driving past the Buffalo Head as Mount Head peaked at them through low clouds. On over the Highwood Pass they went, only to encounter the scene of devastation at the dam at the headwaters of the Kananaskis River. "What a hell of an encampment that is at the N.E. corner of the Upper K. Lake! If you haven't seen it, don't go," Patterson wrote Pocaterra. "To me the shores of a dam, with its varying levels, are dead; no lovely beaches, no game trail, no small wind-twisted spruce & Labrador tea & wild roses—just an

Upper Kananaskis Lake shoreline after logging in preparation for flooding.

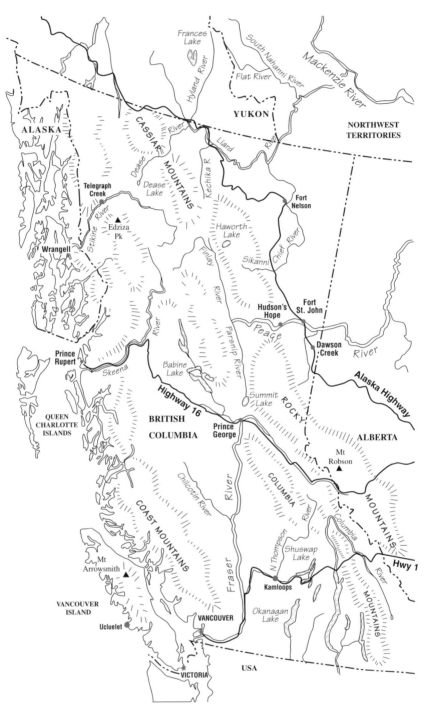

PATTERSON'S TRAVELS IN YEARS 1947 TO 1973

unnatural mess of stones."[83] Pocaterra's reaction was much the same, even though it had been almost a decade since Calgary Power had built the abomination and named it after him without his permission. "The most beautiful mountain scenery in the world, as far as I'm concerned, was at these lakes but now is completely spoiled by the power dams, the drowning of the marvellously beautiful islands and exquisitely curving beaches, the cutting down of centuries old trees, and the drying up of the twin falls between the two lakes, and of the falls below the lower lake."[84]

Back on the coast that fall, Patterson dove into another writing project he tentatively titled "Four Rivers." For a diversion he gave a slide show and talk about the Liard and Nahanni rivers to a group in Vancouver on June 2, 1964. Then it was back to his writing. The book concentrated on the story of the Stikine, Dease, Upper Liard and Finlay rivers. He had travelled them all, and knew their history and that of the fur trade in the area well. The diaries of the explorers were old friends and included "the most fantastic incidents, carefully set down in surveyor's script." Interspersed were tales told by Indian agents, prospectors and others. Patterson was resolved "Their stories should not be allowed to die or rot in Provincial Archives. There is fascinating material, if I can put it properly together. And nobody concerned, bar me, is under eight-five. The tough live long—that's a dead certainty." Fall found him still busy with the project, and owing Pocaterra a letter as well as a visit. "I am busy with a book—tentatively titled Four Rivers but I think it may end up being Three—& it is giving me hell.... I want every fact to be indisputable...."[85]

In the summer of 1965, as part of this research, Patterson joined a trip to the Parsnip and Finlay rivers with Palmer Lewis, Art van Sommer and others. Lewis took along lots of film, still and moving, to record the rivers "realising that much of this wilderness will be drowned forever (or nearly so) by the waters impounded by the Portage Mountain Dam."[86]

The material for the Four Rivers project was too much for one book, so in 1965 he split up the subject matter. The first volume, *Trail to the Interior*, covered the Stikine and Dease rivers in the northern reaches of British Columbia and was written in six parts. Two 1946 diaries in his daughter's handwriting formed the basis for Part One. Just out of high school, Janet had helped drive sixty-two head of horses from Hazelton in west-central B.C. up the abandoned Yukon Telegraph Trail to Telegraph Creek. En route they had lost twenty-three horses and taken forty-four days instead of thirty, but all the bipeds had survived.

The other research source was Patterson's own diary written in 1948. Plans for Patterson's solo canoe trip had come to the attention of his old friend and hunting partner, Colonel Harry Snyder of Sundre, who offered the following advice, "Buy a copy of 'Raw North' by Charles E. Gillham...and sit down and read it instead. Then come here for a visit. I think we still have enough Bacardi for one good drink or two.... For God's sake, Raymond, don't do it. Be your age. If you try to make this contemplated trip alone, just as sure as hell you are never coming back, and we cannot afford to lose such a valuable friend. Just remember this, young fellow my lad, you are now dancing attendance around the fifty mark, and the things you could do and stand fifteen to twenty years ago are now among, or should be among your cherished memories. Just what in hell would happen to you if, five hundred miles from nowhere, you were to have another attack of that lumbago of yours?" With Marigold on a trip back to England, Patterson was free to travel. "...While you are footloose and fancy-free, why not come over, and I will damn well talk you out of this crazy trip you are projecting up north. Instead we will invent some other kind of devilment."[87]

Not easily dissuaded, Patterson boarded the CPR ship *Princess Norah* in Vancouver on July 17, and settled into upper berth #108 on his way to Alaska.[88] From Wrangell he ascended the Stikine to Telegraph Creek, then freighted over to Dease Lake, his diary recording each step of the way in great detail. August found him and the 14-foot Chestnut canoe running 200 miles down the Dease to its mouth and up the Liard to the Lower Post. Plans called for an ascent of the Hyland to Frances Lake and a hike over the watershed to the headwaters of the Flat River. But it "was late in the year owing to the strike, my wife not getting back from England till mid July etc. etc. Also the canoe was too small for upstream work, so, what with one thing and another, I called it a day at the Lower Post & flew out." By that time he had a badly inflamed paddling wrist that convinced him to pack it in for the year. Leaving the canoe for the post manager to sell, he left for Victoria on Saturday, August 29. During the trip the colonel's worst fear had almost come true. "I did pack away a go of flu from Telegraph Creek which came to a head on Third Lake—a lovely spot, & there I lay around camp for nearly three days, living on tea, chocolate, oranges & aspirin, & groaned & read Black Mischief by Evelyn Waugh, & somehow cured myself."[89]

Trail to the Interior reached welcoming readers in 1966 and that fall Patterson made a rare book tour. In a letter to Janet dated October 10, 1966, he wrote that he had been to Calgary "where I conducted a book

The colonel—Harry Snyder, 1949.

R. M. Patterson at Dease Lake,
August 11, 1948.

Camp at Third Lake, Dease River, looking north. August 14, 1948.

party—which personally I didn't think was worth the effort, but after which I was told I had had 'much more success than Pierre Berton.' Sold more books, I gathered." It is of interest that *Trail to the Interior* included endnotes, the only Patterson book to do so. It also shared the added academic feature of a bibliography with Patterson's fifth book.

Sadly, Stikine River old-timer and friend T. F. Harper Reed, to whom he had dedicated the book, died on December 20, 1965. The death of his friends and acquaintances was becoming a recurring sadness.

Alan Patterson head washing, camp style, Finlay River, 1949.

The jacket of his fifth book included a synopsis: "A vivid account of a wild and beautiful river in British Columbia and the men who have explored it." Dedicated to Marigold and completed in December, 1967, *Finlay's River* was also a lament for the death of a river. As he wrote the final text, workmen were completing the W. A. C. Bennett Dam, a hydroelectric facility that would restrict the flow of the Peace River to which the Finlay and the Parsnip are the major tributaries. Today, most of the territory described in Patterson's longest published manuscript (315 pages) lies flooded under the massive Williston Lake reservoir. Without apology, he quoted at the front of the book a caustic condemnation of careless progress from Norman Douglas' book, *In the Beginning*: "I forsee the day when...every fair spot has been scarred by their hands and deformed to their mean purposes, the rivers made turbid and hills and forests levelled away and all the wild green places smothered under cities full of smoke and clanking wheels."

Colonel Harry Snyder also ranted against his 1949 expedition to this northern tributary to the Peace. "You take my tip" the colonel broke in, "and leave the Finlay alone. A bad river. You'll go fooling with a canoe once too often."[90] They argued playfully on into the night with the same result as before. The Pattersons—Alan would accompany his father for the first month and Marigold for the second—made preparations for an extended voyage from Summit Lake north of Prince George in British Columbia, down the Crooked, Pack and Parsnip rivers to the town of Peace River.

The forty-eight-page diary began on July 27 with a piece of canoe culture every paddler can appreciate.

SONG: THE CANOE MAN'S LAMENT

Why do we never see,
At five o'clock,
The places that we see
At three.
Oh, no, we never do!
We just go howling on!
Until my tummy rumbles so,
And thunder comes & goes,
"Boom, Boom, Boom, Boom!"
Inside & out.
And "Ovaltine" the crew does shout.
I wish I were
At home in bed.
The window shut, a candle at my head.
(cres.) I'll Roam No More!
(Tune adapted from Fred Astaire's "Just keep on dancing")

The diary contains a variety of information. On July 31, for example, "Left my hat stuffed into a willow at the Warrens—damn, I like that hat." August 19 records a climb to a mountain top for pictures and the usual letdown experienced when returning from on high: "Day not good for pictures but damned good for mosquitoes & every other pest." August 23: "Sorted outfit & completed the interrupted laundry—did camp chores—&, above all, patched one pair of navigatious bags [trousers] with the other so as to have one wearable pair.... By the way—after running sideways down that rapid yesterday—I fished in an eddy at the foot. Was absorbed in my fishing & was surprised, on looking up, to see a black bear swimming across & very close to me. He was v. scared & ran up the cutbank as soon as he landed—why animals will swim rivers when human beings are floating on them beats me. They seem to lose all their judgement."

On September 6 the Pattersons arrived at Peace River Gap. "George New, when cutting out some new trapline this spring, had a feeling that somebody was watching him. He turned, & there was a grizzly, standing on its hind feet, right behind him. He raised his axe for one desperate swipe, but the grizzly smacked him over sideways, bit him in the ribs, turned round & scratted earth & leaves over him & departed, leaving him for dead. Anybody had a closer one?"

On September 8 Patterson prepared for his wife's arrival. "Perfect again, thanks be to Allah, the Merciful, the Compassionate. Faint mares' tails floating in a blue sky. Marigold not due till the 10th so shall stay here one more day for one more fish supper (or is it for the golden afternoon light on the green water of the canyon?). Completed laundry & then took wood ashes & cleaned all cooking pots till they sit now (9:30 a.m.) shining like bridesmaids at a wedding (the wedding we shall never have, now.) Camp now respectable enough to face Marigold."

The next day Patterson "...floated into Finlay Forks about plane time. No plane—but it turned up about six p.m. with Marigold who had thoroughly enjoyed her flight in from Prince George. We were received with real northern hospitality & made most comfortable in the bunk house behind the store." Decades later Patterson recalled his reputation had preceded him, "When I first got to Finlay Forks, Mrs. McDougall, the trader's wife there, was most hospitable and kind. I said who I was. 'Oh' she said. 'Come inside. We haven't got any wolverine stew for you but we'll do the best we can.'"[91]

September 16: "How it rains! It must be eleven a.m., anyway. Marigold still in bed in her rabbit hutch of a tent, after an early morning cup of tea, while I read & write in warmth & comfort under the lean-to & by the fire. The lean-to is of Willesden canvas, the gift of Sir George Lowndes in 1935. It has seen a thing or two, since then.

"Later—It still rains. Anxious for good pictures we refuse to travel till we can see the hills. A day of gossip, reading, eating—11:30 p.m. saw us still at it by a blazing fire. No characters remained undefamed."

Toward the end of September they rigged a sail and ran before the wind downstream. "The river is now very wide & very magnificent." On September 26 they beached the canoe for the last time that season. "The End. Arrived at Peace River about 3.0 p.m., caching stuff in the H.B. Co. machine shop through the courtesy of Mr. R. F. McConnell. Weather even more perfect—in fact damned hot. Finis."[92]

After his frustrating attempt to connect with Curtis Smith on the Nahanni in the summer of 1955, Patterson and Marigold returned later that year to the Pack, Parsnip and Peace rivers. On Friday, September 9, "M. arrived at 2.0 p.m. looking very exotic in a tailored suit with sausage in hand."

Tuesday, September 13, found them both worse for wear. "Rain. Put up tent & stove & I cut my left hand with the axe. A narrow escape—much blood but nothing serious. Marigold, feeling rotten herself, bandaged me up & we had a late supper & went to bed in a tent that was like old Chaos." Friday of that week found them without an operational outboard—the sheer pins in the toolbox were for a different shaft. "Damn—& we tracked & poled up the Parsnip to our abandoned campsite & re-made it—then sat & drank hot soup with whiskey in it—very good." On Friday, September 23, Patterson scouted the Ne Parle Pas Rapids. "I walked down & looked things over & took what photos I could. Then we lined down with me in the water & M. on the pole-she nearly fell in, shoving the canoe off, several times." That night, "A half moon made a track down the river, all wrinkled & twisted with movement." On October 1 they outdid themselves with laziness. "Slept late—and M. slept 2 hrs. later still, having gone to bed nearly an hour earlier. Good God! Why try to get anywhere? So we didn't try." They arrived at the Alaska Highway bridge over the Peace River on October 3, and flew west the next day, arriving at Vancouver airport at 7.30 p.m. Expenses for the expedition, including freight, airfares, hotels and film, totalled $347.98.[93]

Head of Deserters' Canyon, Finlay River, 1949.

R. M. Patterson at Finlay Rapids, 1949.

That summer was tough on Patterson's body. A dozen years later he admitted to losing twenty-three pounds. Indeed, the photo of him taken at Finlay Rapids shows a scarecrow—a faint shadow of his already thin frame—with pants torn out at the knee. Only his trademark scarf redeems the whole outfit. While writing the book in 1967, he mentioned the image to Pocaterra. "If that book gets published (which I wouldn't bet on) that photograph will do me no good socially. Nobody nice will ever want to know me again."[94]

In 1967, the Pattersons' fall holiday to the Okanagan and Caribou country of the B. C. interior fell by the wayside when publisher William Morrow of New York requested he complete the manuscript by October 1. That proved optimistic, but most of it was in the mail by the end of the month.

The handwritten manuscript of this book has survived. Written into the pages of a 1967 Year Book—the DayTimer of its day—the text begins on Thursday, January 5, and continues on the right-hand pages, with notes and revisions on the opposite page until Sunday, November 12. The text for the foreword and acknowledgements follow, all written in small, neat, legible printing with wild hatted d's and fancy capitals.[95] His typist lived just across the lawn so making corrections was a breeze.

As Patterson explained to Pocaterra, "It was a difficult book to write: so many people going over the same ground (or water) again & again that it could easily have become monotonous. I hope it has not...."[96] As always, Patterson included notes from previous explorers' accounts of the river: reports by R. G. McConnell, Alfred Selwyn and John Macoun of the Geological Survey of Canada, a 1908 Report of the B.C. Minister of Mines and a 1914 Report of the B.C. Minister of Lands. The result is a fine book, well crafted, passionately written and one that places historic personalities and the reader in the same canoe.

In *Finlay's River* he returned to an obsolete method of punctuating geographic names, a choice Patterson made because he considered it "well suited to what is largely an account of old-time travel." As he aged, the author was drifting toward recording older events, this allowing him to shift his focus of research from the mountains and rivers he had so easily negotiated in his youth to more appropriate settings in archives and libraries.

The book was published in 1968. As a reward, the Pattersons booked passage to England for late January 1968 on a twelve-passenger freighter taking the long way round through the Panama Canal. For five months Patterson continued his research on Napoleon's couriers. In England he returned to Oxford—even got his old rooms—-and spent two weeks in the Bodleian Library using only an author index as the library had no guide to subjects. Then on they went to the continent, travelling through Austria, France and Spain. They even wandered into Italy under smoggy skies. On his one day in Paris, Patterson found it hard to get around. "Taxis were rare & almost impossible. Neither of us having looked at a paper or received any mail for a month, how was I to know that this was the second day of the French strike, riots etc? I did run into a few strings of students on the Boulevard St.-Germain, linked arms, clean & smiling. I just stood and smiled at them & they opened up to let me through. Nice kids—no hippies. I must have caught about the last normal train out of Paris & cashed, luckily, the last traveller's cheque." On returning to the British Isles, they boarded ship for Canada—"The distance from ship to door proved to be 3108 miles & it took us a week, averaging 450 m.p.d."—and were back in Victoria by early July. "And now, as you can well imagine, we're bust flat. We just sit & lick our wounds & drink the occasional bottle of vin d'Alsace—& wonder when the next time will be."[97]

But for a few details, the 1968 trip ended the research phase of Patterson's final work he called "The Emperor's Horsemen." He began writing in 1969 and by 1973 had completed the first draft of the 186,000-word manuscript.

At one point Patterson approached the Canada Council with a request for research assistance. "After reading today in The Colonist a further account of the curious antics of the Canada Council, I rather doubt if Horsemen is nutty enough & far enough removed from human interest for the C.C. to wish to have anything to do with it," he wrote Gray Campbell.[98]

Publishers shied away from the project in droves. Some thought the topic too military and others complained about the length. A British house would not get involved unless an American publisher agreed to share the risk. Another feared production costs would price the book out of the market. One of Patterson's previous publishers dismissed the idea of a two-volume work as "old fashioned." Typical of the tactful letters was one from an English publisher: "I am very sorry that I can't bring you better news, but I can say with some certainty that all publishers are different and that it is not at all unlikely that you will find one to accept your work...."[99]

As late as 1980 a few readers were still holding out hope the manuscript would find a publisher. Patterson, fed up with them all, let his friend and retired publisher Campbell in on his conclusion: "Now, if I'd written one more book (to add to the thousands) about Waterloo—it wd. have to be about the swearwords used in that battle in all the half-dozen languages (which must be the only aspect of Waterloo not yet written about) publishers wd. have wagged their tails & grovelled. Any publisher is welcome to this idea."[100]

"The Emperor's Horsemen" is like nothing else Patterson wrote and is arguably his masterpiece. Intellectually, Napoleon was Patterson's first love and one does not easily forget one's first passion. Not all of his days at Oxford in the early 1920s had been filled with women, archery, poling punts and drinking in pubs. In the last term he had applied himself with great resolve and "most persistent of all was my special subject, Napoleon's Jena campaign of 1806."[101] Fifty years later he returned to his passion and the result was a 404-page manuscript—reduced from some 900 pages at the request of his publishers. Thematically, it strays far from home and never touches the western Canadian scene he made famous in his numerous articles and five books. Systematically, however, it builds on the strengths he honed during three decades as a busy author by allowing the reader to experience the thrill of writing a dispatch for his military hero. "Your reports must make me see everything as if I had seen it with my own eyes," commanded Napoleon to his generals at the front. Details matter to a commander who wants to control all of Europe with not only military might, but most of all, through the power of his own incredible mind.

But this manuscript is not just a barely disguised hymn of praise for a great man. Its greatest emphasis is that in the Napoleonic wars, as in the Boer War at the end of the 1800s, "the individual still counted. And it is with these very individual men that this book deals." Patterson dedicated his manuscript "To the memory of those young horsemen who rode across Europe for the Emperor and who wrote of it afterwards 'with pens dipped in champagne.'" He subtitled the book "A Napoleonic Pilgrimage," a phrase that describes his methodology. Knowing full well that tens of thousands of titles already filled the shelves on the subject, he sought a fresh approach by taking us into the lives of the postilions, estafettes, couriers and post-boys of the Napoleonic communications system.

Patterson also brought something relatively new to the historian's perspective on Napoleonic literature: experiential understanding, the "one thing that may, perhaps, be new in modern historical writing on Napoleon's time.... In the years before the machine age...we had to travel as men travelled in Napoleon's day, and the sole motive power was the horse and our own strength and endurance. This post-graduate, extra-mural course (as one might call it) in the ways of the mountains and the wild rivers, and in the vagaries of the horse, has, I hope, helped me to appreciate the hazards that confronted the Emperor's horsemen, and so to set their accounts in living words before the reader." How could historians, he wondered, fully comprehend the courier's role if they set themselves up as ivory tower merchants?

His search for historic truth had taken him to the passes, the rivers and bridges where Napoleon's victories and defeats had unfolded from 1796 to 1815. He and Marigold had parked the car and hiked the old trails through fields where he "found battlefields as they once were...by the gentle murmur of the stream. That is the way a battlefield should remain—far from the turmoil of cities and given over to quietness and heroic memories." He had examined gun placements with his experienced artilleryman's eye, picking apart erroneous accounts and placing in their stead realism and accuracy.

He had visited museums that boasted portraits of these men and describes their character through their images on canvas. He is kind but truthful with his hero: Napoleon was a master strategist as well as a sloppy rider, he could be very hard on his men, but nineteen horses were shot out from under him in a display of fearlessness that made him "a soldier's general."

He had tracked down the original diaries in French, Spanish and German, and in selecting quotes had translated as he wrote. In particular, Patterson considered the diaries of Jean-Baptiste Marbot and Philippe-Paul de Segur masterpieces, even though they did not always agree with one another. "Both Marbot and de Segur were possessed of the same devil: they were writers.... They were not necessarily always writing history: they were writing personal memoirs—and neither one had any intention of writing memoirs that were dull."

As a result of his meticulous research and in perhaps the best prose of his career, Patterson takes the reader along for the ride. We join the courier on hands and knees in the pitch black of a moonless night as the courier crossed narrow log bridges, horse following, in blinding, freezing rain. We cringe when a horse gallops across a field of snow, then suddenly wallows in a snow-covered ravine and catapults its rider. With officers, we make small talk and saunter nonchalantly across an enemy-occupied bridge set with explosives and covered with artillery. We watch in amazement as shepherds in black woollen capes, atop seven-foot stilts, walk boldly alongside the horses, escorting the emperor safely through their land. We gawk when Napoleon finds enemy soldiers hiding behind the curtains in his room. "He just smiled at the Spaniards, making a gesture that was almost one of compassion" as he handed them over to his guards. We are at Niegolewski's side when he falls, only temporarily disabled by two bullets and nine bayonet wounds. In the moonless night we accompany Napoleon's men on a clandestine crossing of the flooded Danube River and sneak into enemy territory in a boat constantly battered by springtime flood debris. We sit with hungry "men to whom a frozen potato and a slice of horse, singed in the flames on the point of a sabre and seasoned with gunpowder, represent the ultimate in gastronomic luxury."

The story ends in 1815, but not before de Segur talks a man with a bullet near his heart into taking courage and living, since he also has a metal ball in his chest. Patterson could empathize with the wounded soldier because he too was nearing the end of his life. Almost eighty years old when he completed this manuscript, he could feel his body aging rapidly. Perhaps it was fitting that Patterson ended his writing career as it began, researching and writing about the Napoleonic period that so inspired him in his youth.

The Twilight Years
1974 to 1984

WHEN eighty-six years old and in frail health, Patterson voted in the 1984 federal election. A staunch Conservative, his ballot undoubtedly helped defeat Liberal Prime Minister John Turner and install Brian Mulroney. Alan drove his father to the polling station and recalls he seemed a bit disoriented when they returned home. Before supper, father and son enjoyed a drink of water and Johnny Walker Red Label—"ranch whiskey" Patterson called it. A good meal revived his spirits and he became bright and cheerful, full of stories. That evening he gave his stetson, purchased at Bradleys in High River, to grandson Jeremy.

That night Patterson suffered a stroke during his sleep. At his mother's request, Alan came over and helped get his father out of bed. A doctor arrived. Could Raymond remember his mother's name, he asked? "Emily" came the reply. The physician held up a pencil, "And what is this?" "Damned if I know," said the octogenarian. A few days later he suffered another stroke in the hospital. Unconscious in the last weeks of his life, he never again opened his eyes or said a word. His wife and children visited often: Alan on his way home from work every day and Janet via plane from Vancouver every weekend. Finally, On October 20, 1984, the soul of Raymond Murray Patterson passed from this world.[1]

PATTERSON'S twilight years included many happy days. Raymond and Marigold lived in a pleasant house in a secluded part of Victoria with no street sign. They tended their garden and enjoyed visits from the grand-children. By the mid seventies all three children were married and rais-ing families of their own. Eldest child Janet Blanchet worked as a secre-tary and administrator, and lived in North Vancouver with husband David

273

Photo John Barnard.

R. M. Patterson in his study in Victoria.

Photo Palmer Lewis.

R. M. Patterson cooking pancakes
at Euchenika Lakes.

and daughter Julia. Alan worked on survey crews in the North for several summers before settling in Victoria, then later Vancouver. He went on to become a lawyer, working his way up to Registrar of the Supreme Court and eventually Master. He married Ann Boys and added three more grandchildren to the Patterson clan: Jeremy, Samantha and Jennifer. Youngest son Robin studied history at the University of Victoria and took a job with the Royal British Columbia Museum in the provincial capital. He and his wife Susan had two children, Mark and Claire. Although none of Patterson's children lived quite as adventurously as their father, they took advantage of the many opportunities life gave them.

They have canoed and rafted many rivers, including the South Nahanni and Tatshenshini, and sailed the waters of the Pacific coast. They have ridden on horseback high into the Canadian Rockies and visited their parents' homeland in the United Kingdom. The grandchildren are still young, but already they have experienced adventures of their own in Canada, Cuba, Australia, England, Europe and elsewhere.

People who lead interesting lives must often respond to the demands of an adoring public. In the half-century since the first article appeared in *The Beaver*, hundreds of thousands of people had read Patterson's stories. Some pilgrims trekked to the house hidden in the trees, surrounded by flower gardens and immaculate lawns, to seek an audience with their hero. Often they brought along a book for the author to autograph. Others wrote, from near and far, with good wishes or to request a book or information. Each received a reply. Not a form letter or short note. Each response from Patterson included another tale, a bit of news or an elaboration on the story of his life and times. Indeed, letters to Mother and his friends had begun his writing career.

Excerpts from his correspondence would fill another volume, but a few examples give the flavour. In a letter to Dr. Harry Jennings and his wife Frances dated October 11, 1966, Patterson wrote thanking them for their fine hospitality—the Pattersons had recently passed through Calgary on the way home. They had consumed copious amounts of fruit and Patterson wondered why they didn't get sick. "Immune, I suppose, through long years of steady munching at all kinds of fruit." They had met the Matthews in the B.C. interior. "Gordon was at Nakusp to meet us & we spent a hilarious evening with him & Mollie there. And, for the second time, Marigold spent her birthday, Oct. 5th at Kootenay Cottages on Kootenay Lake—a perfect day: in the afternoon we gathered a basketful of Italian prunes & sat with our books by the lake shore, waiting till the sun slid behind the mountains, then announcing The Children's Hour. Which we had—by a nice log fire." Commenting on life in England and the prospect of returning there to retire, he wrote, "I could live there happily if the inmates of Britain weren't all insane & were not taxed from cradle to the grave till they can't even call their souls their own. And far too many of them." The northern colony had made a permanent citizen of its adopted son. He ended the letter with one of his enigmatic notes: "1966—the year I made tea in the washing-up water."

Complete strangers received equally warm letters. Patterson wrote Dr. Michael A. S. Jewett of Toronto in late January, 1975, thanking him for his card and the sketch the physician's wife had made of The Gate. "I have been there alone four times & twice with other people—and I always slept on that sandy point." Just before Christmas Steve Stevens had visited from Yellowknife. "Steve says it keeps him fit, packing grub & explosives out to his mine." He apologized for his tardiness in answering Jewett's card and explained that Christmas mail had become "a major hurdle of the year—especially as, around Dec. 15th, I down pen & do not take it up again till January, devoting the days between to parties, friends, our family...and the usual seasonal celebrations. So now I get on with revising a book [The Emperor's Horsemen] & answering those who have been good enough to write to me." He counselled the Jewetts to always avoid the Nahanni and its mosquitoes in June, and ended with a warm salutation, "So, with these various activities, the survivors of that carefree time continue to survive."

In July, 1978, he wrote two letters eleven days apart to James McMarten Jr. of Barton, Vermont. It appears he answered the correspondent's letter once, lost it in his shuffle of papers, and then answered it again. McMartin must have been pleased with the variety of information he received. On July 17, Patterson wrote about his current project, The Emperor's Horsemen. "This has been a study of mine since I was about ten years old (and that is now seventy years ago!), and I found that these young men, travelling in the age before the coming of the machine, had to deal with their obstacles & hazards in exactly the same way as we dealt with ours fifty-six years ago...." He encouraged McMarten to make a trip to the Nahanni even though it had changed since he first saw it in 1927. "But I always felt that, after my old Dangerous River achieved a popularity that I never even dreamed of, to be a National Park was the only safeguard for that wonderful bit of country. The boundaries of that Park are too narrow & skimpily & ungenerously drawn—but at least it's a beginning, & I hope you will find yourself there before long. The canyons are unchanged."

The July 28 letter mentioned Gordon Matthews' death in April, 1976, "thus ending a close friendship of exactly 50 yrs., 1926-76." Albert Faille had died in 1974, and before him, George Pocaterra in 1972 and Fenley Hunter in 1965. The Black Pirate of Nahanni fame in the late 1920s was also gone. "Starke, the old Klondiker, was drowned just where the Coppermine River flows out of Lac de Gras in the Barren Lands. Shot a caribou & ventured out on the rotting spring ice to get it, & the ice let him through." While visiting Dick Turner in March of 1960, he had returned to the scene of one of his near-death experiences. "I snowshoed down the Nahanni from the then trading post (Dick Turner) now I think, the forestry cabin. My object was to gouge out of the log wall of the old La Flair Post the .45 bullet that Stevens just missed me with in May of 1929. The old buildings of La Flair's time were abandoned & derelict, & almost out into the river. I shoved the door open & went in. Alas, all was changed: Jack's 'better half' had evidently wanted more light, & Jack had sawn out that section of the log wall & put a window there! Hence no souvenir for R.M.P. Those buildings are gone now—out into the Nahanni." After his salutation and florid signature he wrote, "'George' to those who live north of 60°."

Among the letters Patterson kept were ones from Palmer Lewis, Dick North, Frank Swanell, the Pocaterras, Nicholas Ignatieff, Vera Burns, W. Kaye Lamb, Bert Sheppard, Harper Reed, Mrs. Crosbie Garstin, Eric Harvie, Sam H. Smith, Norm Caton, Roderick Haig-Brown, Clifford P. Wilson, H. S. Patterson, S. C. Ells, Bert Smith, F. H. Peters, Diamond Jenness and A. M. Narraway. He threw most of the others away.

Luckily, some of his visitors recorded their encounters, which give insight into a modest man. Before writing a review of *The Dangerous River* for the *Victoria Daily Times* in 1954, Tony Dickason visited Patterson and met a "handsome greying man…." When asked how the author covered such incredible distances alone in the North, Patterson replied casually, "I really don't know…. Some people just have a liking for that sort of thing, and I'm one of them." A proponent of outdoor activity, he used the interview to encourage others. "Mr. Patterson, who speaks as softly as his words are interesting, believes northern river travel for sport should be greatly encouraged. The north was made accessible by canoe, yet it is little used today. 'The younger generation is missing a magnificent sport.'"[2]

While on contract to Parks Canada to research the human history of the South Nahanni region, W. D. Addison visited Patterson several times in July of 1974. He found the author quite preoccupied with The Emperor's Horsemen material—more interested in French than Canadian history—but the writer warmed to the discussion as they talked. Canoes surfaced frequently—the writer having little use for ones made of spruce bark. "They're very tippy too because the ones I've seen are very beautifully light but they were little round things like that and if you turned your head the thing started to show the effects of it. I tried one at Hay River or somewhere and I was really glad to get out of it." He casually mentioned a paddle that resided in the house. "I've got a paddle of Faille's in the hall there, that he hewed out for himself. And, in the last two or three years, he sent to me. Said 'I'd like you to have it.'" He opposed a road into the Nahanni and thought the boundaries too tight considering the migration habits of game. Another pet topic was the unsuitability of the name Virginia for the cataract he always called The Falls of the Nahanni. Perhaps, he suggested, they could be renamed after locals or white explorers.[3]

A collection of letters to fellow wilderness aficionado Palmer Lewis of Washington state reveals some of Patterson's other activities during this last decade as well as the effects of aging that he feared would put him into a wheelchair in a nursing home.

In late 1972 he wrote he had been to Woodward's "for one of those ghastly 'author's afternoons.' All things come out in the end, but only Patterson's Poison [rum based] will repair this devilish day."

The next year Patterson quit camping after an outing with Lewis that beat all nights in the woods. "I shall never forget waking up, as I always do, just enough to turn over in my eiderdown, & just at that moment when that meteor, fireball or whatever, passed over, lighting the place like sunset & causing all the horses to make with a clash of bells. All the hills were lit up for a second or two, as by a brilliant sunset. That must have been the sign for the end. 'Patterson, lusisti satis—you have played enough. No more will the stars listen to your snores.'"

By 1974 Patterson was complaining he was feeling "like an old crow sometimes." Odd aches and pains became more pronounced during the late 1970s as did a heart condition that had caused him angina pains since the late 1950s. During these episodes he had "dynamite" pills to put under his tongue. Still, his letters in 1980 state he and Marigold were considering a trip to South Africa by airplane. In another letter he called afternoon tea "the 4 p.m. bun struggle." His apology for not writing more often in 1981 read: "I'm not getting old, but I think I am getting lazy." Through 1982 he continued the ongoing quest to see The Emperor's Horsemen get into print. And his so-called laziness did not prevent him from cutting and splitting wood after his 84th birthday. But, finally, in 1983 his enthusiasm for seeing his last book published began to wane and he wrote, "I do not think that Horsemen book is going to go...." And on October 20, 1983, in one of his last letters to Lewis he closed with the salutation: "May God speed all your endeavours."

American river writer Verne Huser first wrote in 1982 to arrange a visit. "I shall look forward to your proposed visit though I'm afraid all you can hope to find is a very old man, not so very active these days."

Photo Verne Huser.

R. M. Patterson in the last year of his life.

In response to Huser's question about literary influences came the reply, "You ask about books. Well—you can look at my books when you come, & form your own opinion. Mostly books about <u>men doing things</u>. The adventures of the mind seem to have little place. Other people's minds—frequently too long-winded & repetitive…. Authors: Norman Douglas, Kipling, Surtees, and the many who have written one or two good books on the things that I like. About 2000+ books kicking around this house." In August, 1983, he granted Huser permission to extract a section from *The Dangerous River* to use in an anthology titled *River Reflections* that also included extracts from the works of Sigurd Olson, Mark Twain, William Faulkner, John Steinbeck, Roderick Haig-Brown, John McPhee, Norman Maclean, Ann Zwinger, R. D. Lawrence and Edward Abbey. Patterson's September letter to Huser suggested his failing health. "Thanks for your letter—which I might have answered before, but what with impaired vision and *<u>ODTAA</u>, I have come to detest the sight of my own handwriting, especially in the opening bars of a letter." At the bottom of the page was an explanation for the abbrieviation: "One Damn Thing After Another."[4]

Patterson's beautiful handwritten letters had come to an end, but not before he penned a wonderful synopsis of his relationship with Marigold. Letters to friends were often more like a conversation over a drink than formal documents. In one such note to publisher Gray Campbell, he stopped partway through and upon picking up the pen returned to the discussion of trial marriages so common in the late 1970s. "We never had all these advantages—& yet we seem to have somehow made it. Marigold & I, if we make it for another six or seven months, will be celebrating our golden wedding—which will be becoming rarities pretty soon, what with trial runs & changes of partners. I suppose 50 yrs. rather stamps one as unenterprising, or as a stick-in-the-mud—but there is one great bond and advantage in it: you can reminisce with your partner about all the asinine things you did when you were first turned loose, as a pair, on the world. Ours would fill a book—and that is one reason why I have always retained such a strong affection for Alberta. That, and a few subsidiary reasons, too."[5]

Verne Huser's September, 1984, letter elicited no poignant reply from Patterson's pen. Instead, there came a note above Marigold's signature. Her husband had experienced a "stroke two weeks ago, and is still unconscious…we don't know what the outcome will be…." Sad as she was to see him slipping from this world, her advice might have come from her husband's pen: "I have told the family to snatch the day, and use it to the full, and we have done that all our lives; a good ruling I think."[6]

Epilogue
2000

ON August 19, 2000, people gathered from around western Canada to celebrate the naming of a mountain in Alberta's Highwood Range after R. M. Patterson. Patterson's Peak rises to almost 9000 feet to the north of Mount Head and is clearly visible as part of the skyline from many parts of southern Alberta, including the city of Calgary.

R. M. Patterson's widow Marigold, daughter Janet and sons Alan and Robin attended the afternoon party. The day had been a long time coming; Raymond and Marigold had first visited the little lake on the north side of the mountain in 1931. By the late 1930s locals were referring to the mountain as Patterson's Peak after Patterson's curious antics on its northern slopes in 1936. Gillean Daffern began lobbying the Alberta government to name the peak after Patterson in the late 1970s. In 1996 Dave Birrell took up the cause and finally, on March 1, 2000, the name became official.

Photo Marty Dewis.

Patterson's Peak from Sullivan Hill, Highway 541. August 19, 2000.

Photo Tom Van Hardeveld.

Left to right, top row: Cousin Camilla Coates, Alan Patterson, Robin Patterson, Robin's wife Susan. Bottom row: David Finch, Janet Blanchet, Marigold Patterson, Alan's daughter Samantha.

And so, on a sunny summer afternoon, the Patterson family, former neighbours in the Highwood and almost 100 friends—old and new— gathered for a brief ceremony. Politicians and government officials brought greetings and outdoor writers told of the inspiration they had received from reading Patterson's books. A time for visiting followed. As the sun moved across the afternoon sky, ninety-six year-old Marigold Patterson graciously chatted with the many people who had come to celebrate her husband's contribution to the story of the Canadian West.

Acknowledgements

IT TAKES many people to write a book, and even more to convince the author to get it done. Glenn Finch, my father, telephoned one day and said something like "You better go and see that Nahanni country, otherwise, how will you ever write that book?!" Of course, I never had enough money to go North, but that never stopped anyone else from adventure. So North I went and I found the Nahanni as strange, enticing and unpredictable in the mid-1990s as Patterson found it in the late 1920s.

But the story of this book began several years before I headed for the largest tributary of the Liard River. While out canoeing one day I saw a strange apparition, standing up in his canoe and poling up the Bow River in the city of Calgary. Mike McBryan became a good friend and not only introduced me to upstream travel, but to Patterson. "You should really read *The Dangerous River*, about this guy who...."

Another paddler got me hooked on canoes. "Why not build a cedar stripper this winter?" said Bill Anderson, an adventurer and photographer when other duties can be avoided. And so every spare moment of the dark days of the end of one year and the early part of the next became filled with the hundreds of little details that go into making a cedar-strip canoe. Not just any canoe, mind you, but a Prospector—the workhorse of the trapper in the North. And it was through this canoe that I became part of the paddling fraternity in southern Alberta as well as other parts of Canada and the United States.

Three people pointed out the incredible resources that archives and libraries contain. Bill McKee and Doug Cass, archivists at the Glenbow Archives in Calgary, egged me on to do historical research through means both helpful and devious. Lindsay Moir of the Glenbow Library has assisted the research process for this book and countless other projects with limitless enthusiasm, creativity, good humour and professionalism. Archivists at the British Columbia Archives and Records Service were also helpful as were their peers at the Edmonton City Archives, the Provincial Archives of Alberta, the National Archives of Canada, the Royal Opera House in London and many other research centres.

Documents alone cannot provide enough information for a biography of an avid lover of the outdoors and so the research process also took me into the field. Canoeing the South Nahanni was important and for the chance to join their guided tours on that wilderness river I thank Dave Hibbard of Nahanni Wilderness Adventures and his guides Steve McGrath, Miles Davis and Eric Dumont as well as Wendy Grater of Black Feather Wilderness Adventures and her guides Patrick Henry and Matt Bender. The clients on these trips provided important insights into the experience of canoeing Patterson's river and some of them, Blaine and Ron Dalby, have become good friends. Neil Hartling of Nahanni River Adventures has also been an important contact in the research process and his book, *Nahanni: River of Gold...River of Dreams*, is an important resource for anyone considering a trip on this river. Peter Jowett's book, *Nahanni: the River Guide*, is the best single source of information. Trips to the Nahanni typically do not provide the visitor much time to get to know the people of the North, but it is hard to pass through Yellowknife, Fort Simpson, Nahanni Butte and Lindberg Landing without interacting with the special people who live in a land that is challenging most of the year. The way they share a part of their lives during the short summer with visitors is both gracious and sacrificial. Many thanks to pilot Jacques Harvey and his workhorse, a turbo-charged Twin Otter, for safe, reliable and relatively quiet shuttles into the Bunny Bar on the South Nahanni upstream of the park reserve.

Thanks to the people of the stores, shops and the pizza place in Fort Simpson as well as the children and adults who chat shyly, but willingly, with interlopers. Stephen "I was born in England and have never recovered from that" Rowan guided us through the history of the village with knowledge and insight.

Margaret and Paul Jones and their daughter Anne-Marie of Lindberg Landing make each visit special. Edwin and Sue Lindberg, who share their surname with the Landing, are some of the best hosts in the world. Edwin's mother Anna still remembered the day Patterson staggered in on that cold January 1929 day from his cabin up the South Nahanni. She showed us the little sled she and her husband Ole lent Patterson for his snowshoe trip to Fort Simpson. And she still recoiled in terror as she recalled the huge sled dogs Matthews and Patterson returned with a few weeks later, animals that towered over the slight woman when they jumped up on her to play.

The interpreters and staff at the museums in Yellowknife, Fort Simpson and Blackstone Landing all provide additional information on the history, culture, context and current issues in this special part of the North.

In an attempt to ride some of Patterson's trails in Southern Alberta, I spent time with Jean, Kent and Luree Williamson at Elkana Ranch near Bragg Creek, learning to pay attention to horses and to make time in the saddle a harmonious experience for rider and mount alike. Later came the chance to join a cattle drive from the Buffalo Head Ranch up Flat Creek to the high country. The denizens of the Highwood River allowed me into their lives and homes, under various pretexts, and I attended brandings, helped repair fences, ride herd, put out chemical and drink scotch with some of the men and women who keep alive a tradition of feeding stock on natural grass—not in a feedlot. Although I interviewed Bert Sheppard several times in the last years of his life, it was the generation of cowboys and partners that followed his horse—literally and figuratively—that I came to know better: Gaile, Kerri, Trevor and Lisa-Marie Gallup, Larry Gallup and Marlane Cotter, Steve Hoar and Barb Binkley, Bob Spaith, Rich and Jan Roenish, Josephine Bews, Tommy and Rosemarie Bews, Billy Bews, and Joey and Margaret Bews as well as Lenore and Roy Maclean and Tim and Julie Maclean and many more fine folk from this special valley.

Louis and Betty DePaoli moved into the Buffalo Head Ranch in the cold and snowy days of January 1950 and with their son Don and his wife Suzanne keep Pocaterra's matchless property successful as a working ranch, though they have kept plenty busy without the added adventure of taking in dudes.

My first overnight trail ride was with Walter Morris and his wranglers up Evan-Thomas Creek into Pocaterra's coal mining territory as part of Rick and Denise Guinn's operations at Boundary Stables in the Kananaskis Valley. Later, Janet Blanchet and I had the chance to join Dewy and Jan Matthews' Anchor D outfit for a few days in the high country near the headwaters of Sheep Creek. Heather Mills and Cleve Kidd of the Anchor D staff also provided important insights into the complexity of providing riding tours to the mountains of southwestern Alberta.

There are many other special people who contributed to this story with their recollections of the moments they bumped into either the person or the writings of R. M. Patterson: W. D. Addison, Merrily Aubrey, Adolf Baumgart, Dave Birrell, Wendy Bush, Gray and Eleanor Campbell and their son Dane Campbell, Craig and Sandra Cassidy, Paul, Elva, Michael, Tania and Mark Dennis, Marty Dewis, Betty Donaldson, Simon Evans, Jenny Feick, Alastair Ferries, Carol Fullerton, Donny and Joan Gardner, Ted Grant, Linda Hanley, Stan Harding, Marion Harrison, Ted Hart, Fenley Hunter, Verne Huser, Bill and Dorothy Jackson, John and Nicola Jennings, Norm Kagan, Arnor Larson, Joel Lipkind, Keith and Sandy Logan, George Luste, Kenzie and Faye MacLeod, Joyce Mason, Dick, Mike and Carol Matthews, Wayne McGonigle, the late Vern Millard, Keith Morton and Mary Enright, Ruthie Oltmann, P. K. Page, Ken and Laurie Powell, Jim Raffan, Phillipa Rispin, Brian Rusted, Wally Schaber, Mike and Glennys Schintz, George Scotter, Doc Seaman, Earl Shaw, Chuck Stormes, Anne Swiderski and Mark Dagenais, Ron and Elaine Tessolini, Alister Thomas, J. P. Thomas, Rob Toller and Heather Wattie, the late Pierre Trudeau, Bob Turner, Dick Turner, Linda Wiggins and Steve Herrero, Brian Young and many, many others who helped in important ways.

Thanks also to the publishers who continue to keep Patterson's books in print: Boston Mills Press for *The Dangerous River* and Horsdal & Schubart Ltd. for the other four titles. For permission to quote briefly from *The Buffalo Head* and *Far Pastures* we give credit to Horsdal & Schubart Ltd. here as well as in footnotes to the relevant passages.

Without the cooperation of the Patterson family this biography could not have been written. In particular I offer my deepest thanks to Mrs. R. M. Patterson who kindly and accurately answered many questions over the years and provided access to important materials. Many of its sources still remain with the family and are not part of the archival or public record. Robin Patterson suggested I contact his mother and arrange for an interview and I appreciate the help he and his wife Susan have provided for this project. Alan Patterson has also supplied important information and allowed me to interview him several times. His children Jeremy, Jennifer and Samantha have also commented on their recollections of their grandfather. The eldest grandchild, Julia Blanchet, provided a written account of her impressions of Patterson.

The late Robert Coates, Patterson's cousin, provided information regarding his business relationship with Patterson when they ranched together in southern Alberta in the early 1950s. Further afield, during a research trip to England in 1998, Tom and Sally Fenwick graciously hosted Janet Blanchet and me during a visit to the northeastern part of England and showed us around the massive country house called Foresters Lodge where Patterson spent many happy childhood days with lifelong friend Edwin Fenwick. Andrew Forbes of Tisbury in the south of England also supported the research for this project by offering hospitality as well as his own recollections of his distant relative.

And finally, of the Patterson clan and friends there is Janet Blanchet. As the eldest child and only daughter born to Raymond and Marigold Patterson, she became my contact with the family. What started out as a cordial business relationship between a biographer and an official contact with the estate turned into a friendship that has grown to include my wife Jeannie and daughter Annie. Janet helped arrange photographs for the book from the family photo albums, answered dozens of detailed questions about life as a member of the Patterson family, and read the manuscript several times and made helpful comments and suggestions. She and I also visited England together, doing research at Patterson's boarding school, at Oxford, in London and other places her father loved. One memorable day we hiked Red Pike, High Stile and High Crag in the Lake District, an adventure that allowed us afterwards to appreciate a supper of locally harvested fish at a pub in the village of Buttermere. Janet is, without a doubt, the world's most gracious travelling companion and an excellent driver in spite of the fact that she brakes—without warning—for every bunny that crosses the road on the foggy moors of northern England.

Bruce Morrison introduced me to literary agent Joanne Kellock and I thank them both for their assistance in helping find the publisher for this book. Dinners with Joanne are one of the highlights of life that help keep otherwise perennially discouraged writers dedicated to their craft.

The staff at a publishing house are always professional, overworked and incredibly dedicated to the task of creating books from the manuscripts that wander through the front door. But Rocky Mountain Books, which began publishing outdoor guidebooks in 1979, adds to these qualities a genuine interest in the men and women who research and write books. Tony Daffern is the co-publisher, Marcelle MacCallum is the graphic artist, Ana Tercero creates the maps, Janice Redlin is an outstanding editor, Joanne Godziuk is the distribution department and Claire Moller creates the publicity and promotional opportunities that move the books from the warehouse into the reader's hands. And finally there is co-publisher Gillean Daffern, who also researches and writes the best guidebooks for hikers and skiers in southern Alberta. To this biography, Gill brought her incredible knowledge of western Canadian outdoor history and served as a most thorough substantive editor. Her interest in Patterson, his life, times and adventures encouraged me in many ways. I even reached the top of Patterson's Peak with Gill and Tony on August 14, 2000. Thanks so very much.

My mother Anne Finch, sister Sylvia Adams and late sister Glenys Finch Hardock also took an interest in this project and I thank them for their love.

Jeannie Finch and our daughter Annie have been very special to me during the years spent researching and writing this story. They did not suffer, to the best of my knowledge, most of the usual injustices perpetrated by obsessive authors on their families. Instead, I believe they benefited from the process of creating this book when they joined in on hiking, camping, canoeing and horseback trips to experience some of the wonder and majesty of the territory that Patterson loved so much. Jeannie and Annie have also helped me balance this passionate quest for the story of Patterson's life with a life full of adventures of our own. I love you both from the bottom of my heart.

In spite of all the help from this host of friends and acquaintances, I take responsibility for any errors of fact, omission or interpretation that appear in this text. Feel free to contact me through the publisher with comments and I will make corrections in a future edition of this biography.

David Finch
October, 2000

List of Works by R. M. Patterson

1933—Patterson self-published an eight-page booklet *The Flat River Country North West Territories of Canada*.

1947—First article, "River of Deadmen's Valley" printed in the June edition of *The Beaver*.

1950—"A Thousand Miles by Canoe" printed in July 28 edition of *Country Life*.

1951—Patterson self-published *Dear Mother: A Collection of Letters Written from Rossall Between May 1911 and March 1917*.

1952—"Nahanni Revisited" printed in the June edition of *The Beaver*.

1954—*The Dangerous River* published in New York and London. More than twelve editions have been released by various publishers since; one in Dutch, another in Spanish.

1955—"Fort Simpson, McKenzie's River" printed in the March edition of *Blackwood's Magazine*.
—The Hudson's Bay Records Society published Samuel Black's *A Journal of a Voyage From Rocky Mountain Portage in Peace River To the Sources of Finlay's Branch And North West Ward In Summer 1824* with a major introduction by Patterson.

1957—"The Beaches of Lukannon" printed in the September edition of *Blackwood's Magazine*.

1958—"Springtime in the Rockies" printed in the October edition of *Blackwood's Magazine*.

1960—"The Calgary Road" printed in the May edition of *Blackwood's Magazine*.
"The Foothill City" printed in the November edition of *Blackwood's Magazine*.
"The Bow River" printed in the December edition of *Blackwood's Magazine*.

1961—*The Buffalo Head* published.

1963—*Far Pastures* published.

1966—*Trail to the Interior* published.

1968—*Finlay's River* published.

1969—Began writing "The Emperor's Horsemen."

Chronology

1898, May 13 Born to Henry and Emily Patterson ... p. 8

1911-1917 Attended Rossall Public School in northwest England ... p. 10

1918 Served in artillery in France. Captured on March 21 ... p. 25

1919-1924 Attended Oxford and worked at the Bank of England ... p. 32

1924-29 Homesteaded in Alberta ... p. 40, canoed the South Nahanni ... p. 64

1929, July 4 Married Marigold Portman ... p. 153

1930 Bought sheep ranch, Buckspring. Daughter Janet born May 21 ... p. 155

1933 Sold Buckspring and bought the Buffalo Head Ranch ... p. 155

1936 First son Alan born on October 15 ... p. 183

1939, May Patterson's mother, Emily Taylor Patterson, died ... p. 206

1944, May 15 Second son Robin born ... p. 219

1945, July 16 Sold Buffalo Head and moved to Vancouver Island ... p. 221

1947 Began writing articles for *The Beaver* magazine ... p. 230

1948 Took 14-foot canoe on the Stikine, Dease and Liard rivers ... p. 262

1949 Took 17-foot canoe on the Parsnip, Finlay and Peace rivers ... p. 264

1954 Canoed northern rivers with cousin Christopher Paterson ... p. 245

1955 Explored the Pack and Parsnip rivers, researching *Finlay's River* ... p. 266

1959 St. John's College, Oxford, conferred M.A. degree in his absence ... p. 254

1960 Sold Vancouver Island house and took up residence in England ... p. 254

1961-1962 Travelled in Europe researching Napoleon's horsemen ... p. 256

1962 Returned to Canada and settled in Victoria, Vancouver Island ... p. 256

1969 Began writing "The Emperor's Horsemen" ... p. 269

1979 Celebrated fifty years of marriage to Marigold ... p. 280

1984 October 20 Died in hospital in Victoria ... p. 280

Endnotes

THE EARLY YEARS—1896 TO 1916

1. Interview with Patterson by W. D. Addison, July 23-25, 1974, British Columbia Archives and Records Service, Victoria/Add.MSS. 2762, box 6, file 1, p. 123.
2. Ibid., p. 10 and email from Janet Blanchet, September 30, 1996.
3. R. M. Patterson, *The Buffalo Head*. New York: Sloane, 1961, p. 7.
4. Ibid., pp. 6-7.
5. Ibid., pp. 7-8.
6. Ibid., p. 9.
7. Ibid., pp. 10-11.
8. C. S. Lewis, *Surprised by Joy*. New York: Harcourt Brace & Company, 1956, pp. 80-81, 89.
9. *The Buffalo Head*, pp. 11-13.
10. R. M. Patterson, *Dear Mother: a Collection of Letters Written from Rossall Between May 1911 and March 1917*. Victoria, B. C.: self-published, 1951, p. 10.
11. Ibid., p. 20.
12. Ibid., p. 5.
13. Ibid., July 16, 1911, p. 6.
14. Ibid., October 6, 1912, p. 17.
15. Ibid., November 24, 1912, pp. 18-19.
16. Ibid., May 7, 1911, p. 5.
17. Ibid., July 5, 1912, July 21, 1912, p. 16.
18. Ibid., November 7, 1914, p. 35.
19. Ibid., October 1, 1911, p. 8.
20. Ibid., February 25, 1912, p. 12.
21. Ibid., March 25, 1912, p. 13.
22. Ibid., May 19, 1912, p. 13.
23. Ibid., November 24, 1912, pp. 18-19.
24. Ibid., May 28, 1912, p. 14.
25. Ibid., November 29, 1913, pp. 26-27.
26. Ibid., May 31, 1913, pp. 21-22.
27. Ibid., November 8, 1913, p. 26.
28. Ibid., February 15, 1914, pp. 30-31.
29. Ibid., June 12, 1914, p. 33.
30. Ibid., December 13, 1914, pp. 37-38.
31. Ibid., November 18, 1914, p. 36.
32. Ibid., November 23, 1914, p. 36.
33. Ibid., December 13, 1914, pp. 37-88.
34. Ibid., January 30, 1915, p. 39.
35. Ibid., February 5, 1915, p. 39.
36. Ibid., February 7, 1915, pp. 39-40.
37. Ibid., November 27, 1915, p. 53.
38. Ibid., February 26, 1915, pp. 41-42.
39. Ibid., March 6, 1915, pp. 42-43.
40. Ibid., p. 44.
41. Ibid., pp. 48-49.
42. Ibid., November 13, 1915, pp. 51-52.
43. Ibid., March 14, 1915, p. 43.
44. Ibid., March 21, 1915, pp. 43-44.
45. Ibid., November 25, 1915, pp. 52-53.
46. Ibid., December 4, 1915, p. 54.
47. Ibid., November 26, 1911, p. 10.
48. Ibid., October 11, 1915, pp. 49-50.
49. Ibid., November 8, 1915, p. 51.
50. Ibid., March 11, 1916, p. 59.
51. Ibid., June 16, 1916, pp. 60-62.
52. Ibid., October 1, 1916, pp. 63-66.
53. C. S. Lewis, *Surprised by Joy*, pp. 147-150.
54. *Dear Mother: A Collection of Letters…*, p. 67.
55. Ibid., January 22, 1917, p. 70.
56. Ibid., January 29, 1917, pp. 70-71.
57. Ibid.
58. Ibid., March 7, 1917, p. 73-74.
59. Ibid., April 4, 1917, p. 77-78.
60. Ibid., June 6, 1951, p. 77-78.

WAR AND A SORT OF PEACE—1917 TO 1923

1. *The Buffalo Head*, p. 21.
2. Letter from Sgt. Harold J. Rabon to Emily Patterson, April 9, 1918, BCARS/Add.MSS. 2762, box 5, file 10.
3. *The Buffalo Head*, pp. 13-19.
4. Ibid., p. 20.
5. Ibid., p. 22.
6. Ibid., p. 26.
7. Ibid., p. 33.
8. Letter from George R. I. to Patterson, BCARS/Add.MSS. 2762, box 5, file 11.
9. *The Buffalo Head*, p. 47.
10. Ibid., p. 49.
11. Ibid., p. 51.
12. Ibid., p. 53.
13. Interview with Janet Blanchet and Alan Patterson, October 12, 1995.
14. *The Buffalo Head*, p. 56.

HOMESTEADING—1924 TO 1926

1. R. M. Patterson, *Far Pastures*. Sidney, B. C.: Gray's Publishing, 1963, p. 8.
2. Interview with Patterson by W. D. Addison, BCARS/Add.MSS. 2762, box 6, file 1, p. 10.
3. Letter from Patterson to Mother, BCARS/Add.MSS. 2762, box 3, file 6.
4. Ibid., May 19, 1924.
5. Ibid., May 22, 1924.
6. Howard Palmer with Tamara Palmer, *Alberta: A New History*. Edmonton: Hurtig, 1990, pp. 187, 198-202.
7. Letter from Patterson to Mother, Sunday, June 28, 1924, BCARS/Add.MSS. 2762, box 3, file 6.
8. *The Buffalo Head*, p. 61.
9. Ibid., p. 62.
10. *Far Pastures*, p. 8.
11. Ibid., pp. 9-12.
12. Letter from Patterson to Mother, September 14, 1924, BCARS/Add.MSS. 2762, box 3, file 6.
13. *The Buffalo Head*, pp. 65-67.
14. *Far Pastures*, p. 25.
15. Ibid., p. 16.
16. Ibid., pp. 18-31.
17. Letter from Patterson to Mother, October 24, 1924, BCARS/Add.MSS. 2762, box 3, file 6.
18. Ibid., November 26, 1924.
19. Ibid., December 7, 1924.
20. Ibid., December 21, 1924.
21. *Far Pastures*, pp. 36-37.
22. Ibid., pp. 34-36.
23. *The Buffalo Head*, pp. 79-80.
24. Letter from Patterson to Edwin Fenwick, July 28, 1925, BCARS/Add.MSS. 2762, box 3, file 5.
25. Ibid., November 21, 1925.
26. Ibid., November 23, 1925.
27. Ibid., February 8, 1926.
28. *Far Pastures*, p. 54.
29. Letter from Patterson to Mother, May 4, 1926, BCARS/Add.MSS. 2762, box 3, file 7.
30. *Far Pastures*, p. 56.
31. Letter from Patterson to Edwin Fenwick, February 8, 1926, BCARS/Add.MSS. 2762, box 3, file 5.
32. Ibid., March 27, 1926.
33. Ibid., May 29, 1926.
34. Letter from Patterson to Mother, May 4, 1926, BCARS/Add.MSS. 2762, box 3, file 7.
35. *Far Pastures*, p. 58.
36. Letter from Patterson to Mother, July 7, 1926, BCARS/Add.MSS. 2762, box 3, file 7.
37. Ibid., July 10, 1926.
38. Interview with Dick Matthews, October 13, 1995.
39. Ibid., R. M. Patterson, *The Dangerous River*. London: Allen and Unwin, 1954, p. 258 and *The Buffalo Head*, p. 79.
40. Interview with Patterson by W. D. Addison, BCARS/Add.MSS. 2762, box 6, file 1, pp. 66-67.
41. Interview with Dick Matthews, October 13, 1995.
42. Letter from Patterson to Edwin Fenwick, August 1, 1926, BCARS/Add.MSS. 2762, box 3, file 5.
43. *The Buffalo Head*, pp. 7-10.
44. Edgar Christian, *Unflinching: A Diary of Tragic Adventure*. London: John Murray, 1937.
45. *The Buffalo Head*, p. 73 and *The Dangerous River*, p. 13.

HARD TO KILL—1927

1. Edgar Christian, *Unflinching: A Diary of Tragic Adventure*, p. 10.
2. Ibid., p. 19.
3. Ibid., pp. 23-24.
4. Ibid., pp. 136-142.
5. Letter from Patterson to Mother, May 24, 1927, BCARS/Add.MSS. 2762, box 3, file 8.
6. *The Buffalo Head*, p. 54.
7. *The Dangerous River*, p. 14.
8. *The Buffalo Head*, p. 73.
9. Letter from Patterson to Mother, May 24, 1927, BCARS/Add.MSS. 2762, box 3, file 8.
10. *The Dangerous River*, p. 14.
11. *The Buffalo Head*, p. 74.
12. Letter from Patterson to Mother, May 24, 1927, BCARS/Add.MSS. 2762, box 3, file 8.
13. Eric Morse, *Fur Trade Canoe Routes of Canada/Then and Now*. Toronto: University of Toronto Press, 1969, p. 95.
14. *The Dangerous River*, p. vii.
15. Ibid., p. 43.
16. Letter from Patterson to Mother, June 9, 1927, BCARS/Add.MSS. 2762, box 3, file 8.
17. R. S. Surtees, *Jorrock's Jaunts & Jollities*. London: Eyre & Spottiswoode, 1931, p. 212.
18. Letter from Patterson to Mother, June 17, 1927, BCARS/Add.MSS. 2762, box 3, file 8.
19. Ibid., June 24, 1927.
20. Ibid., July 3, 1927.
21. Ibid., July 7 and 8, 1927.
22. *The Buffalo Head*, p. 76.
23. *The Beaver*, March, 1924, pp. 237-238.
24. Ibid., June, 1927, p. 47.
25. *The Dangerous River*, p. 47.
26. *The Beaver*, March, 1928, pp. 164-165.
27. *The Dangerous River*, p. 32.
28. Interview with Patterson by W. D. Addison, BCARS/Add.MSS. 2762, box 6, file 1, p. 70.
29. *Far Pastures*, p. 235.
30. *The Dangerous River*, p. 16.
31. *The Buffalo Head*, pp. 75-76.
32. Dick Turner, *Nahanni*. Saanichton, B. C.: Hancock House, 1977, pp. 113-114.
33. Ibid., pp. 115-116.
34. Ibid., p. 120.
35. *The Dangerous River*, p. 31.
36. *The Buffalo Head*, p. 78.
37. Interview with Patterson by W. D. Addison, BCARS/Add.MSS. 2762, box 6, file 1, p. 21.
38. *The Dangerous River*, p. 35.
39. Interview with Patterson by W. D. Addison, BCARS/Add.MSS. 2762, box 6, file 1, p. 123.
40. Ibid.
41. Ibid., p. 122
42. *The Dangerous River*, p. 61.
43. Email from Janet Blanchet, December 13, 1995.
44. *The Dangerous River*, pp. 69-71.
45. Ibid., p. 73.
46. Interview with Patterson by W. D. Addison, BCARS/Add.MSS. 2762, box 6, file 1, p. 117.
47. Interview with Patterson by W. D. Addison, BCARS/Add.MSS. 2762, box 6, file 1, p. 57.
48. *The Dangerous River*, p. 77.
49. Ibid., pp. 93-94.

GOLD AND FUR—1928 AND 1929

1. Letter from Patterson to Mother, February 17, 1928, BCARS/Add.MSS. 2762, box 3, file 8.
2. *Far Pastures*, p. 77.
3. Letter from Patterson to Mother, March 29, 1928, BCARS/Add.MSS. 2762, box 3, file 8.
4. *Far Pastures*, pp. 80-84.
5. Ibid., pp. 61-92.
6. *The Dangerous River*, pp. 111-114.
7. Ibid., p. 106.
8. Ibid., p. 107.
9. Letter from Patterson to Mother, August 11, 1928, BCARS/Add.MSS. 2762, box 3, file 8.
10. *Far Pastures*, p. 7.

11. *A Trip to the Western Arctic—1928* by Fenley Hunter, August 9, 1928, National Archives of Canada/reel A-863, at head of Canyon Camp (First White Sheep Camp).
12. Letter from Fenley Hunter to Patterson, April 12, 1951, BCARS/Add.MSS. 2762, box 1, file 9.
13. Letter from Fenley Hunter to Curtis Smith, March 14, 1951, BCARS/Add.MSS. 2762, box 1, file 9.
14. Bruce W. Hodgins & Gwyneth Hoyle, *Canoeing North Into The Unknown: A Record of River Travel: 1874 to 1974.* Toronto: Natural Heritage/Natural History Inc., 1994, pp. 128, 141, 196.
15. *A Trip to the Western Arctic—1928* by Fenley Hunter, NAC/reel A-863. This material is based on the diary for the dates July 26 to August 27, 1928.
16. Letter from Patterson to Mother, August 11, 1928, BCARS/Add.MSS. 2762, box 3, file 8.
17. Ibid., August 11, 1928.
18. *The Flat River Country North West Territories of Canada*, BCARS/NW/972.16/P318f.
19. *The Dangerous River*, pp. 145-148, 154, 163, 165, 167, 200, 239.
20. Ibid., p. 157.
21. Ibid., pp. 100, 178, 182, 207, 228.
22. Ibid., p. 177.
23. Ibid., p. 187.
24. Ibid., pp. 200, 206.
25. Ibid., p. 192.
26. *The Buffalo Head*, p. 58.
27. *The Dangerous River*, pp. 201-227.
28. Ibid., p. 214.
29. Ibid., pp. 216-217.
30. *Dear Mother, A Collection of Letters…*, pp. 48-49.
31. *The Dangerous River*, p. 220.
32. Ibid., pp. 223-224.
33. Ibid., pp. 227-230.
34. See chapter titled "Fort Simpson, Mackenzie's River" in *Far Pastures* for more details.
35. *The Dangerous River*, p. 232.
36. Ibid., p. 186.
37. *The Buffalo Head*, pp. 79-80.
38. Interview with Patterson by W. D. Addison, BCARS/Add.MSS. 2762, box 6, file 1, p. 97.
39. *The Dangerous River*, pp. 250-251.
40. Ibid., p. 251.
41. Ibid., pp. 176, 187.
42. Ibid., p. 257.
43. *The Buffalo Head*, pp. 81-82.
44. *Far Pastures*, p. 111.
45. Ibid., p. 235.
46. Lorne Manchester, *Canada's Aviation Industry.* Toronto: McGraw-Hill Co. of Canada, 1968, pp. 46, 54.
47. *Canadian Annual Review of Politics and Public Affairs.* Downsview, Ontario: University of Toronto Press, *1928-29*, pp. 214-215, *1929-30*, p. 334.
48. Kenneth M. Molson, *Pioneering in Canadian Air Transport.* Winnipeg: James Richardson & Sons, Ltd., 1974, p. 22.

THE BUFFALO HEAD YEARS—1929 TO 1946

1. Rafaelle Kennedy, Duchess of Leinster, *So Brief a Dream.* London and New York: W. H. Allen, 1973, pp. 29-31.
2. Interview with Marigold Patterson, July 12, 1991.
3. Interview with Marigold Patterson by Janet Blanchet, February 21, 1999.
4. *The Buffalo Head*, p. 72.
5. Letter from Gordon Matthews to Patterson, February 4, 1931, BCARS/Add.MSS. 2762, box 1, files 11-12.
6. Interview with Marigold Patterson, July 12, 1991.
7. *Far Pastures*, p. 116.
8. Glendale Women's Institute, Alta., *Taming the Prairie Wool: A History of the Districts of Glendale, Westminster and Bearspaw.* Glendale Women's Institute, 1965, p. 158.
9. Letters from Gordon Matthews to Patterson, February 4, 1931, March 11, 1931, June 8, 1931, BCARS/Add.MSS. 2762, box 1, files 11-12.
10. Interview with Marigold Patterson, November 2, 1995.
11. *Far Pastures*, p. 186.
12. Cochrane and Area Historical Society, *Big Hill Country: Cochrane and Area.* Cochrane: The Cochrane and Area Historical Society, 1977, p. 340.
13. Letters from Patterson to G. W. Pocaterra, July 28, 1942, April 15, 1962, Glenbow Archives, M6340, file 111.
14. Letter from Patterson to Edwin Fenwick, September 28, 1929, BCARS 93-6227.

15. Ibid., November 19, 1929.
16. Letter from G. W. Pocaterra to Patterson, February 12, 1937, BCARS/Add.MSS. 2762, box 1, file 14.
17. Letter from Patterson to Edwin Fenwick, November 1, 1931, BCARS 93-6227.
18. *The Buffalo Head*, pp. 87-88.
19. Ibid., p. 88.
20. Ibid., pp. 106-107.
21. Ibid., p. 109.
22. Ibid., p. 111.
23. Ibid., pp. 113-115.
24. Ibid., p. 107.
25. Letter from Patterson to Edwin Fenwick, August 18, 1932, BCARS 93-6227.
26. Interview with Marigold Patterson, November 2, 1995.
27. Letter from Patterson to G. W. Pocaterra, December 15, 1930, Glenbow Archives, M6340, file 111.
28. *Far Pastures*, p. 116.
29. T. W. Blakiston, *Further Papers Relative to the Exploration by the Expedition under Captain Palliser of that portion of British North America which lies between The Northern Branch of the River Saskatchewan and the Frontier of the United States; and between the Red River and the Rocky Mountains, and thence to the Pacific Ocean.* London: G. E. Eyre and W. Spottiswoode, 1860, pp. 66-68.
30. Interview with Adolf Baumgart, June 18, 1992.
31. Unpublished manuscript: "Son of the Mountains: the Story of George W. Pocaterra, Pioneer Alberta Rancher, Explorer, and Friend of the Stoney Indians," by Norma Piper Pocaterra, Glenbow Archives, M6752.
32. Interview with P. K. Page, November 7, 1995.
33. Interview with Adolf Baumgart, June 18, 1992.
34. *Far Pastures*, p. 4.
35. Interview with Mike Schintz, February 17, 1996.
36. Agreement to Purchase, BCARS/Add.MSS. 2762, box 5, file 1, April 7, 1933.
37. G. W. Pocaterra papers at Glenbow Archives, M6340, file 161, October 14, 1933.
38. Interview with Marigold Patterson, July 12, 1991.
39. Letter from Pocaterra to Patterson, April 19, 1938, BCARS/Add.MSS. 2762, box 1, file 14.
40. Interview with Adolf Baumgart, June 18, 1992.
41. Information provided by Janet Blanchet, August 23, 1999.
42. Interview with Marigold Patterson, July 12, 1991.
43. Ibid.
44. Letters to Patterson from J. C. Hargrave, 1940, BCARS/Add.MSS. 2762, box 5, file 1.
45. Interview with Marigold Patterson, July 12, 1991.
46. Bert Sheppard, *Just About Nothing: The Hardest Part of Doing Nothing is Knowing When to Quit.* Calgary: McAra Printing, 1977, p. 121.
47. Ibid., pp. 22-23.
48. Ibid., p. 33.
49. Food orders for May 2 & 11, 1936, and October 16, 1941, from Western Grocers, Calgary, BCARS/Add. MSS. 2762, box 5, file 1.
50. Email from Janet Blanchet, December 13, 1995.
51. Interview with Marigold Patterson by Janet Blanchet, February 21, 1999.
52. Invoice, BCARS/Add.MSS. 2762, box 5, file 6.
53. Ibid., BCARS/Add.MSS. 2762, box 5, file 8.
54. Ibid., BCARS/Add. MSS. 2762, box 5, file 6.
55. Interview with Alan Patterson and Janet Blanchet by author and Verne Huser, October 12, 1995.
56. Ibid.
57. Email from Janet Blanchet, November 13, 1995.
58. Interview with Alan Patterson and Janet Blanchet by author and Verne Huser, October 12, 1995.
59. Letter from Patterson to G. W. Pocaterra, January 27, 1937, Glenbow Archives, M6340, file 111.
60. Letter from G. W. Pocaterra to Patterson, February 12, 1937, BCARS/Add.MSS. 2762, box 1, file 14.
61. Interview with Alan Patterson and Janet Blanchet, July 11, 1991.
62. Interview with Alan Patterson and Janet Blanchet by author and Verne Huser, October 12, 1995.
63. Interview with Dick Matthews by author and Verne Huser, October 13, 1995.
64. Interview with Alan Patterson and Janet Blanchet, July 11, 1991.
65. Ibid.
66. Letter from Patterson to Janet Blanchet, Janet Blanchet's private collection.
67. *Far Pastures*, p. 190.
68. Letter from G. W. Pocaterra to Patterson, February 12, 1937, BCARS/Add.MSS. 2762, box 1, file 14.
69. Letter from Patterson to G. W. Pocaterra, August 29, 1937, Glenbow Archives, M6340, file 111.
70. Letter from Patterson to G. W. Pocaterra, March 14, 1939, Glenbow Archives, M6340, file 111.
71. *Far Pastures*, pp. 189-190.
72. Ibid., pp. 203-204.
73. *The Buffalo Head*, p. 158.

74. Ibid., pp. 159-160.
75. Ibid., pp. 162-163.
76. Letter from Patterson to Edwin Fenwick, November 8, 1934, BCARS 93-6227.
77. *The Buffalo Head*, p. 164.
78. Ibid., pp. 164, 170-173.
79. Ibid., pp. 184-186.
80. *Far Pastures*, pp. 127-128.
81. *The Buffalo Head*, p. 156.
82. Ibid., p. 151, and interview with Marigold Patterson, July 12, 1991.
83. Invoice, BCARS/Add.MSS. 2762, box 5, file 1.
84. Interview with Marigold Patterson, July 12, 1991, and interview with Janet Blanchet and Alan Patterson, July 11, 1991.
85. Interview with Janet Blanchet and Alan Patterson, July 11, 1991.
86. *Far Pastures*, pp. 119-120.
87. Interview with Marigold Patterson by Janet Blanchet, February 21, 1999.
88. Letters from H. S. Chestnut to Patterson, April 4, 1936, and September 2, 1936, BCARS 78-206.
89. Letter from Patterson to Pocaterra, January 27, 1937, Glenbow Archives, M6340, file 111.
90. *The Buffalo Head*, pp. 218-226.
91. Letter from Patterson to G. W. Pocaterra, January 27, 1937, Glenbow Archives, M6340, file 111.
92. Letter from Patterson to G. W. Pocaterra, February 15, 1956, Glenbow Archives, M6340, file 111.
93. Letter from Diamond Jenness to Patterson, August 19, 1937, BCARS/Add.MSS. 2762, box 2, file 1.
94. Letter from Patterson to G. W. Pocaterra, August 29, 1937, Glenbow Archives, M6340, file 111.
95. *The Buffalo Head*, p. 240.
96. Invoice, BCARS/Add.MSS. 2762, box 5, file 6, September 17, 1936.
97. Interview with Alan Patterson and Janet Blanchet by author and Verne Huser, October 12, 1995.
98. *The Buffalo Head*, p. 136.
99. Ibid., pp. 191-192.
100. Letters from Patterson to Arnor Larson, February 15, 1972, and January 24, 1979.
101. Letter from Patterson to G. W. Pocaterra, August 29, 1937, Glenbow Archives, M6340, file 111.
102. Letter from Patterson to Edwin Fenwick, July 14, 1940, BCARS 93-6227.
103. Interview with Marigold Patterson by Janet Blanchet, February 21, 1999.
104. Interview with P. K. Page, November 7, 1995.
105. Letters from Carl Rungius to Patterson, November 18, 1943, January 16, 1944, July 4, 1944, October 18, 1944, September 1, 1945, BCARS/Add.MSS. 2762, box 1, file 15.
106. The Ranchmen's Club, Calgary, July 29, 1954, BCARS/Add.MSS. 2762, box 2, file 3.
107. Letter from Pocaterra to Patterson, April 19, 1938, BCARS/Add.MSS. 2762, box 1, file 14.
108. Letter from Adolf Baumgart to Patterson, 1938, BCARS/Add.MSS. 2762, box 1, file 2.
109. *The Buffalo Head*, p. 124.
110. G. W. Pocaterra Papers, October 24, 1946, Glenbow Archives, M6340, file 14.
111. Letter from Patterson to G. W. Pocaterra, January 27, 1937, Glenbow Archives, M6340, file 111.
112. Letter from G. W. Pocaterra to Patterson, April 12, 1937, BCARS/Add.MSS. 2762, box 1, file 14.
113. Ibid., February 5, 1938.
114. Letter from Patterson to G. W. Pocaterra, March 14, 1939, Glenbow Archives, M6340, file 111.
115. Ibid., May 26, 1940.
116. Letter from G. W. Pocaterra to Patterson, probably February, 1940, Glenbow Archives, M6340, file 11.
117. Letter from G. W. Pocaterra to Patterson, June 8, 1940, Glenbow Archives, M6340, file 13.
118. Letter from G. W. Pocaterra to a doctor, July 9, 1941, Glenbow Archives, M6340, file 13.
119. Letter from G. W. Pocaterra to Norma Piper Pocaterra, January 28, 1941, Glenbow Archives, M6340, file 13.
120. Ibid., February 1, 1941.
121. Letter from The War Office, April 30, 1940, BCARS/Add.MSS. 2762, box 2, file 1.
122. Letters from Sir Edward Peacock to Patterson, August 14 & 25, 1941, BCARS/Add.MSS 2762, box 1, file 13.
123. Rafaelle Kennedy, Duchess of Leinster, *So Brief a Dream*, pp. 119-121.
124. *The Buffalo Head*, pp. 138-139.
125. Letter from Patterson to Edwin Fenwick, November 5, 1943, BCARS 93-6227.
126. *The Buffalo Head*, pp. 242-243.
127. Letter from Patterson to Edwin Fenwick, November 5, 1943, BCARS 93-6227.
128. *The Buffalo Head*, pp. 245-246.
129. Ibid., p. 247.
130. Letter from Patterson to Edwin Fenwick, November 5, 1943, BCARS 93-6227.
131. *The Buffalo Head*, pp. 247-248.
132. *Far Pastures*, p. 224.
133. Interview with Mike Schintz, February 17, 1996.
134. *The Buffalo Head*, p. 141.

135. Letter from Patterson to G. W. Pocaterra, March 14, 1939, Glenbow Archives, M6340, file 111.
136. Ibid., November 18, 1948.
137. Interview with Marigold Patterson, July 12, 1991.
138. Contract, BCARS/Add.MSS. 2762, box 5, file 1 (no date but evidence indicates July 16, 1945).
139. G. W. Pocaterra Papers, February 14, 1946, Glenbow Archives, M6340, file 14.
140. Interview with Louis, Betty and Don DePaoli, March 16, 1994.
141. G. W. Pocaterra Papers, May 24, 1946, Glenbow Archives, M6340, file 14.
142. Ibid., n.d. but probably 1947, to Dick Wright of Cochrane.
143. *The Buffalo Head*, pp. 254-255.
144. Ibid., pp. 256-257.
145. Ibid., pp. 260-261, 266-267.
146. Ibid., pp. 268-270.
147. Ibid., pp. 272-273.

GONE WEST: A WRITING LIFE—1947 TO 1973

1. Letter from Patterson to G. W. Pocaterra, June 8, 1946, Glenbow Archives, M6340, file 111.
2. Ibid., June 8, 1946, and February 16, 1956.
3. Patterson's introduction to Samuel Black's Diary for the H.B.C. Records Society, p. lxi .
4. Letter from Fenley Hunter to Patterson, July 17, 1947, BCARS/Add.MSS. 2762, box 1, file 9.
5. Letter from Clifford P. Wilson to Patterson, September 11, 1947, BCARS/Add.MSS. 2762, box 6, file 5.
6. Letter from Julia Blanchet, December 9, 1996.
7. See page 287 for full list of Patterson publications.
8. Letter from Sir Edward Peacock, August 5, 1950, BCARS/Add.MSS. 2762, box 1, file 13.
9. Ibid., March 26, 1947.
10. George & Barbara Perkins & Phillip Leininger, *Benet's Reader's Encyclopaedia of American Literature*, ed. New York: HarperCollins Publishers, 1991.
11. Letter to Patterson from G. D. Blackwood, March 7, 1950, March 12, 1952, BCARS/Add.MSS. 2762, box 6, file 5.
12. Letter from E. E. Rich to Sir Edward Peacock, July 4, 1950, BCARS/Add.MSS. 2762, box 1, file 13.
13. Letter from Patterson to G. W. Pocaterra, December 23, 1955, Glenbow Archives, M6340, file 14.
14. Letter from Patterson to Gray Campbell, May 21, 1978, private collection of the author.
15. Letter from Sir Edward Peacock, March 26, 1947, BCARS/Add.MSS. 2762, box 1, file 13.
16. Letter from Fenley Hunter, March 14, 1951, BCARS/Add.MSS. 2762, box 1, file 9.
17. Ibid., April 12, 1951.
18. Letter from Patterson to Curtis Smith, April 11, 1950, BCARS/Add.MSS. 2762, box 3, file 9.
19. Ibid., undated, probably 1951, BCARS/Add.MSS. 2762, box 3, file 9.
20. Interview with Patterson by W. D. Addison, BCARS/Add.MSS. 2762, box 6, file 1, p. 195.
21. *Far Pastures*, p. 235.
22. Ibid., p. 239.
23. 1951 notes on trip to South Nahanni BCARS/Add.MSS. 2762, box 4, file 5.
24. Letters from George Allen & Unwin Ltd., June 26, 1952, July 18, 1952, July 25, 1952, BCARS/Add.MSS. 2762, box 6, file 5.
25. Letter from William Morrow & Co., Inc., October 23, 1952, BCARS/Add.MSS. 2762, box 6, file 5.
26. Letter from G. D. Blackwood to Patterson, August 25, 1952, BCARS/Add.MSS. 2762, box 6, file 5.
27. Letter from George Allen & Unwin Ltd., May 22, 1953, BCARS/Add.MSS. 2762, box 6, file 5.
28. Letter from Gordon and Mollie Matthews, July 1, 1953, BCARS/Add.MSS. 2762, box 1, files 11-12.
29. Letter from Jim Bennett to Patterson, February 26, 1958, BCARS/Add.MSS. 2762, box 2, file 5.
30. Letter from Sir Edward Peacock, June 21, 1954, BCARS/Add.MSS. 2762, box 1, file 13.
31. Letter from G. W. Pocaterra to Patterson, October 27, 1955, Glenbow Archives, M6340, file 15.
32. Letter from Patterson to G. W. Pocaterra, February 16, 1956, Glenbow Archives, M6340, file 111.
33. Letter from Dick and Vera Turner, January 4, 1955, BCARS/Add.MSS. 2762, box 1, file 18.
34. Letter from Curtis Smith, January 20, 1954, BCARS/Add.MSS. 2762, box 1, file 16.
35. Letter from Albert Faille to Patterson, August 14, 1955, BCARS/Add.MSS. 2762, box 1, file 7.
36. Letter from Eric Morse to Patterson, October 11, 1956, BCARS/Add.MSS. 2762, box 2, file 5.
37. Letter from P. E. Trudeau to Mrs. G. C. F. Dalziel, November 16, 1970, BCARS/Add.MSS. 2762, box 1, file 6.
38. Letter from P. E. Trudeau to author, March 19, 1996.
39. Invoice from Chestnut Canoe Co., July 12, 1954, BCARS 78-206, microfilm copies 1978.
40. Letters from Dick and Vera Turner, January 4 and 10, 1955, BCARS/Add.MSS. 2762, box 1, file 18.
41. Letter from G. W. Pocaterra to Patterson, April 12, 1937, BCARS/Add.MSS. 2762, box 1, file 14.
42. Letter from G. W. Pocaterra to Patterson, November 17, 1955, Glenbow Archives, M6340, file 14.
43. Letter from Patterson to G. W. Pocaterra, December 23, 1955, Glenbow Archives, M6340, file 14.
44. Letter from Curtis Smith to Patterson, May 18, 1955, BCARS/Add.MSS. 2762, box 1, file 16.
45. Ibid., June 13, 1955.
46. Diary of Flat River trip, July, 1955, BCARS/Add.MSS. 2762, box 4, file 7.
47. Interview with Patterson by W. D. Addison, July 23-25, 1974, BCARS/Add.MSS. 2762, box 6, file 1, p. 101.

48. Diary of Parsnip/Peace trip September & October, 1955, BCARS/Add.MSS. 2762, box 4, file 7.
49. Letter from Patterson to G. W. Pocaterra, April 22, 1956, Glenbow Archives, M6340, file 111.
50. Letter from G. W. Pocaterra to Patterson, April 25, 1956, BCARS/Add.MSS. 2762, box 1, file 14.
51. Ibid.
52. Letter from Helen King to Patterson, March 29, 1960, BCARS/Add.MSS. 2762, box 6, file 5.
53. Letter from Patterson to Gray Campbell, December 8, 1961, author's private collection.
54. Letter from Patterson to G. W. Pocaterra, September 5, 1961, Glenbow Archives, M6340, file 17.
55. Letter from Dick and Vera Turner, December 30, 1961, BCARS/Add.MSS. 2762, box 1, file 18.
56. Review in *The New Yorker*, November 25, 1961, BCARS/Add.MSS. 2762, box 6, file 7.
57. *Far Pastures*, pp. 289-290.
58. Letter from Dick and Vera Turner, January 10, 1955, BCARS/Add.MSS. 2762, box 1, file 18.
59. Ibid., November 21, 1958.
60. Letter from Patterson to C. Sproule, April 12, 1959, Faille file, BCARS/Add.MSS. 2762, box 1, file 7.
61. Letter from C. Sproule to Patterson, March 13, 1961, Faille file, BCARS/Add.MSS. 2762, box 1, file 7.
62. Letter from Dick and Vera Turner, September 25, 1961, BCARS/Add.MSS. 2762, box 1, file 18.
63. Letter from Patterson to C. Sproule, April 12, 1959, Faille file, BCARS/Add.MSS. 2762, box 1, file 7.
64. Shuswap canoe trip October 1-15, 1956, BCARS/Add.MSS. 2762, box 4, file 7.
65. Letter from Roderick Haig-Brown to Patterson, July 30, 1959, BCARS 78-206.
66. Letter from Patterson to G. W. Pocaterra, March 7, 1963, Glenbow Archives, M6340, file 111.
67. Letter from D. A. Russell, October 15 and 23, 1959, BCARS/Add.MSS. 2762, box 5, file 2.
68. Letter from Helen King, June 27, 1960, BCARS/Add.MSS. 2762, box 6, file 5.
69. Letter from Patterson to G. W. Pocaterra, April 18, 1960, Glenbow Archives, M6340, file 111.
70. Interview with Alan Patterson and Janet Blanchet by author and Verne Huser, Oct. 12, 1995.
71. Ibid.
72. Letters from Patterson to Gray Campbell, July 14 and 15, 1977, author's private collection.
73. Letter from Sir Edward Peacock, June 27, 1962, BCARS/Add.MSS. 2762 box 1, file 13.
74. Letter from Gray Campbell to Patterson, January 16, 1963, BCARS/Add.MSS. 2762, box 6, file 5.
75. Letter from G. D. Blackwood to Patterson, December 10, 1962, BCARS/Add.MSS. 2762, box 6, file 5.
76. Letter from Malvina Bolus to Patterson, June 5, 1963, BCARS/Add.MSS. 2762, box 6, file 5.
77. Letter from Patterson to Gray Campbell, December 29, 1978, author's private collection.
78. Patterson obituary by Gray Campbell for *The Review*, October 31, 1984, p. B1.
79. Letter from Patterson to Gray Campbell, December 29, 1978, author's private collection.
80. Letter from Patterson to G. W. Pocaterra, September 17, 1963, Glenbow Archives, M6340, file 111.
81. Ibid., March 7, 1963.
82. Ibid.
83. Ibid., September 17, 1963.
84. "Among the Nomadic Stoney" by G. W. Pocaterra, *Alberta Historical Review*, V. 11, No. 3, Summer, 1963, p. 13.
85. Letters from Patterson to G. W. Pocaterra, March 24 and October 29, 1964, Glenbow Archives, M6340, file 111.
86. Diary of Parsnip-Finlay trip, June 24, 1965, BCARS 78-206.
87. Letter from Col. Harry Snyder to Patterson, March 17, 1948, BCARS/Add.MSS. 2762, box 2, file 2.
88. Diary of Stikine/Dease trip, July 17, BCARS/Add.MSS. 2762, box 2, file 2.
89. Letter from Patterson to G. W. Pocaterra, November 18, 1948, Glenbow Archives, M6340, file 111.
90. R. M. Patterson, *Finlay's River*. Toronto: Macmillan, 1968, p. 10.
91. Interview with Patterson by W. D. Addison, BCARS/Add.MSS. 2762, box 6, file 1, p. 105.
92. Diary for Finlay River trip, July 27 to September 25, 1949, BCARS/Add.MSS. 2762, box 4, file 5.
93. Diary of Parsnip/Peace trip September & October, 1955, BCARS/Add.MSS. 2762, box 4, file 7.
94. Letter from Patterson to G. W. Pocaterra, October 20, 1967, Glenbow Archives, M6340, file 111.
95. *Finlay's River* rough draft, BCARS/Add.MSS. 2762, box 6, file 2.
96. Letter from Patterson to G. W. Pocaterra, October 2, 1968, Glenbow Archives, M6340, file 111.
97. Ibid., December 2, 1967.
98. Letter from Patterson to Gray Campbell, March 10, 1977, author's private collection.
99. Letter from Hart-Davis, MacGibbon Limited to Patterson, July 9, 1974, BCARS/Add.MSS. 2762, box 6, file 5.
100. Letter from Patterson to Gray Campbell, February 27, 1980, author's private collection.
101. *The Buffalo Head*, p. 46.

THE TWILIGHT YEARS—1974 TO 1984

1. Interview with Alan Patterson and Janet Blanchet by author and Verne Huser, October 12, 1995.
2. *Victoria Daily Times*, Thursday, October 21, 1954, p. 6, BCARS/Add.MSS. 2762, box 6, file 7.
3. Interview with Patterson by W. D. Addison, BCARS/Add.MSS. 2762, box 6, file 1, p. 139.
4. Letter from Patterson to Verne Huser, November 19, 1982, August 8, 1983, September 10, 1983.
5. Letter from Patterson to Gray Campbell, December 29, 1978.
6. Letter from Marigold Patterson to Verne Huser, September 18, 1984.

Index

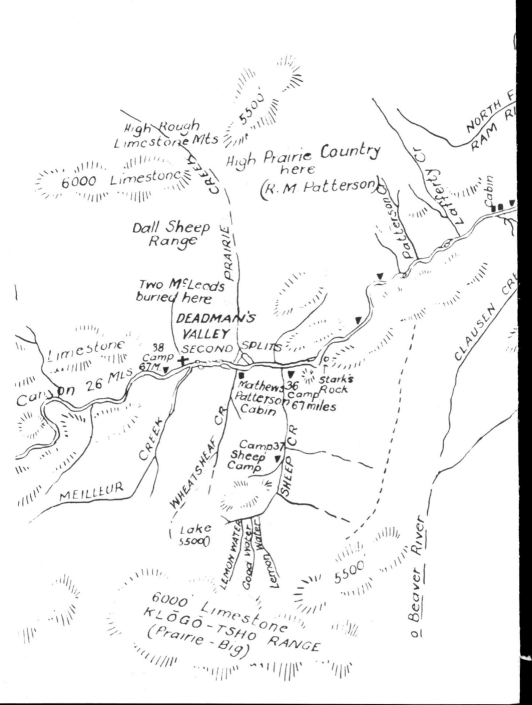

FENLEY HUNTER'S 1928 MAP
OF THE SOUTH NAHANNI